Women in America

FROM COLONIAL TIMES TO THE 20TH CENTURY

Women in America

FROM COLONIAL TIMES TO THE 20TH CENTURY

Advisory Editors
LEON STEIN
ANNETTE K. BAXTER

A Note About This Volume

This biography, containing many letters and personal documents, is a warm account of the life of a woman who was the wife of a distinguished scientist, a loving mother to the children she inherited when she married him and a founder of Radcliffe College. In 1850, Elizabeth Cabot Cary Agassiz (1822-1907) married Louis Agassiz, the famous Swiss naturalist who had become a professor at Harvard. She kept his home and, although self-schooled, his notes. She collaborated with his son in writing a book on marine biology and started a school for girls, involving Harvard professors as teachers, in order to help augment family income. She travelled with her husband wherever his work led— to teaching in Charleston, S.C., on an expedition to Brazil, through the Straits of Magellan and to Buzzards Bay. She kept records of his work and travels, and he remained devoted to her until his death when she was 51. Thereafter she became involved in the events that led to the establishment of a women's college at the "Harvard Annex" in 1879 and the chartering of Radcliffe College in 1894. She lived a full life as woman, as scholar, as her husband's companion, and she insisted on the highest standards, equal to those at Harvard, for the school she helped create.

ELIZABETH CARY AGASSIZ

A BIOGRAPHY

LUCY ALLEN PATON

ARNO PRESS
A New York Times Company
NEW YORK – 1974

Reprint Edition 1974 by Arno Press Inc.

Reprinted from a copy in
 The Newark Public Library

WOMEN IN AMERICA
From Colonial Times to the 20th Century
ISBN for complete set: 0-405-06070-X
See last pages of this volume for titles.

Manufactured in the United States of America

Library of Congress Cataloging in Publication Data

Paton, Lucy Allen.
 Elizabeth Cary Agassiz.

(Women in America: from colonial times to the 20th century)
 Reprint of the ed. published by Houghton Mifflin, Boston.
  1. Agassiz, Elizabeth Cabot Cary, 1822-1907.
 2. Agassiz, Louis, 1807-1873. I. Series.
QH31.A19P3 1974   378.744'4 [B]   74-3969
ISBN 0-405-06117-X

ELIZABETH CARY AGASSIZ

ELIZABETH CARY AGASSIZ

A BIOGRAPHY

BY

LUCY ALLEN PATON

WITH ILLUSTRATIONS

BOSTON AND NEW YORK
HOUGHTON MIFFLIN COMPANY
THE RIVERSIDE PRESS
1919

COPYRIGHT, 1919, BY RADCLIFFE COLLEGE

ALL RIGHTS RESERVED

PREFACE

A FEW words in regard to the circumstances under which this book has been written are necessary. In the spring of 1917, the Council of Radcliffe College appointed Mrs. William G. Farlow, Miss Alice M. Longfellow, and Professor William E. Byerly a committee, to which Professor Fred N. Robinson was later added, to arrange for the publication of a biography of Mrs. Louis Agassiz, the first President of the college, in order that the future students might have some knowledge of her character and of what Radcliffe owes to her. It was decided that the earlier portion of the memoir, treating of Mrs. Agassiz's youth and married life (1822–73), should be written by Miss Emma F. Cary, her youngest and only surviving sister, and the remainder (1873–1907) by myself.

From the time when the biography was first planned, Miss Cary devoted herself to its preparation and gave it constant thought. It was to be not only the crowning labor of her long life, which already numbered eighty-three years, but also a final tribute of devotion to a dearly loved sister. Her friends earnestly hoped that she might live to see the book completed, but she had made only a preliminary selection of letters and had written merely a few sections of her narrative, when in August, 1918, her work was ended by her death.

Her heirs kindly placed at the disposal of Radcliffe College her material for the biography and thus made it possible for the book to be written. The title that Miss Cary had expected to give to her part of the work — "Memories of Elizabeth Cary Agassiz, by One who Looked On" — expresses very well the character of the brief portion that she had prepared. This consisted largely of a description of the Boston of her own and Mrs. Agassiz's youth, for memories crowded so thick and fast upon her as she wrote that she was diverted from the account of Mrs. Agassiz's individual girlhood, and had herself concluded that probably much of her narrative might prove irrelevant to the memoir. I have, therefore, selected from her manuscript the sections that convey an impression of Mrs. Agassiz's immediate environment in her earlier years and have published these with very few and unimportant verbal changes. Of the material dealing with Mrs. Agassiz's ancestry Miss Cary left too incomplete a draft for publication, but her notes have served as a basis for the first chapter and have been amplified from other family papers. From the letters that she had collected for possible use I have made a selection and have added to these many from other sources. If Miss Cary could have finished her part, the book would have had a unique character that would have enhanced its interest. As it is, the admission must sadly be made that it contains but little of her writing.

The resources for the biography have been ample for some chapters, scanty for others. Mrs. Agassiz had

PREFACE

comparatively few correspondents, for with the exception of her Swiss and German connections, she lived so surrounded by her family and her most intimate friends that she had little need for the exchange of letters with them. Much of her correspondence has been destroyed; much that remains is too personal for publication or is not available. Consequently the letters published here are addressed to a limited circle and are by no means representative of her friendships. In the narrative also there are gaps. The deepest privacies of love and faith, joy and sorrow have the most profound influence upon character, but they are holy ground to be passed by in silence. The canvas, therefore, is unfinished in parts, but it serves to depict the most important externals of Mrs. Agassiz's life and to portray her character through the medium of her own words.

Two minor points remain to be mentioned. In the account of Mrs. Agassiz's part in the growth and development of Radcliffe College, it has seemed best, for the sake of clearness and interest, to treat the story as a unit, interrupted merely by a chapter containing letters written by Mrs. Agassiz during a year in Europe, although this necessitates a departure from the chronological arrangement followed in the rest of the book and anticipates some of the years that form the subject of a later chapter. It should also be said that many omissions from letters and other quoted passages have been made, which in deference to Miss Cary's wishes are in general not indicated by the use of asterisks.

PREFACE

The book owes much to the interest of friends who have lent letters for publication, and whom I have the pleasure of thanking in behalf of Radcliffe College. Material kindly given by Mrs. Cornelius Conway Felton is at her request specified: the letters on pages 180 and 276 and the manuscript from which selections appear on pages 277 to 279. Warm thanks are also due to friends and various members of Mrs. Agassiz's family for advice and suggestions, and especially to Mrs. Henry L. Higginson and Mrs. Robert Shaw Russell for material and information generously supplied. The Commemoration Addresses in Chapter XV are republished from the *Harvard Graduates' Magazine* for March, 1908, by the courtesy of its editor.

LUCY ALLEN PATON

CAMBRIDGE, MASSACHUSETTS
October, 1919

CONTENTS

I. ANCESTRY	1
II. TEMPLE PLACE	9
III. CAMBRIDGE — CHARLESTON — THE AGASSIZ SCHOOL — EUROPE	30
IV. LETTERS FROM BRAZIL	68
V. CAMBRIDGE — A Journey in Brazil	103
VI. THE VOYAGE OF THE HASSLER	118
VII. PENIKESE ISLAND — THE DEATH OF AGASSIZ	165
VIII. CHANGED CONDITIONS — THE BIOGRAPHY OF AGASSIZ	171
IX. THE SOCIETY FOR THE COLLEGIATE INSTRUCTION OF WOMEN: THE HARVARD ANNEX	192
X. THE PASSING OF THE HARVARD ANNEX	230
XI. EUROPE	275
XII. RADCLIFFE COLLEGE	310
XIII. THE RADCLIFFE TRADITION	358
XIV. THE LAST YEARS	367
XV. COMMEMORATION ADDRESSES	394
INDEX	413

ILLUSTRATIONS

ELIZABETH CARY AGASSIZ . . . . . *Frontispiece*
  From a photograph taken in 1872
MR. AND MRS. THOMAS GRAVES CARY 4
THE CARY COTTAGE AT NAHANT 16
ELIZABETH CARY AGASSIZ IN 1852 44
LOUIS AGASSIZ AND COUNT FRANÇOIS DE POURTALÈS 118
ELIZABETH CARY AGASSIZ IN 1872 166
THE FAY HOUSE IN 1887 222
THE AGASSIZ HOUSE AT NAHANT 278
ELIZABETH CARY AGASSIZ HOUSE, RADCLIFFE COLLEGE 354
THE AGASSIZ GATE, RADCLIFFE COLLEGE . . . 394
  Erected to the memory of Mrs. Agassiz by her children and grandchildren in 1916.

ELIZABETH CARY AGASSIZ

CHAPTER I
ANCESTRY

IT is preëminently true of Elizabeth Cary Agassiz that the memory of what she was possesses an even greater permanent value than what she did, and that indications of her character are of more importance in her biography than a record of her achievements, notable though some of these were. Not a complex nature, it was marked by strong individuality, of which the principal elements were singularly pronounced — the influences of a New England ancestry extending over almost two centuries and of an inherited environment in Boston, blended with inborn gifts of mind and spirit schooled by the discipline of experience. But in her personality there was throughout her life a distinctive quality — the light of pure sweetness and truth — which should not be forgotten in estimating the value of her presence, yet which eludes analysis and, although it is reflected in her letters and diaries, can be no more faithfully reproduced than the changing beauty of a dawn or sunset.

The background of Mrs. Agassiz's life always remained practically unchanged and was formed by her family connections and associations. On both her father's and her mother's side she came of excellent Massachusetts stock, which provided her not only with the practical and moral equipment characteristic of such an heritage, but also with a line of ancestors among whom one after another was conspicuous for effective and interesting traits. The first of her father's family to emigrate from England to America was James Cary, who in 1639 left Bristol, where his father and great-grandfather each in his day and generation had been first Sheriff and then Mayor, and came to Charlestown, Massachusetts. Here he spent the rest of his life, a person of sufficient importance to be made Clerk of the Writs, Recorder, and Tithingman. In Charlestown and its vicinity his descendants continued to live for generations and by marriage became connected with some of the families who were well known among the early settlers of Massachusetts. His great-grandson, Samuel Cary, for example, in 1741 married Margaret Graves of Charlestown, a descendant of John Winslow, the brother of Governor Winslow, and Mary Chilton, the daughter of James Chilton, one of the founders of Plymouth Colony. Through Margaret Graves there came into the possession of the Cary family an extensive piece of property in Chelsea, originally part of a royal grant to Governor Bellingham, which was bequeathed to her by her stepmother, who had inherited it from her sister, the daughter-in-law of Governor Bellingham. In this way Chelsea became the centre of the family life, and the "Retreat," as the Bellingham estate was called, remained the Cary homestead until 1911.

For Mrs. Agassiz the interest and attractions of the "Retreat" were enhanced by its immediate associations as her father's birthplace and early home. His father, Samuel Cary, the eldest child of Samuel and Margaret Cary, had a chequered career, which for a time led him far away from the seclusion of Chelsea. Handsome, gay, and fond of so-

ANCESTRY

ciety, he was no favorite with his serious-minded father, who gave him his patrimony and despatched him to the island of Grenada in the British West Indies, where he became a prosperous planter. He married, however, a Bostonian, Sarah Gray, the daughter of the Reverend Ellis Gray, and after eighteen years in Grenada, they felt New England tugging at their heart-strings, and believing that they had means sufficient to bring up their large family of children as they desired, they returned in 1790 to the "Retreat." But four years later, during political disturbances in Grenada, Samuel Cary lost his entire fortune and was reduced to the resources of the Chelsea farm for the support of his household. His prosperity proved a valuable school for adversity, and the fortitude with which he and Mrs. Cary met the situation admirably illustrates the moral calibre under the influence of which their children were brought up. A picturesque description of the family life in Chelsea has been left by Mrs. Agassiz in a brief manuscript memoir of her father, Thomas Graves Cary, who was only four years old at the time of his father's reverses:

Under the changed aspect of affairs the family life was restricted within the closest possible limits, and these conditions were never essentially changed until the children had grown up and entered the world to fight its battles for themselves. And yet to those who know the records of this life it was not wanting in the elegance and refinement which cultivated tastes and dignity of character may give to the narrowest circumstances. One hears, for instance, of the oldest daughter, who had already received her education at an expensive school in England, turning the dining-room into a schoolroom where her flock of little brothers and sisters became her scholars, a duty in which an older brother also returned from foreign lands joined her. The old family journals tell of the play of Shakespeare or the novel of Walter Scott read aloud in the winter evenings when the snow outside had shut them in, by "Mama," who added to her gracious presence and sweet voice the gift of admirable reading, or the minuet danced by the younger members of the family, while "Sister Margaret" played the harpsichord and the mother and father looked on from their straight-backed stately armchairs in the corner of the parlor. Nourished on good literature, trained in the manners of the old school, drawn closer in family affection and intercourse by the absence of other society, and taught to reverence and love the hard-won institutions of their country so recently secured, these young people grew up valuing their education the more, perhaps, because they owed it in so large a degree to their own personal efforts and those of their parents.

Such were the surroundings in which Mrs. Agassiz's father lived until he entered Harvard College. After his graduation he studied law and in 1820 married Mary, the daughter of Thomas Handasyd Perkins of Boston. By 1821 he was established as a lawyer in Brattleboro, Vermont, and had he continued to practise his profession there, Mrs. Agassiz's life would doubtless have run in very different channels from those that it followed. But not long after her birth, in 1822, he decided to give up his legal practice and cast in his lot with his brothers who were already

MR AND MRS. THOMAS GRAVES CARY

ANCESTRY

engaged in business in New York. In 1832 he brought his family from New York to Boston and entered the firm of his father-in-law, Perkins and Company, which had long been successfully engaged in the China trade. Six years later, however, the business was dissolved, and after a brief interval, Mr. Cary became treasurer of the Hamilton and Appleton Mills in Lowell, a position which he held until his death in 1859. His life, as Mrs. Agassiz describes it in the memoir quoted above, was that "of a quiet business man, never brilliantly successful so far as his own fortunes were concerned. His purity of character and unselfishness of conduct alone gave him the honored place he held in the community. Truly a good citizen and deeply interested in the charities and educational interests of the state, he was always ready to render unpaid service and was therefore often called upon to act as trustee or director of public institutions. He was for many years a most active trustee of the Institution for the Blind endowed by his father-in-law. He was also the indefatigable friend of the Boston Athenaeum, the affairs of which possessed the greater interest for him because he had marked literary tastes, for the pursuit of which his busy life allowed him little time. His memoir of Colonel Thomas H. Perkins, printed only for private circulation was a very spirited biographical sketch and he left also a number of short, well-written papers on matters of finance and manufacturing interests."

Through their mother, Mary Perkins, his children had an ancestry no less stamped by individuality than through him. The Perkins family was first established in America at Ipswich, Massachusetts. Here John Perkins, who emigrated to New England with Winthrop and Saltonstall settled in 1630. He was joined later by his god-daughter, Alice Perkins, who although a Puritan had married, in spite of family displeasure, her Roman Catholic cousin, Edmund Perkins of Ufton Court, and being left at his death with scant provision for her three children, came with them from England to her god-father for support. From her son, Edmund, the branch of the family to which Mrs. Agassiz belonged was descended. In his grandson, James Perkins, a highly respected merchant of Boston, the great-grandfather of Mrs. Agassiz, qualities appear that acquire a significance in her biography. Grave and courteous in manner and upright in principles he found his friends among such men as Samuel Adams, James Otis and Paul Revere. He is associated to his own advantage with Paul Revere in a flattering family tradition, according to which they came home one day after a hard gallop on horseback, Revere as mud-stained as he had reason to be after his famous ride in a better cause, and Perkins the pink of neatness, for, the record adds, "dirt, moral or physical, could not stick to him." His wife, Elizabeth, the daughter of Thomas Handasyd Peck of Boston, a dealer in furs, was fully his equal in strength of character and when at his death she was left with the care of a large family of children, she not only brought them up admirably, but assumed the management of her husband's business and conducted it with such efficiency that her sex was not suspected by her commercial correspondents in Holland, who used to address her as Mr. Elizabeth Perkins. Many tales are also told of the good works that she did, not only in connection with various charitable associations of Boston, but independently, lodging, for instance, an insane woman in her cellar till she had nursed her back to sanity, and tending the wounded, even British soldiers, during the troublous times of the Revolution.

Her son, Thomas Handasyd, the grandfather of Mrs. Agassiz, married Sarah Elliot, the daughter of Simon and Sarah Wilson Elliot of Boston, and brought a strain of Scotch blood into the family through his wife's mother, who was born in Scotland and had come to America in her girlhood. She was as interesting for her lovable qualities as Elizabeth Perkins was for her executive capacity, and her house was long remembered by her grandchildren as the scene of many youthful frolics in which their grandmother was an active sympathizer. The marriage of Thomas Perkins and the daughter of so excellent a mother fulfilled its promises of happiness. In the sixty-three years of their life together they were favored by fortune, and Colonel Perkins, as he was always called after being appointed lieutenant-colonel in the "Lancers," became one of the influential and wealthy citizens of Boston, prominent for the wise and philanthropic purposes for which he used his means, especially as a generous contributor to the Boston Athenaeum and the Massachusetts General Hospital, and as the founder of the Perkins Institution for the Blind.

His daughter, Mary, Mrs. Agassiz's mother, was therefore brought up amid more easy circumstances than her husband, Thomas Cary, in a household where public local interests and benefactions were of consequence, and under the simple social conditions of early nineteenth-century Boston. It is interesting to read of the impression that she made upon her future brother-in-law, William Cary, during a visit in Boston in 1818. He reports to Thomas, who was out of town at the time, that he had met Miss Perkins at a tea-party and had heard her sing. "I can't tell you how charmed I was with her voice (which is really divine)," he continues, "with her conversation, with her manners, — indeed I thought her possessed of every quality which man could possibly wish for in woman. Then her little laugh is killing." "I last saw her at the ball given by herself," he writes later, "where she walked among her friends, imparting pleasure and gayety to all the young and cheerfulness to those of the 'matured.' The next morning I called to say *Adieu jusqu'au revoir!* She came down dressed in a red crape, with a handkerchief round her neck; looked all goodness and benignity as usual; gave me her hand, and I took my leave, saying to myself, 'What a happy fellow is this brother of mine!'" The sparkling wit and vivacity of her youth characterized Mary Perkins throughout her life no less than her "goodness and benignity," and her cheerfulness and affectionate sympathy were among the traits that always endeared her to her friends and were transmitted by her to her children.

It is evident that as in generation after generation of the Cary and Perkins families during two hundred years these distinctive personalities developed, there was accumulating for their descendants a heritage of elevated moral ideals, refinement of taste, executive ability and family affection — qualities that continued to live in Mrs. Agassiz. How fine a strain in her character she also inherited directly from her parents, especially from her father, we shall see as we follow the story of her life.

CHAPTER II
TEMPLE PLACE
1822-1850

ELIZABETH CABOT CARY was born on December 5, 1822, at the house of her grandfather, Colonel Perkins, in Pearl Street. It was a dignified street in those days, lined with handsome dwellings and shaded by fine trees, offering many attractions to merchants as a quarter for residence because of its proximity to Fort Hill where from a grassy park on the Revolutionary fortifications, still unlevelled, they could survey the harbor and watch their ships from India or China coming into port. But ten years later the neighborhood of the Common was considered more desirable, and in 1833 Colonel Perkins moved to Temple Place where he had built a new house, — now occupied by the Provident Institute for Savings, — and established in the Pearl Street residence the school for the blind that afterwards bore his name. At that time the Cary family were living in Brookline, where they had gone on their return to Boston in the previous year, but Colonel Perkins speedily began to gather his daughters about him in Temple Place and built a house for Mrs. Cary next his own on the side toward the Common. Of the earlier years of Elizabeth Cary's childhood, while her parents were living in Brattleboro and New York and her grandparents in Pearl Street, we have no record. Our first impressions of her begin in Temple Place, and since she knew no other home until her marriage, it is with this house that her youth is completely identified.

Temple Place, known as "the Court," presented conditions altogether typical of the Boston of that period. On the opposite side of the street from the Cary dwelling two other married daughters of Colonel Perkins lived, Mrs. William H. Gardiner and Mrs. Samuel Cabot. "Grandchildren in Temple Place were commonplace facts," Mrs. Agassiz's sister, Mrs. Charles P. Curtis, says in her *Memories*, a family manuscript from which there will be frequent occasion to quote below. There were twenty-one all told, eight Cabots, six Gardiners and seven Carys — Mary (Mrs. Cornelius Conway Felton), Elizabeth (Mrs. Louis Agassiz), Thomas, Caroline (Mrs. Charles P. Curtis), Sarah, Emma and Richard. The Perkins connection, accordingly, may be said to have dominated the Court, and the constant intercourse and intimacy between the sisters and their children kept the family feeling strong and the traditions unbroken. Such a gathering of a clan into a single limited district was in complete accordance with the Boston custom of those days, when families had the habit of congregating in one street and not only claimed it as their own, but also looked somewhat askance upon the unblest world without. "I dare say they are wrong; they do not live in Temple Place," Mr. Cary used to remark with a little twinkle in his eye, when the opinions of outsiders were called into question by his daughters. A picture of the family environment in Temple Place has been left by Miss Emma Cary among the papers mentioned in the Preface.

The house of our grandfather in Temple Place was an attractive house in the solid style of that day with a heavy stone portico and stone steps leading up to the front door. Ah, that door! It was of black oak made of wood from the famous old man-of-war, the Constitution. It opened heavily and closed with a great thud and crash that could be heard in all the houses round about. The vestibule was very pretty with marble statues on each side, and steps again led up to the door opening into the hall. From the hall a broad spiral staircase wound up to the top of the house and was crowned with a cupola, from which we could see the comet of the time, or watch meteors trail their mysterious light across the sky. Two stories below was a spacious hall with grandfather's suite of rooms on the left side; on the opposite side our grandmother held sway. The elder grandchildren were very intimate with their grandfather, but we younger ones never ventured into these sacred precincts unless the rooms were empty. To our grandmother's parlor we always had access. She was usually sitting by a bright fire in a thickly upholstered rocking chair with arms and ears. She received us kindly, but usually said, "Where is your mother?" — a rather disconcerting question, but I don't remember being repelled by it. At dusk of a winter's day when the astral lamps were lighted, John Tevin, the old butler, drew out and opened a mahogany table with claw feet, spread a white cloth, put on the hissing kettle, and we had tea with grandmother. A particular kind of toast dwells in the memory of the participants, some East India preserve or other delicacy, and our favorite gingerbread marked, no doubt, with a fork, to our taste superior to any other luxury.

Downstairs on the *piano nobile* on our right as we came down into the hall, was the dining-room, its walls hung with rare engravings. Here at two long tables we used to have our Thanksgiving dinner when most of us were children or very young men and maidens. The little people were at a long side-table with Aunt Sally and my mother to preside. The elders, however, sat at the table of ceremony where grandfather and grandmother presided in state. How gravely John Tevin served us young folks, though ready enough to crack a joke with us on ordinary occasions! How the tables groaned under the glorious productions of Hannah Allen's genius, who was surely a high priestess in the culinary art, of which we youngsters were devotees! In later years the Thanksgiving feast was spread in the two large drawing rooms with folding doors that stood always open. They were handsome, spacious rooms, hung with interesting paintings, chiefly of the English school and strongly influenced by the genius of Constable. There were two beautiful bas-reliefs by Thorwaldsen, and some exquisite ornaments in Sèvres and other precious materials, but the furniture was of the plainest, covered with horsehair and the carpet was of sober brown Brussels. Two relics of a departed glory we regarded with awe: an armchair of Napoleon that he sat in at St. Helena, gnawing his heart out, one may guess, — also a small copy of his tomb with sword and *chapeau bas* laid upon it.

Next to this pleasant mansion was the smaller house where Thomas Graves Cary was watching over his seven children, a task shared by the mother of the family with cheerful serenity.

Temple Place was a court, connected with Washington Street only by a flight of steps leading down to a short and narrow pavement that opened on the thoroughfare. The name of Temple Place came from the Masonic Temple, a substantial stone building fronting on Tremont Street. In this temple there was a hall used for concerts, and many were the delightful hours we spent there making our first acquaintance with the best music, for our household was devoted to music. Lizzie and Mary sang delightfully together, and each younger child was expected to play or sing or do both to add to the domestic pleasure.

This taste for music led to many valuable friendships, and I often wonder how all these amateurs learned to sing and play so well. I fancy that there was a convenient supply of political exiles who brought the fine arts of Europe to New England. Exiles were greatly in fashion in the early nineteenth century, and I remember one who taught my sisters and their friends to sing some of the noble Italian compositions sung in the Sistine Chapel in Rome. This was Signor Gambardella, a man of versatile talents. He painted several beautiful portraits during his stay in Boston, and became famous in later years after his return to Europe, as assistant of Lord Ross in his astronomical studies and in the making of his wonderful telescope.

But, however acquired, there was much talent for

music in Boston and refined taste in selection. An orchestra of twenty-three musicians, some of them amateurs, gave concerts in the Odeon and among other great compositions rendered Beethoven's Fifth Symphony. All Boston went to hear these concerts, and the æsthetes from Brook Farm took possession of the gallery and listened no doubt to the music of the spheres. Their generous experiment in democracy was then at the full tide of its hopes for humanity. Margaret Fuller's talks were the wonder of the times; Alcott and Thoreau were trying experiments in living, and Emerson looked on, sympathized and held himself aloof from all that savored of exaggeration or bad taste. Transcendentalism was at its height, indignation at the negro slavery was surging in many hearts, and meanwhile alongside of all these enthusiasms a most conventional social world moved on as placidly as if nothing in Boston would ever change.

Boston was then a small and very pretty city. The Common was in its perfection, a charming little park. The streets around it were picturesque with houses individual in style and of a comfortable character. The Back Bay was still a bay. There was an odd attempt made to turn the Public Garden into a private park owned in shares, where there was a conservatory, an aviary, and a faint attempt at a menagerie. I remember my boundless pride when our grandfather gave to me among others, a life ticket to this infant Jardin des Plantes, but our lives would have been short indeed, if we had not survived the utility of our tickets, for this enterprise was soon given up and the enclosure became the Public Garden. Out towards Brookline stretched the Mill-Dam, and on the other side of the city "The Neck" led to Roxbury and also was connected with South Boston by a bridge. The Neck and the Mill-Dam afforded space for long walks for the pedestrians of the time. People walked in those days and were the better for it.

Between the two divisions of Boston, the conservatives and the transcendentalists, Elizabeth Cary passed her youth and like a wholesome plant, drew the best from all these elements.

The winter life in Temple Place passed under the conditions that Miss Cary has described was to a great extent continued for the Cary household during the summer, which they always spent at Nahant. Here they occupied a stone cottage built by Colonel Perkins not long after the marriage of Mrs. Cary and said to have been the first house in the place built by a Bostonian, for Nahant had not yet won the name of "cold roast Boston," bestowed upon it later by a famous wag, and was little more than a resort for fishing and bathing parties. Here Mrs. Agassiz spent her summers with few exceptions from her earliest years until 1904, and Nahant never knew a rival in her affections. Her life there was gay and happy in her girlhood, for the cottage was overflowing with young people and echoing with their music and merriment. "How well I remember in our house at Nahant," Miss Cary writes, "a line of young people tramping abreast round the broad piazza singing glees and catches and all sorts of ditties, their fresh young voices ringing out on the evening air. Or in our plain little parlor with nothing pretty in it but an exquisite China paper on the wall, there would be a circle of young people around the piano preparing hymns for the coming Sunday; for under my father's direction they made the choir at the Nahant church, singing without accompaniment and with perfect accuracy."

Of Elizabeth Cary herself, as she grew up in the surroundings afforded by Temple Place in winter and Nahant in summer, the most vivid picture that we have is contained in Mrs. Curtis's *Memories*.

Lizzie was the second child born to my father and mother, and as there was not two years' difference between her and her sister Mary, they grew up together and the tie between them was very close. I remember at Mary's death Lizzie said to me, "I have lost my twin." Though unlike in appearance and character there was one interest equally strong in both, and that was their love of music, which brought them the closer that Mary's contralto and Lizzie's soprano seemed made the one as companion to the other. Their music was partly from Italian operas, but with a mingling of English songs — and these were not English words set to music by German composers, but simply romantic love stories. I remember especially a favorite which was often asked for, in which the first verse ended: "Sister, since I saw thee last, O'er thy brow a shade has passed." The second wound up with, "Gentle sister, thou hast loved"; and the climax was reached with, "Sister, thou hast loved in vain." This was among what you might call the "popular" songs of that day. Another cheerful one of the kind

THE CARY COTTAGE AT NAHANT

began, "Love not, love not, The thing you love may die." But there was really beautiful music aside from these, *Semiramide*, *I Puritani*, *Somnambula*, now belonging to the middle ages.

Lizzie's youth was delicate, and in the few years before she was twenty there was some anxiety about her lungs. We always had our dear Miss Lyman [the governess] with us. As each one reached the age of fourteen or so, we passed on from her teaching to a larger school, where more branches could be taught, — all except Lizzie, and for her it was thought wiser that she should stay at home, taking lessons in languages, drawing and music. It was curious enough in consideration of the life before her that she had not as solid an education as the others. But this was balanced by her love of reading in general, perhaps not reading of the most solid kind, but wider than it would have been if she had had to bring lessons home from school to study, and when the intimacy with her brother-in-law, Mr. Felton, came, she read a great deal under his direction.

Lizzie's personality was very charming. She was of good height, slender and graceful, with pretty delicate features, hair arranged in little curls on each side of her face according to the fashion of the day, hazel eyes of the color some one has described as like the water of a brook running over a bed of brown autumn leaves, and her expression was in keeping with her character — always sweet and unruffled. The nursery name given her by her little brother Richard, when she said, "Whom do you love best,

Mary or me? Do say me," and he answered, "Dear Me," was very appropriate; and "Dear Me," we younger ones used to call her.

The earliest anecdote told of Elizabeth Cary chronicles the nearest approach to a misdemeanor that is recorded against her in the course of her eighty-five years. Her companion on the downward path was her cousin, Lizzie Cabot (afterward Mrs. Henry Lee), who was of about the same age and with whom she was so identified that they were called by the family "The Lizzies." Mrs. Curtis tells the story.

The Lizzies had been reading aloud a very interesting novel and had arrived at such an intense point that they agreed it would be impossible to sleep with the doubt of the heroine's fate on their minds; so it was arranged that Lizzie Cary was to return to her uncle's house after tea for the end, and it was thought more prudent in case of an interruption, that Lizzie Cabot should be found in bed and so a little nearer going to sleep. The plot of the book hung on a misunderstanding which started between the hero and heroine from the very church door after their marriage, and their sorrows filled the first two volumes, but in the third volume they met over the dying bed of an old servant. As they bent to receive his last words, one of Lady Mary's long curls caught on her husband's coat button, their eyes met — and at that point the Lizzie in bed sprang up with a shriek of excitement, old Nannie rushed from the nursery, my Uncle Cabot from his library, and the Lizzie from across the way hurried home to be very coldly received by her father, who had come down to unlock the door.

A more serious side of Elizabeth Cary's occupations is shown in the following letter to her father, written when she was not quite sixteen years old, in which she appears as an irreproachable youthful Bostonian — of her day.

TO THOMAS GRAVES CARY

Boston, November 16, 1838

MY DEAR FATHER: I have decided to take lessons in singing of Mrs. Franklin, as Mother has given me my choice between her and Mr. Paggi. I think that I shall prefer her, as she instructs in English as well as in Italian. She gives lessons to Lizzie Cabot, who is very much pleased with her.

I suppose that you will like to hear how I spend the money which you left me. Two of the five dollars have been expended on lectures.

Mr. Catlin has given three lectures on the Indian tribes which he has visited, all of which I have attended with Uncle Cabot. I found them very interesting and am glad to have heard them, as he gave us such information, as would not easily be found in books, or learnt from any one who had not associated with, and become familiar with the Indians.

I have also bought tickets to Mr. Buckingham's course of lectures on Palestine, of which there are to be only four. I think that they will be entertaining, as you know he has travelled all through that country himself and must therefore be thoroughly acquainted with it.

Mother has been proposing to us today a little alteration in our plan of reading. She thinks that a variety of reading would be better and wishes us to read every other day Combe on the Constitution of Man. Mary is not much pleased with the plan, as she is so much interested in Ferdinand and Isabella that she does not like to go to anything else. I think that it is a very good idea, because Mr. Combe's book would be perhaps a better exercise for the mind than such interesting histories as we are now engaged in.

We are having quite remarkable weather here. Day before yesterday was so warm that we had the windows open and the blinds closed in our room as if it had been a hot day in summer. And yet it is but a fortnight before Thanksgiving. How strange it will seem to have you gone, at that season of pies and puddings! How much we shall miss you!

An entertainment was given to Mr. Combe and his wife last evening. Its expenses were paid by subscription. An elegant collation was given at the end of the evening. About a hundred went and speeches were addressed by several gentlemen to Mr. Combe to which he replied. It was altogether a very elegant party.

Caddie and Mary send their love, but Sallie wishes me to write in her name, "Love me, Papa, for I love thee."

    Yours affectionately,
        E. C. CARY

The following letter written by Elizabeth Cary to a cousin, Dr. Samuel Cabot, while he was in Paris, to whom gossip was reporting that she was engaged, shows her in a gayer mood and gives an early glimpse of her life-long passion for flowers and music. Little did she dream that seventeen years later she would write to her mother the letter given below on page 55, telling of her husband's refusal of a professorship at the Jardin des Plantes, of which she speaks here with such enthusiasm to her cousin.

TO DR. SAMUEL CABOT

Boston, March 21, 1840

WELL, my dear Sam, and how do you find yourself, set down, as you are, in the midst of the great metropolis of Europe? Have you learned to waltz yet? But no, I fear that I must not hope that. Your disposition, I think, was never quite volatile enough to enjoy the whirling dance, thou', if you had lived in the time of *minuets*, I doubt not you would have made a famous dancer, when you could have paced slowly and gracefully across the room and made a low bow at a *proper distance* from your partner, then gently taking the tips of her fingers paced back amidst the admiring gaze of the multitude. Ay, the minuet would have been the dance for your sober *legs* (excuse me!) to have joined in.

Think of Edward's being engaged — actually in love! Shall I congratulate you or not? I hardly think it a subject of congratulation — to lose a brother, for certainly it is losing a friend to a certain degree when they take upon themselves the awful *responsibilities* of matrimony. Is it not? Take care, my dear, how you involve yourself in such a *slough of despond*. Won't you? By the way I heard a very funny report the other day concerning who do you think? — Why, your stately self and your harum-scarum cousin Lizzie. You did not know that this good-natured world, which is so fond of giving away what does not belong to it, has given you and me to each other. Shall I confirm the idea? Pray write me word — perhaps it would be better to bring out our engagement at once before you return — do inform me of your wishes on this subject.

You little wretch! how dare you be going to the opera every night when you know that I am pining here at home for the sounds which you have been hearing all winter. Oh! if I could spend one whole evening in the Italian opera house at Paris and hear the finest European singers, I do think that at the end of it I should be perfectly content to die on the spot. What bliss could exceed it?

Do you know (as of course you don't know) that we had the most delightful party at the Cushings' the other day. Don't you think the millennium must be coming when Mr. Cushing gives a party? I must tell you, to explain this wonder, that there has been a Pole here lately, called Kowsowski, who plays most delightfully on the piano. All the world have been distracted about him, and as the Cushings are very fond of music they determined to give him a party. The day was expected by their guests with impatience,

TEMPLE PLACE

as, you know, a party in the country at this season is quite a novelty, and most fervent wishes were made for propitious weather. But alas! for the disappointments of human life — the morning was ushered in by a violent snow storm. However, the most adventurous of the party went undaunted by the difficulties which met them, and by eight o'clock quite a numerous assembly had arrived. The rooms were perfectly crowded with flowers so that the air seemed loaded with the most delicious scents (you know that somehow or other Mr. Cushing's flowers do smell better than any one's else), the music was as beautiful as Boston can offer, the supper was handsome, the host and hostess were most hospitable, and the whole thing went off as well as you can imagine it to, with so many outward circumstances to aid it, and to crown the whole at 11 o'clock the snow storm was over, the clouds had broken away, and we rode in by moonlight. Oh! but I forgot to tell you that notwithstanding the weather we went out to the green-house, and though the rooms had been so perfectly supplied with flowers from it, you would not from the abundance remaining have supposed that any had been taken. I never saw so beautiful a display of hot-house plants in my life — but the idea of telling you of the Cushings' flowers, who have been in the "Jardin des Plantes," and yet I think that were I in France a little blue violet that came from Boston would have at least the beauty of association in my eyes, however inferior it might be in appearance to what would surround me there. So perhaps it is the same with you.

I always think of you, *mon ami*, when we meet together on Sunday evenings and miss your face and your voice very much indeed, and very, very often when Mary and I learn something that is new and pretty, I think of you, and wonder whether you will be too wise to enjoy our uncultivated music when you return. But no! I will not believe any such thing. I am sure it will at least have the power of association like the violet, and that you will value it, if it is only for being *home music*.

And now I must ask a thousand pardons of you for boring you with such a long epistle; but somehow or other I have been going on without much thinking, and having a hundred things to say to you, till I really have inflicted upon you much more than I meant to when I began, and can only beg that if you find it stupid, you will not consider yourself at all obliged to read the whole.

Your affectionate cousin,
LIZZIE CARY

Our next reminiscence of Mrs. Agassiz's youth is supplied by Miss Cary.

One of my earliest recollections of my sister Lizzie is of a dancing party given by my father for his elder daughters. I was eight or nine years old, and this was the first ball I had ever seen, a simple affair compared to the splendid balls of today, but to me it seemed sumptuous. The flowers came from the greenhouses at Brookline and made our small rooms very pretty, and they looked to me very spacious with the furniture removed and the carpets covered with white cloth.

Our eldest sister, Mary, must have been twenty-one at that time, a stately, dignified girl, with beautiful eyes and teeth, handsome hands, a heavenly singing voice, and a charming voice in speaking. She was not handsome, but she was not a person to be overlooked in any company.

Lizzie was a very pretty girl of nineteen in the style of beauty that belonged to that day, — graceful, gentle, rather languid in her movements, but bright and animated in conversation. She was a very attractive girl, but one for whom I should not have predicted a career that would give her a wide reputation. When I look at the massive building at Radcliffe, named for her, it seems to me a strange monument to have been raised to the gentle sister whom I remember at the ball I am describing.

Caroline was then about fourteen years old, straight as a dart, and promising to be the fine girl that she was at eighteen, a graceful dancer and very witty and attractive. Sallie was a round, plump, pretty child. Our eldest brother, Tom, was an elegant young man, and quite aware of the fact. Richard and I were the children and allowed to come to the party and look on. And thence came a sad adventure for me. Mr. Richard Greenough invited me to dance, and I, seized with a sudden panic, ran away and hid myself. Alas, poor me! I thought I was disgraced for life. But to my aid came the dear Lizzie, always kind and full of feeling for others. She came in search of me, took me downstairs, made my excuses to kind Mr. Greenough, and smoothed life for me once more.

The outline of Mrs. Agassiz's girlhood that we form from these various reminiscences and letters is filled in by a few of her letters written in 1843 and 1844. The affectionate elder-sisterly tone of interest and pride in the voice of Sallie, eight years her junior, — a just pride that never waned, as will be seen later, — her high spirits, her joy in music, all give a pleasant conception of the atmosphere in which she lived and which she helped create. It should be said by way of preface to these letters that the interest in dramatics and *tableaux vivants* was very keen among the young Carys and their "set," and that they had formed a theatrical company of their own which won great éclat among their friends. A diary kept by Mrs. Agassiz's brother, Thomas, gives a lively picture of the animated doings at the performances, not to mention the rehearsals. Mrs. Agassiz figures on only one occasion in the diary. In February, 1847, her brother none too cordially records: "We were forced to make an acquisition to our female force in Lizzie Cary and Mary Gardiner." The addition seems to have proved satisfactory, however, for a fortnight later when the company had given *The Waterman*, he reports that "the debutante, Lizzie, being new, deserves a word; her whole performance was one of great merit, correct without being stiff, and very easy on the stage without being familiar with the audience. She was much admired by all and won the hearts of the old gentlemen generally." This story has a sequel, for *The Waterman* was repeated with the original caste after all the members had reached middle life, and Mrs. Agassiz took her former part, to the intense delight of her children, who thought her very charming in it.

TO MISS SARAH G. CARY

Boston [1843]

I SHOULD have written to you long ago, my darling Sallie, before Mother left New York, if I had not supposed it would only be a bore to you to receive a letter, because you might feel obliged to answer, and when to my great delight Father brought me one from you the other day, it was so late in the week that I did not send a reply, because it was very uncertain whether you would get it before you left. But now, that I find you are to be gone so long and that you do not dislike writing, I shall send you a letter very often, and you, my precious, must write twice a week, won't you, to let us know what you are about.

I suppose that today you will receive a letter from Father, giving you leave to take lessons from Bagioli while you are with Aunt Nancy; my only fear is that as he is so popular a teacher, all his time will be engaged and he will not be able to give you an hour. You must write at once and let me know if you have succeeded and when you are to begin; and, dear Sallie, do take every pains to profit by these lessons and to practice carefully, so that you may make the most of the advantage. . . .

Good-bye, my darling, and don't forget to write often.

Your
LIZZIE

Boston [1843]

I suppose, dearest Sallie, that you all know before this that the grand explosion has taken place and Lizzie [Cabot] "is another's," but if anything can console us for having her carried off in this unceremonious manner, it is that "another" can appreciate her and is fully aware of the blessings he is appropriating to himself.

I suppose that all this will have but little interest for you, now that heart and soul are taken up by Macready, as I suppose yours must be. You can imagine Caddie's state of heart-rending despair when she received your letter this morning; it arrived about breakfast time and in vain did we offer her pressed beef, cut in thin, sentimental slices, hot rolls and coffee — she refused to be comforted until the dinner hour, when roast beef and Yorkshire pudding recalled her wandering senses and reminded her that her duty to her friends forbade her to starve. Nothing will console her but your writing constantly about all that happens in the theatrical line, and for my especial benefit do send us word of Altrochi's opinion of you and how your music comes on. High treason as you will think it, that interests me more than anything about Macready or his performances, though I am very glad to hear of him too.

New York [1844]

I have had such intense enjoyment of the *Giuramento*, going every night till I have learned exactly where to listen for the parts I like, and it is full of beautiful things. I have bought a small copy and shall insist upon your getting up a slight rave with me for sympathy's sake, when I return. Tonight we hear *Il Giuramento* once more, and on Friday I go again with the Ruggleses, when they will repeat this opera, or — "bear with me, Mrs Porter," it is only a possibility — or — *Ernani*.

New York, Wednesday night, 11.30 [1844]

I MUST add a line, dearest, on my return from the opera to mention that I am just now in that miserable state of excitement when all seems stale, flat and unprofitable but the scene we left behind. This is the last time we shall hear *Giuramento*, which adds to my melancholy, and there is a fearful report about tonight that on Friday evening we have *Lucia* instead of *Ernani*, on which I had set my heart.

Mother sends much love to Father, whose letter she was delighted to receive this afternoon. I don't send love to anybody, because after writing every spare moment, I only get blackguarded for my pothooks, which, thank Heaven, are appreciated in New York, if not elsewhere. Tell Father and Tom that Aunt Nancy avers, among all the letters she has received from me she has never had the least difficulty in deciphering one. Don't let them see this one if they want to ever so much.

We shall come home on Monday without an escort, if none offers, as we are not in the least timid about taking care of each other. Good-night.

Your
LIZZIE

CHAPTER III
CAMBRIDGE — CHARLESTON — THE AGASSIZ SCHOOL — EUROPE
1850-1865

THE girlhood of Elizabeth Cary as we have followed it in the preceding pages differed little from the usual existence of a Boston girl of the time, growing up in a large circle of relatives linked by intermarriage with other Boston families whose names were more or less conspicuous in the commercial interests of the place — especially trade with East India or China. Into this provincial community there flashed a brilliant element in 1846 with the arrival of Louis Agassiz, already well known as an able naturalist and a gifted professor in the University of Neuchâtel. He had left his delicate German wife with their two daughters at Carlsruhe and his son at school in Neuchâtel, and had come to America with scientific exploration as his primary object, for which he had received a grant of money from the King of Prussia. But previous to sailing, in order to eke out his slender income, he had arranged under the auspices of Mr. John Lowell to deliver a course of lectures for the Lowell Institute in Boston. The effect that he produced upon his audience, composed of scientific and cultivated hearers side by side with working-men, is best described by Mrs. Agassiz in his biography:

Never was Agassiz's power as a teacher, or the charm of his personal presence more evident than in his first course of Lowell Lectures. He was unfamiliar with the language. . . . He would often have been painfully embarrassed but for his own simplicity of character. Thinking only of his subject and never of himself, when a critical pause came, he patiently waited for the missing word, and rarely failed to find a phrase which was expressive if not technically correct. . . . His foreign accent rather added a charm to his address, and the pauses in which he seemed to ask the forbearance of the audience, while he sought to translate his thought for them, enlisted their sympathy. Their courtesy never failed him. His skill in drawing with chalk on the blackboard was also a great help both to him and to them. When his English was at fault he could nevertheless explain his meaning by illustrations so graphic that the spoken word was hardly missed. . . .

After the first lecture in Boston there was no doubt of his success. He carried his audience captive.

Agassiz's popularity in the lecture-room opened for him agreeable social relations, the pathway to which his genial personality made all the more easy. That he was uncommonly prepossessing is illustrated by the story of the cruel blow that Mrs. Cary received when on coming home from church one Sunday morning shortly after his arrival in Boston, she said to her daughter Elizabeth, "I should like to know who it was who sat in the Lowells' pew this morning, for he's the first person I ever saw whom I should like you to marry," only to be informed that the stranger was none other than the popular Agassiz, who already had a wife and children in Europe.

Eventually Agassiz established himself in East Boston, and in 1848 after the canton of Neuchâtel ceased to be a dependency of the Prussian kingdom and he had been honorably discharged from the service of the King of Prussia, he accepted the chair of Natural History at the Lawrence Scientific School, then a newly organized department of Harvard University. The spring of that year, accordingly, found him established in Cambridge in a small house on Oxford Street. But the favorable prospects that were opening before him were soon shadowed by the death of his wife, and his sense of loss was intensified by the separation from his children, whom he considered too young to bring to America. A sketch of his life at this time has been given in his biography by Mrs. Agassiz, which is quoted here as her own description of the community in which she was soon to take her place.

The college was then on a smaller scale than now, but upon its list of professors were names which would have given distinction to any university. In letters, there were Longfellow and Lowell, and Felton, the genial Greek scholar of whom Longfellow himself wrote, "In Attica thy birthplace should have been." In science, there were Peirce, the mathematician, and Dr. Asa Gray, then just installed at the Botanical Garden, and Jeffries Wyman, the comparative anatomist, appointed at about the same time with Agassiz himself. . . .

In connection with these names, those of Prescott, Ticknor, Motley, and Holmes also arise most naturally, for the literary men and scholars of Cambridge and Boston were closely united; and if Emerson, in his country home at Concord, was a little more withdrawn, his influence was powerful in the intellectual life of the whole community, and acquaintance readily grew to friendship between him and Agassiz. Such was the pleasant and cultivated circle into which Agassiz was welcomed in the two cities, which became almost equally his home, and where the friendships he made gradually transformed exile into household life and ties.

In Cambridge he soon took his share in giving as well as receiving hospitalities, and his Saturday evenings were not the less attractive because of the foreign character and somewhat unwonted combination of the household. Over its domestic comforts now presided an old Swiss clergyman, Monsieur Christinat. He had been attached to Agassiz from childhood, had taken the deepest interest in his whole career, and . . . had assisted him to complete his earlier studies. Now under the disturbed condition of things he had thrown in his lot with him in America. . . . To Agassiz his presence in the house was a benediction. He looked after the expenses, and acted as commissary in chief to the colony. . . . In short, so far as an old man could, "Papa Christinat," as he was universally called in this miscellaneous family strove to make good to him the absence of wife and children.

The make-up of the settlement was somewhat anomalous. The house though not large was sufficiently roomy, and soon after Agassiz was established there he had the pleasure of receiving under his roof certain friends and former colleagues, driven from their moorings in Europe by the same disturbances which had prevented him from returning there. . . .

The house stood in a small plot of ground, the cultivation of which was the delight of Papa Christinat. It soon became a miniature zoölogical garden where all sorts of experiments in breeding and observations on the habits of animals were carried on. A tank for turtles and a small alligator in one corner, a large hutch for rabbits in another, a cage for eagles against the wall, a tame bear and a family of opossums, made up the menagerie, varied from time to time by new arrivals.

Among the many friends whom Agassiz made in Cambridge he had few more intimate than Professor Cornelius Conway Felton, later president of Harvard University, but at that time professor of Greek. He had married Mary Cary, and it was at his house that Agassiz first met her sister Elizabeth. The occasion was a dinner given by Professor Felton to Agassiz and a few other Cambridge men, and Elizabeth and Caroline Cary had come out from Boston to help Mrs. Felton entertain her guests after dinner. No reminiscences from an evening that had such important consequences have been preserved beyond the reply made by Agassiz to a question from one of the company about the curious formation of the head of the sculpin, — "Oh, God must have His leetle joke," — an answer that recalls his habit of referring to any fish that he happened to be describing in his lectures as "this leetle indiveedual."

Two people more unlike in their previous environment than Agassiz and Elizabeth Cary it would not have been

CAMBRIDGE

easy to find in the Cambridge college circle of that day — Agassiz, born in his father's parsonage in the little village of Motier, in sight of the Bernese Oberland, spending his boyhood among the mountains of Switzerland, inured to scanty means, passing from the varied and absorbing life of a young naturalist in Germany and Paris to that of a professor at Neuchâtel, and then, essentially a son of the Old World, "accustomed to draw Europe's freer air," transplanted to Boston; and Elizabeth Cary, the child of New England ancestry, born into a sufficiency of this world's goods, reared, as one of her sons-in-law has said, "among silks and spices and cotton shirtings and sheetings," brought up as a Bostonian of the Bostonians, having spent her years between Temple Place and Nahant in a placid ebb and flow of conventional circumstance in the midst of a happy family life. Yet in her sincerity and sweetness the simple, genial nature of Agassiz found its level, and his eager, buoyant temperament was balanced by the quiet steadiness of her own.

On April 25, 1850, they were married in Boston in King's Chapel, a church with which the Cary family had been connected for more than a century. "Lizzie looked lovely," Mrs. Curtis writes in her diary, "dressed in a green silk, white camel's hair shawl, straw bonnet trimmed with white, [with] feathers on each side. After the ceremony they drove directly out of town." They began their married life in the house on Oxford Street, of which we have read Mrs. Agassiz's description. In a few letters that she wrote to Agassiz in one of his absences on a lecturing tour just before their marriage — letters which reveal her habitually high-minded attitude toward all the relations and purposes of her life —

she had told of her preparations for turning the extraordinary establishment into a home and making it "cheerful and comfortable." Her plans had been complicated during this same absence of Agassiz by "Papa Christinat," who believing that it would be best to leave the newly married couple to manage the household, had suddenly taken his departure to a French parish in New Orleans. His decision was a matter of deep regret to the bride elect, for such was his familiarity with all the details of Agassiz's daily life that his presence would have lifted many responsibilities from her shoulders after she became the mistress of the house in Oxford Street. "I have assured him," she writes characteristically to Agassiz after having had a long talk with Mr. Christinat, "that he will never find me tenacious of my rights, that I should be not only willing but glad to give up to him the occupations that he has had at your house; but all I urge in argument or affectionate persuasion is useless." "You must not be quite in despair at the thought of my ignorance and inexperience in household matters," she says in another letter, "for I hope to convince you that I can be quite an efficient person on occasion; but I know that the loss of Mr. Christinat as a useful assistant in your household will be but a small part of your regret and in other things I cannot so easily fill his place." Her difficulties were simplified, however, by the scattering of several of the foreign members of the establishment and many assistants. Mr. Jacques Burkhardt, an artist friend of Agassiz, his fellow-student at Munich and now his draughtsman, alone remained, and continued to live in the family until his death seventeen years later at the house of Agassiz's younger daughter, Mrs. Shaw. In the summer preceding Agassiz's marriage, his son, Alexander, a boy thirteen years of age, had joined him, and in the autumn of 1850 his two daughters, Ida and Pauline, both some years younger than their brother, came to America. Thus the family in Oxford Street was made complete.

The relation between Mrs. Agassiz and her step-children was most unusual and singularly happy. Her judicious tenderness won their affection, and her devotion to them and theirs to her in sickness and in health until death parted them knew scarcely a shade of difference to that existing between a mother and her own children. "She showed us and taught us, just by being herself, only good and lovely things," one of them wrote of her many years afterward. Close and enduring as was the tie soon formed between Mrs. Agassiz and her little step-daughters, the intimacy which speedily developed between Alexander and herself was still more remarkable. He had come to America less than a year after the death of his own mother, who had been his adored companion and the object of his tender devotion during her final illness, when he had assumed the care of the household. Quiet and thoughtful beyond his years, with his mother's place forlornly empty, speaking only French and German, he offered in his boyish heart ready soil for the flower of affection that sprang up at his first sight of his father's future wife, and that never ceased to blossom. She remained, as he said at her death, for sixty years his mother, guide and friend. How closely their lives became entwined will in a measure be seen in later chapters, but has best been expressed by Alexander himself in a letter written shortly after his stepmother's death and published in his biography by his son

George: "Our relations were so peculiar that I don't know what to style them. She was my mother, my sister, my companion and friend, all in one.... From the time that I first saw her at Mr. Felton's house as Miss Cary, and I only a small boy of thirteen, there never was a word of disagreement; she belonged to me and I to her; it could not have been otherwise; she learned to know me through and through and placed in me the most unbounded confidence, and entrusted me with the keeping of her sorrows."

Thus the beginning of Mrs. Agassiz's married life was occupied with the care of the three children and the regulation of Agassiz's amazing establishment. Although many of the human inmates had disappeared, the animate zoölogical specimens still had to be reckoned with. Many a stirring incident of their varied doings is related, one by Mrs. Agassiz herself in a letter written to her mother not long after her marriage.

TO MRS. THOMAS G. CARY

[Cambridge]

BY the way, I must tell you something that happened to me today, in solemn warning to any woman who thinks of becoming the wife of a naturalist. In a hurry this evening to prepare for church, I ran to my cupboard for my boots, and was just going to put my hands upon them when I caught sight of the tail of a good-sized snake, which was squirming about among the shoes. I screamed in horror to Agassiz, who was still sound asleep, that there was a serpent in my shoe-closet. "Oh, yes," he said sleepily, "I brought in several in my handkerchief last night; probably (yawning) they have escaped. I wonder where the others are." This is a true tale. The rest of the pleasing monsters were secured, and Agassiz had the audacity to call upon me to admire their beauty, when he had caught them again.

Let us hope that it was one of the same family of snakes and not the member of still another colony that once provided Miss Emma Cary with a *mauvais quart d'heure* in the course of a night that she was passing in Oxford Street, when she woke to remember on discovering no matches for her candle by her bedside that a lost snake was gliding about the house, and to wait in terror for daylight, expecting every moment to feel something cold and slimy wriggle across her face. The snake turned up later on the stairs and was forthwith consigned to a jar of alcohol. The hero of a still more disquieting adventure was a bear cub which had been sent to Oxford Street from Maine and was kept in due subjection in the cellar, until one day he arose in his might, and breaking his chain decided to join the family and some guests at dinner. As he entered the dining-room by one door, the company at the table left by the other, and he was given *carte blanche* to devour the dinner. He was summarily banished to a livery stable in retribution for this escapade and before long was found worthy of a dose of prussic acid.

Agassiz's marine specimens lent a fresh color also to the summers at Nahant, which took on a new character for Mrs. Agassiz after her marriage. Mr. Cary then arranged a home for her and for Mrs. Felton by moving to his land a cottage of four or five rooms, to which additions were made so that it could be comfortably shared by the two sisters and their households. A laboratory for Agassiz was also built on a little later. Here in large and small glass receptacles he kept his marine specimens, generally medusae whose soft yet brilliant colors and delicate structure made them an ornamental acquisition in the eyes of Mrs. Agassiz. The doors of the cottage were never shut to guests, old or young, famous or obscure, and the same intimate family intercourse that formed so large an element in the winter's pleasure knew scarcely a break in the summer.

An agreeable interlude came in Mrs. Agassiz's life a little more than a year after her marriage. In 1851 Agassiz was called to a professorship in the Medical School at Charleston, South Carolina, which demanded lectures only during the three winter months, and since in those days the winter vacation of Harvard extended over six weeks, thus permitted him to give his autumn and spring courses at the Lawrence Scientific School. He held this position for two years, when he was obliged to resign it on account of ill health. Mrs. Agassiz was with him during both winters, which, since they brought her lasting friendships, were by no means unimportant in her experience. Southern hospitality and attractive surroundings combined to make the conditions congenial. A part of the time was spent on Sullivan's Island, where a friend, Mrs. Rutledge, had given Agassiz the use of her cottage, which he turned into a laboratory. He and Mrs. Agassiz were also received with the utmost cordiality by Dr. John E. Holbrook, a well-known scientist, and his gifted wife, who opened to them their country-place, of which Mrs. Agassiz has left a delightful picture in her memoir of Agassiz. "The woods were yellow with jessamine, and the low, deep piazza was shut in by vines and roses; the open windows and the soft air full of sweet, out-of-door fragrance made one forget, spite of the wood fire on the hearth, that it was winter by the calendar. The days, passed almost wholly in the woods or on the verandah, closed with evenings spent not infrequently in discussions upon the scientific ideas and theories of the day, carried often beyond the region of demonstrated facts into that of speculative thought."

The few characteristic letters which follow were written during these winters at Charleston and on the journey home in 1852 when Agassiz went to Washington to deliver a course of lectures at the Smithsonian Institution.

TO MRS. THOMAS G. CARY

Charleston, December 22, 1851

WE have just returned from a visit at Sullivan's Island, where I have left Agassiz very busy and happy with some exceedingly thin, scrawly looking monsters with no bodies, and amazingly long legs, which afforded him immense satisfaction. He had intended returning to town with me, till these emaciated gentlemen were brought in from the beach, and of course against such attractions I had nothing to plead. We passed, however, a very charming day there, with reading, gathering shells, sketching a monster, hunting, according to the different tastes of the company.

The town is as empty as Boston in the middle of August — everybody gone to the plantation for the Christmas festivities, and we expect to leave tomorrow or the next day for Belmont, where we shall pass the week. During Christmas the town is absolutely given up to the blacks, and if any of the white population are so unfortunate as to have no refuge for the holidays in the country, they can scarcely go through the streets in safety for the firing of crackers, the shooting of pistols, playing with fire balls, and other mad pranks of the negroes.

It is odd that just when you wrote to me to read Carlyle's life of Sterling, I was deeply interested in another life of him by Hare, which you must try to get now that you have finished the other, and which includes a large selection from his writings. The two lives will go well together, and I mean to get Carlyle's, who was induced to write his, as explanatory of Hare's, who though most friendly to Sterling, is a tremendous churchman and represents every intellectual process in his friend's religious views after his health obliged him to leave the active ministry of the church, as a sinful and much lamented fall, to be spoken of, however, with pity rather than condemnation. His language with respect to these spiritual errors, is so ambiguous that one is almost in doubt whether Sterling had really committed some crime, or merely learned to differ from Hare's religious views. I hope you will read it, if you have not already commenced it.

Sullivan's Island, January 2 [1852]

I SHOULD have answered your letter, which was so very welcome, earlier, but I wanted to write from our new home, and have been waiting till we should enter upon the honors and responsibilities of housekeeping.

CHARLESTON

How I wish you could look in upon us this first evening that we pass here, and see how auspiciously our honeymoon begins. You must imagine a small parlor, with a large fireplace, in which the cheeriest wood fire dances and sparkles. I have been out on the beach, gathering drift-wood this afternoon and whenever we throw on a bit, it is so dry that it breaks into the brightest flame, and lights up our little room most brilliantly.

For furniture we have a sofa, rocking chair, dining table, writing table, a number of common chairs, and what I value most, a little oval, three-legged mahogany stand exactly like one that Grandma used to use, on which she almost always had her workbasket, and the last new novel. On this stand tonight, there is a dish of flowers, that I brought from town. We have just done tea, I have cleared away the teathings, drawn the table near the fire and sit down to write to you, while Agassiz writes at the other side, beginning his winter work, and Burkhardt is contentedly smoking his pipe in the chimney corner. The wind moans mournfully outside and threatens a storm tomorrow, which will disappoint me in having my piano which I have ordered from town. When that comes, I shall feel fully established.

We have given up the idea of trusting to luck or Providence for our meals, and have breakfast, dinner and tea in the most orderly manner, though our table service is not the most magnificent. No one leaves on the Island anything but the most common crockery.

I forgot to tell you that Agassiz has had little stoves ("second-handed") put into the upper chambers of the house so that his people can work there, and he has everything going on under his own eye while I am not in the least disturbed by his scientific establishment. If he is only well, I think he will be able to accomplish a great deal this winter, but it seems to me impossible he should finish *all* he has marked out for himself, in three months, especially as he must have so many interruptions. He is obliged to go to town to lecture three times a week, and does not get back till eleven o'clock the next day.

I hope you will try to write often, though my letters will not be a worthy return, for happy as I hope to be here, nothing can be more intensely quiet than the life, and my walk on the beach with an occasional expedition to town, will be the greatest events that I shall have to write about.

TO MISS SARAH G. CARY

Washington, March 22 [1852]

I suppose, my dear, now that you are mistress of a watch you will stand more in dread of fortune hunters than Charles Curtis did, when his grandmother left him the scissors. Poor Ida has told you, no doubt, how much she took to heart the loss of mine, which was, just now, quite a family misfortune, as, when Agassiz was out of the way, it was our only guide about time. But she was so broken-hearted, poor little soul, that I have tried to seem as if I had been wishing all my

ELIZABETH CARY AGASSIZ
1852

life to have an opportunity of learning to judge of the time, by watching the shadows, and to seem really gratified at entering upon this new branch of study.

Shortly after his return to Cambridge from Charleston, it became evident as Agassiz's library grew larger and his children older that the quarters on Oxford Street were too limited, and in 1854 the family moved into a house built for them by the College on the corner of Quincy Street and Broadway, which continued to be Mrs. Agassiz's home for the rest of her life. "The house on Quincy Street was a most delightful and homelike place," Miss Cary writes. "At the right on entering was Lizzie's charming parlor. On the left was Agassiz's fascinating, shabby library, full of orderly disorder. Common wooden book-cases lined the walls, filled with valuable books in shabby bindings. A rickety ladder leaned against one side of the room, a fire burned brightly in the grate, and brighter and more cheerful than any fire, Agassiz sat at the long table, happy in his studies. Behind the library was a study, and behind Lizzie's parlor was the dining-room. There was in this delightful house no luxury, but every comfort. Alex, Ida and Pauline were young, handsome creatures, great favorites with every one, full of life and gaiety; and their friends came freely to the house, which rang with young voices, with laughter and with cheerful talk." Its walls proved elastic and adaptable to the many and varied plans that were made under its roof. Of these none demanded more radical changes than one which materialized in 1856. By the spring of that year the public lecturing by which Agassiz had endeavored through the winter to supplement his all too narrow salary of fifteen hundred dollars was proving so exhausting for his health that it became necessary to find some other means of adding to his resources and relieving him from a heavy debt contracted for the publication of his work on fossil fishes and for other scientific investigations. These perplexities were solved by Mrs. Agassiz, who met the situation with as great adaptability as Elizabeth Perkins had displayed when she was left a widow, and Samuel and Sarah Cary when they lost their Grenada property. As she lay awake one night anxiously turning over ways and means for repairing the family purse, there suddenly flashed into her mind the idea of establishing a school for girls in the upper part of the Quincy Street house with the assistance of her two older step-children. Quickly the scheme built itself up in her ready imagination, and she no less promptly proceeded to carry it out. A note to her father shows that she first consulted him and then secured the coöperation of her step-children.

TO THOMAS G. CARY

Cambridge [*March*, 1855]

I FIND that Ida feels exactly as I expected about our plan. It seems that the thought is not a new one to any of us; we have had it in our minds under different forms. I must say that the hearty pleasure with which both Alex and Ida enter into the project gives me new confidence in it, and I trust the end will show that it was the right and wise course to take. I shall be in again to-morrow to have another talk before you go to New York. Your approbation and sympathy about the plan have made me really strong, and indeed if you had not listened to it so promptly, I should never have dared to propose it to any one else.

THE AGASSIZ SCHOOL 47

Mrs. Agassiz's own words in the *Life* of Agassiz give the story of the foundation of the school and the picture of it that she desired to have transmitted:

In consultation with friends these plans [for the school] were partly matured before they were confided to Agassiz himself. When the domestic conspirators revealed their plot, his surprise and pleasure knew no bounds. . . . He claimed at once an active share in the work. Under his inspiring influence the outline enlarged, and when the circular announcing the school was issued, it appeared under his name, and contained these words in addition to the programme of studies: " I shall myself superintend the methods of instruction and tuition, and while maintaining that regularity and precision in the studies so important to mental training shall endeavor to prevent the necessary discipline from falling into a lifeless routine, alike deadening to the spirit of teacher and pupil. It is farther my intention to take the immediate charge of the instruction in Physical Geography, Natural History, and Botany, giving a lecture daily, Saturdays excepted, on one or other of these subjects, illustrated by specimens, models, maps and drawings." . . . [Agassiz] never had an audience more responsive and eager to learn than the sixty or seventy girls who gathered every day at the close of the morning to hear his daily lecture; nor did he ever give to any audience lectures more carefully prepared, more comprehensive in their range of subjects, more lofty in their tone of thought. . . . The lecture hour was anticipated as the brightest of the whole morning. It soon became a habit with friends and neighbors, and especially with the mothers of the scholars, to drop in for the lectures, and thus the school audience was increased by a small circle of older listeners. The corps of teachers was also gradually enlarged. The neighborhood of the university was a great advantage in this respect, and Agassiz had the coöperation not only of his brother-in-law, Professor Felton, but of others among his colleagues, who took classes in special departments, or gave lectures in history and literature.

It has seemed worth while to quote the above passage not merely because it describes the school to which Mrs. Agassiz devoted eight busy years and from which she regarded Radcliffe College as an outcome, but especially because her effacement of herself in the description is peculiarly characteristic. That it is a case of Hamlet with Hamlet left out, so far as she is concerned, is apparent from Mrs. Curtis's narrative, which serves as a supplement to the above passage:

Lizzie's own share, as I remember it, was to hold the position of the head of the school with a general oversight of the pupils in all the branches. Even without teaching much care devolved upon her with the sense of responsibility in the schoolroom, added to the direction of her own household under these novel conditions. But all inconveniences were met by her with tact and sweet temper, and when at my father's death in 1859, she found that my mother dreaded returning from Nahant, where he had died, to [their house in] Pemberton Square, Lizzie arranged that she with my sister Sallie should spend the winter at Quincy Street. She could not have done this without Agassiz's approval, which he gave most willingly, for he had made himself absolutely one of us and was like a son to my mother; but then all duties devolved upon the housekeeper.

Mrs. Agassiz's part in the school is still more fully described by Miss Schuyler, one of her pupils, in the address published below in Chapter XV. The term, "Hostess of the School," that Miss Schuyler applies to her is significant of the unusual atmosphere that she gave the schoolroom. "She was always to me an ideal gentlewoman," one of the former pupils wrote long after the school days were ended, "an American lady whom any nation might be proud to claim as queen. I always recall her voice, remembering it with the admiration I felt at the time when she reproved her schoolgirls for their boisterous manners and troublesome behaviour in the hours when they should have been quiet, ending — 'I expect you to behave as you would in your mothers' drawing-rooms.'" It was in such wearisome matters of discipline and in the general supervision and direction of the whole that Mrs. Agassiz's principal share of the work lay. But one habit which became of great consequence to both her and Agassiz was formed in these days in the schoolroom. She always attended Agassiz's lectures and took faithful notes of them, which she afterwards wrote out. The practice thus gained proved of inestimable value to him for the preservation of later and more important lectures. It is true that having had no previous scientific training Mrs. Agassiz had to pass through a period of apprenticeship, in the course of which, as she often recalled with enjoyment in a laugh at her own expense, Agassiz one day on looking over her notes, said, "My dear, these are most gracefully expressed, but from the point of view of science they are such nonsense as I never uttered." But that she learned not to sacrifice scientific truth for the sake of a happily turned phrase and became a remarkably proficient assistant of Agassiz we shall see later in the account of the *Journey in Brazil* and her other writings.

Beyond her appearance in Agassiz's lecture-room some of the pupils have few recollections of Mrs. Agassiz in their school days. Yet, as she told them, she was "always there," ready to give them help, counsel, affection, and to do for them a thousand services that at the time they did not realize she was rendering them. A pleasant picture of her part in the school life is afforded us in a letter written to her on the fiftieth anniversary of the opening of the school by one of the first comers, who fifty years earlier had described her as "very pretty and sweet looking and very kind to us." "I have been recalling with joy," she says, "that beloved day fifty years ago when your school began. . . . I must thank you once more for us all for your great thoughtfulness in sending up to us in the schoolroom between two and three when we were eating our dinners there steaming plates of the best mutton broth I ever saw. How kind it was! And how welcome it was! You never taught me, but you often let me pronounce French to you. I wonder if you remember what you usually said after it — 'Surprising — the perfectly Yankee sound of it, though

THE AGASSIZ SCHOOL 51

you keep all the rules in pronouncing.' I think that remains true to this day."

By 1863 the purpose for which the school had been established was accomplished, and owing to the uncertainties occasioned by the Civil War it was given up. As Agassiz's income from his salary was at that time also increased, the pecuniary anxieties that had been so heavy a burden were permanently lightened. From occasional references in the letters given below it will be seen that the closing of the school was a great relief to Mrs. Agassiz. But by means of it she had been instrumental in freeing her husband from indebtedness and providing a sufficient wherewithal for the expenses of his family. Apart from the care and bringing up of her step-children, the school is her first important achievement. She was its originator and guiding star, although the brilliant light of Agassiz gave it perhaps its more distinctive lustre.

In order to keep unbroken the story of the school, some significant events of the period while it was in progress have been omitted. During these arduous years Agassiz's career as a naturalist was expanding, and he was entering upon one scientific undertaking after another, in all of which Mrs. Agassiz was his constant companion and helper. Her existence, in fact, from 1855 to 1865 cannot be understood without reference to the chapters in his memoir in which she has traced his activities through this decade of unremitting toil, when solicitude for his health, which suffered from the strain to which he was subjecting it, became an ever present element in her life. A few letters, however, selected from these years illustrate some of her more personal interests and also the spirit that continually animated her.

The first were written at the time of Agassiz's fiftieth birthday (May 28, 1857), which his students celebrated by a serenade on the birthday eve, arranged with the advice of Mr. Otto Dresel, — an occasion for which Longfellow's well-known verses, *The Fiftieth Birthday of Agassiz*, were written. Mr. Dresel's name deserves more than a passing mention here. A favorite pupil of Liszt and an intimate friend of Robert Franz, he had come with an established reputation to Boston, where he became an important influence in musical circles. Pupils quickly sought him for both vocal and instrumental lessons, among others Mrs. Agassiz and her sisters. In their case the friendship which usually developed between himself and his pupils was made the closer by his marriage with one of their friends, Miss Anna Loring, which led to his being a welcome and frequent visitor in the Agassiz and Cary households, where he usually added the pleasure of good music to that of his presence. It was, perhaps, in the course of the lessons mentioned by Mrs. Agassiz in this letter, that once when she was trying to take a very high note, Mr. Dresel exclaimed, "Ah, Mrs. Agassiz, keep that note for a fire." But her voice, a soprano, was considered very sweet and blended delightfully with Mrs. Felton's deep contralto and Miss Sallie Cary's mezzo-soprano when the three sisters sang, as they often did, in trio.

TO MISS SARAH G. CARY

Cambridge, May 24 [1857]

... Anna has promised to come and hear the serenade. As I wrote to you, Longfellow's words do not work very well for concert music, and Dresel was uncertain when I saw him last whether to make a song of it or adhere to his original plan of a quartette. Longfellow says he has written himself out on the subject with the first effort and his music will not come again at his call; so we must do with those words or none at all.

Did Dresel ever give you a song of Schumann's, the words being the instructions of the Scotch widow of the chief of some Highland Clan teaching her little boy how to steal when he should grow up to manhood like his father? It is the oddest song and of a decidedly questionable morality. Dresel likes it most exceedingly, principles and all. I was afraid he would give me the same songs you have, in which case I should have been greatly disgusted with my own performance of them, and had very little satisfaction in singing them. But he says the songs that are a little too high for you are just about right for me, so that I have quite a different set. I enjoy my lessons very much though often I find it impossible to practice at all between times.

I wish you would write me a little news of Mrs. Gaskell, if you see her. Her life of Jane Eyre [Charlotte Brontë] has interested me intensely. I have been living for the last week in that lonely parsonage with the populous graveyard before it, and the wild moor shut in by hills all around. When you read of Charlotte Brontë's uneventful life, pressed upon by a colorless monotony almost from the beginning to the end you understand for the first time what a volcano must have been pent up in her, that out of such an unvarying sort of existence as hers was, she should have given such a passionate expression both of happiness and suffering. Perhaps if she had found the natural food for her capacities, and her heart and head had not been so starved for want of nourishment from without, her imagination would not have gone on "weaving endlessly for her that story" which, as she tells us in *Jane Eyre*, she was never tired of listening to as she walked up and down the gallery at Thornfield Hall on cold and snowy afternoons. After reading her life I took up *Jane Eyre* again, and I could not help thinking what a delight it must have been to her to get out of the tedious realities of her Haworth home and live for a few hours Jane Eyre's tremendously exciting life. If I knew where to get them I should like soon to read the books of her sisters. I never finished them because they were so distasteful, but now that I know more of the women and their strange way of life, I feel an interest in their books.

TO MISS SARAH G. CARY FROM PAULINE AGASSIZ

June 2, 1857

You can't imagine what a pleasant week this last one has been, only it did not seem quite right, because the celebration of Father's birthday was a sort of thing at which you ought to have been present. Mother has probably given you a long description about it in her letters, so I shall only say that it would have done you good merely to look at Mother's and Father's faces during the serenade, because they both looked

THE AGASSIZ SCHOOL

so happy. . . . Mother and I arranged a quantity of flowers in Father's library. She put a large inkstand that she had bought for him, in the middle of that long table, then on one side of it was a bunch of lilies of the valley, on the other a vase of roses. Behind it was a large dish of flowers and back of that was a large bunch of flowers that Mr. Parkman had brought Mother the evening before, with just fifty kinds of flowers in it. Then on one of the tables near the window there were three more dishes and one bunch. It looked very pretty.

A little later in the same year Agassiz declined an offer of the chair of paleontology in the Museum of Natural History in Paris, preferring, as he said, "to build anew in America rather than to fight his way in the midst of the coteries of Paris." An extract from a letter written by Mrs. Agassiz to Mrs. Cary on this occasion is given here; it is striking because of her complete silence as to any preference that she may have had in regard to her husband's acceptance or rejection of this enviable position. Her personal wishes were entirely merged in his professional interests and responsibilities.

TO MRS. THOMAS G. CARY

Nahant, September 19, 1857

I MUST tell you that yesterday Agassiz received a letter which if it had come two years and a half ago before the scheme for the book [*Contributions to the Natural History of the United States*] and the schoolroom was formed would have taken us out of this country at once, and I should have been living in Paris to receive you when you came out this spring. The letter was an official appointment to a professorship in the Jardin des Plantes. It seems strange that Agassiz should be in a position to decline a thing which when he was a young man he looked upon as the very brightest summit of his most ambitious dreams of success; for there are no higher scientific positions in Europe than those of the professors at the Jardin des Plantes. Even now I think it cost him something to resign it, but he can do unquestionably more for science here than there and his domestic relations here are so delightful that he does not hesitate. It would give him a house in the Jardin, the command of the best museums in Europe, for all care and expense assistants and appointments of all kinds provided, and a salary much better for Paris than that he has here, — about $2000.00, I believe, and the only work exacted is twenty lectures a year. It has a very tempting side, but he intends to refuse it at once, so don't be frightened.

In the following year partly as a result of Agassiz's tacit implication by his refusal to leave Cambridge for Paris that America was the chosen field of his labors, the Museum of Comparative Zoölogy (better known as the Agassiz Museum) was established in Cambridge. The organization and development of this Museum became one of the most absorbing works of his life and of his son's, and consequently occupied an engrossing place in that of Mrs. Agassiz. "I wish," she wrote once from Brazil, "I could find a gold mine in Brazil and carry it home and plant it in the Museum grounds and dig up a great lump as big as my head whenever anything is wanted there." That her interest was not purely sentimental, but was highly intelligent as well is shown by the letter given below on page 93, and also by the following quotation from an article in the *Boston Evening Transcript* for April 23, 1907, by her old friend Colonel Thomas Wentworth Higginson:

Nature had made [Agassiz] a delightful lecturer and art had added a skilful adaptation to his audience which secured an annual appropriation for his Museum for years after the Massachusetts Legislature had stopped all similar appropriations, except this. I once watched him in this process of persuasion when I went in with a large committee of that honorable body to observe his ways. Asked to address them he would begin in the simplest manner and shoot on and on, charming all with his heartiness; and when after a moment's pause some veteran country member would stumble in with the shy question, "This is most interesting, but may we not interrupt the professor to give us from a practical view some illustration of the actual value of all this that we may carry to the Legislature?" . . . Agassiz would eagerly say, "O, I thank the gentleman for his suggestion; that is just what I was coming to. I am glad to inform you that we have just in hand a new experiment which would alone be a sufficient vindication of this whole appropriation. . . ." This being explained with zest, they would break up the meeting and look about the Museum, when Mrs. Agassiz, as gracious and inexhaustible as her husband, would glide about among the members and where two were studying out the scientific drawings in utter hopelessness, would glide up behind them and say sweetly, "Oh, I think I am lucky to be able to explain that one drawing, for I happened to be near by when the Professor was explaining it yesterday. I think it represents, etc.," till both the inquirers felt forever armed with knowledge especially when supplied from the lips of a lovely woman.

It is no wonder that Agassiz once said with deep emotion to his friend, Professor Burt G. Wilder of Cornell University, "Without her I could not exist."

Immediately after the corner stone of the Museum was laid, in June, 1859, Agassiz sailed with Mrs. Agassiz and his younger daughter for a few weeks in Europe, where they made brief visits in Ireland and England upon his scientific friends, the Earl of Enniskillen and Sir Philip Egerton, and at Herbesthal in Rhenish Prussia upon Maximilian Braun, the brother of Cecile Braun, the first wife of Agassiz. The tie that connected Agassiz with her family had been created even before his marriage by his friendship with her brother Alexander (later Director of the Botanical Gardens in Berlin), which began in their student days at Heidelberg, led to his meeting with Cecile, and notwithstanding separation knew no diminution to the end of Agassiz's life. It is significant of Mrs. Agassiz's charm and her power of sympathy that during her stay at Herbesthal the brothers and sister of Cecile Agassiz formed an attachment for her that marked the beginning of a rare and lasting relationship. For long years she regularly exchanged letters with the daughter of Alexander Braun, Frau Cecile Mettenius of Berlin, although they never met until 1895, when Mrs. Agassiz was making her second visit to Europe. "The cousins of my children are to me like nieces and nephews of my own," she wrote to Frau Mettenius, and from the letters quoted below on pages 187 and 188 it can be seen how completely she appreciated and shared the admiration of Agassiz for Braun.

The summer abroad closed with a visit to Agassiz's mother at Montagny in Switzerland, where Mrs. Agassiz first learned to know personally the Swiss relatives, whose affection she speedily won and returned, and who always remained her intimate correspondents. The following letter was written from the house of Agassiz's sister, Olympe, Madame Marc Francillon, at Lausanne. His other sister, Cécile, Madame Wagnon, lived on a beautiful estate among the vineyards at the foot of the Jura, not far from Yverdon, in the little village of Montagny, which was also the home of Agassiz's mother. It is noticeable that in this letter Mrs. Agassiz refers to Agassiz as Louis, as she usually did in speaking of him to his own kindred, whereas in America she habitually called him Agassiz, the name by which he was invariably known among his American friends.

TO MRS. THOMAS G. CARY

Lausanne, July 30, 1859

HERE we are, dear Mother, in Olympe's house, where we arrived yesterday noon. I think I told you that on Sunday we had a visit at Montagny from Marc Francillon, who received me exactly like a brother, and on Monday Louis went to pass the day with Olympe at Lausanne. I thought it quite as well to let him go alone that they might have their good long talk together. We passed the day, Cécile, her mother and I, tranquilly together at Montagny. Indeed, I cannot tell you how delightful that absolutely quiet life at Montagny has been to me, and Louis has rested so completely there — truly rested for the first time since I have known him, and he shows it already in his appearance. People here seem astonished to find him so young and so unchanged. They all attribute it to my good care of him.

On Thursday we went on an excursion with Cécile and the girls. We went to the foot of the Jura in a carriage and leaving it at the entrance of a deep gorge that seems to go into the very heart of the Jura, we followed a narrow and picturesque pass that brings you after a two hours' scramble through superb scenery to one of those green cultivated spots that look so enchanting on the slopes of the Jura as you look up at them from below. There we found two or three houses, a little village where we stopped to rest and take some refreshment, a rural repast of Swiss cheese, bread and wine. I will not describe the view; you know the Swiss views and they defy description, but I will tell you something of the life of the people there that I think will interest you.

Cécile and I observed some women making lace at the door of the cottages and we stopped to examine their work. I don't know whether you have ever seen any of the beautiful lace that some of the peasant women make here, but it is exquisitely fine and of very graceful patterns. I wanted to buy some, and while we were making our purchase Cécile and I went into one of the houses where one of the lace workers lived. We came first into a little kitchen, where everything looked poor as poverty, but as neat as wax; a little fire burned in the chimney, and they were preparing their scanty supper. Out of that led another room not much larger, where we found the father of the family with two daughters working at different parts of music boxes. They worked before a window through which they looked out over the slopes of the Jura to Mt. Blanc, but I believe if Paradise lay before them they would not raise their eyes to look at it, they are so afraid of losing time; and the father told me that in beginning their work at four o'clock in the morning and never ceasing till nightfall they found it difficult to earn thirty cents a day. They were in rags, but they looked perfectly clean. In that little chamber slept the whole family, six in all, the father and mother, two daughters, and two old men, the grandfathers, and yet everything was as clean and neat as possible. One of the beds was not made and the father apologized, saying, "The two old men sleep there, and we like to let them rest, so (that) we cannot make their bed before daybreak as we do our own, and not to lose time during the daylight, we leave it till it is too dark to work." The mother worked at the lace, of which I purchased three yards, but only two and a half were finished. I said to her, "Never mind, I will pay you now and you will send it to me." As we left the cottage, Cécile said, "You will not fail to send the lace," and the woman answered with so much dignity, "We are very poor, but we are also honest." Afterwards we went to other cottages where they all looked excessively poor, but at the same time with a sort of self-respect and propriety that I could not help admiring in the midst of so much poverty. We saw one poor woman, a lace worker, that had twelve children, two of whom were paralyzed; but on the wall of her poor little room hung her white wedding wreath, framed, and kept as a precious souvenir of younger days. I feel that in going about with Swiss people I get a glimpse into Swiss life that strangers, travelling through the country as foreigners, do not often have.

TO MRS. THOMAS G. CARY

I WRITE you of everything that happens and sometimes I am so surrounded with new things and new people that all that has passed at home seems to me like some dim and distant dream. Perhaps for that very reason when it comes upon me like truth it overwhelms me even more than if I were at home. Still you must think of me as having a great deal of pleasure. It is a happiness such as I have seldom had in my life to see Agassiz united to all his relations and friends again, and they are so fond of him, so happy in having him that I cannot but fully sympathize with him and have my share too of happiness.

The "overwhelming" event to which Mrs. Agassiz

refers in this letter was the death of her father. The words with which she began one of her letters to him earlier in the summer, "You are to me the central point in the family picture," are a comment on their relations. Her affectionate reliance upon his judgment, which led her to consider his approval of her plan for the school as the first essential to the undertaking, will be recalled as well as her tribute to him quoted in the first chapter. There were in fact many resemblances in character and manner between them, and some of the traits that Mrs. Agassiz says were most marked in her father were also her own — purity of character, unselfishness of conduct, readiness to render unpaid service to public institutions, and facility of expression in writing; in Mrs. Agassiz, too, there were reflected Mr. Cary's habitual courtesy of manner and his tenderness to his children and grandchildren. His relations with his step-grandchildren were peculiarly charming. When, for example, at the time of Agassiz's second visit to Charleston, Ida and Pauline Agassiz were left with Mr. and Mrs. Cary for the winter, he showed himself the same attentive host to the two little girls that he would have been to older guests, giving them his company at breakfast and dinner, which their school hours prevented them from taking with the family, speeding them on their way to school and always ready with a welcome for them on their return; and a few years later, when he and Mrs. Cary were in Paris and were joined by Ida Agassiz on her way to visit her grandmother, he accompanied her to Montagny and completely captivated Madame Agassiz by the old-fashioned elegance of his manners, in spite of the fact that neither spoke the language of the other. Again and again in the life of Mrs. Agassiz there are examples of her devotion to her step-children and grandchildren, which bring vividly to mind these delightful reminiscences of her father.

Another event of the year 1859 that should be recorded here is the publication of Mrs. Agassiz's first book, *Actaea, a First Lesson in Natural History*, prepared under the direction of Agassiz. It appeared in two editions in one year and in a revised edition twenty years later. Here in the form of letters to her niece and nephew, "Lisa and Connie" Felton, written in clear and simple language, she tells of sea-anemones and corals, hydroids and jelly-fishes, starfishes and sea-urchins, and succeeds as she relates the fundamental scientific facts concerning them in conveying also the imaginative charm that attends their life. Its modest pages give promise of the flowing style that made her later writings on scientific subjects agreeable and successful. To appreciate any of these books it should be remembered that she had had no technical scientific training whatever, and that practically all the information conveyed in her published works had been acquired not by study of her own but by association with Agassiz. They are admirable expressions of her peculiar ability, which lay in the power of presenting second-hand knowledge accurately and with as much animation and authority as if it were the result of her own scientific observations.

Before the school closed the household in Quincy Street had seen changes, for the children of Agassiz had been married, Alexander to Miss Anna Russell, Ida to Major Henry L. Higginson and Pauline to Quincy A. Shaw of Boston, and as Mrs. Agassiz, with a pardonable mixture of metaphor, wrote to one of her sisters, she was already beginning

CAMBRIDGE 65

to see a cloud of children and great-grandchildren loom up before her as the support of her old age. In the following letter we see her exercising the functions and privileges of a grandmother, in which she became a past mistress as the years went by. Her grandchild, Louis, to whom she refers not only here but in many subsequent letters, was an unusually intelligent and interesting boy, the eldest son of Mr. and Mrs. Shaw, who fulfilled the bright promises of his younger years in his manhood, cut short all too soon by his early death. A few months before this letter was written the happy family circle in Quincy Street had been broken by the death of President Felton, to which Mrs. Agassiz refers.

TO MISS SARAH G. CARY

Schoolroom, April 29, [1862]

I STILL live and love you, though you may doubt the fact from my silence; but the days are so full, that night comes and finds half the things undone we mean to do in the morning. The children have occupied me a great deal lately, for they have found a very fascinating occupation that absolutely requires an older hand than theirs. There are pictures to be cut out and pasted on pasteboard, farms, mills, castles, country houses, paper architecture of all sorts and kinds, and it has furnished an endless entertainment for rainy and cloudy days. But they cannot get on without me as I have made a study of it and learned to put them up quite nicely, and it costs me a great deal of calculation to arrange my day so that I can save an hour or two for them and see the baby also.

You will find Louis wonderfully changed; he is full of fun and frolic, but I am very sorry to say very much afraid of strangers, so that unless he takes you for his grandmother (not impossible, my dear) you may find him a little shy.

I was delighted to get your letter about the *Atlantic Monthly;* every now and then I am seized with doubts and fears about the articles by Agassiz [*Methods of Study in Natural History*], and I like to be propped up with a friendly word about them. Agassiz says at his club Whipple, Lowell and Holmes praised him highly.

About this last May article I was especially anxious. You know the coral reefs are very attractive to me, and perhaps I have not understood any of his investigations better than those upon the Florida reefs; but I am conscious that what is beautiful and picturesque in his studies interests me more than what is purely scientific, and sometimes I am afraid that in my appreciation of that side of the subject I shall weaken his thought and give it a rather feminine character. It grows every month more fascinating to me to write them, and I hope we shall make another arrangement with Ticknor and Fields next year.

The school draws to a close, and a sense of freedom begins to come in upon us already. . . . You will not fully feel how blank a place Felton has left till you come home. Oh, Sallie, when I remember his constant little visits, half an hour for a chat, and feel that he will never come in again, cheerful, genial, affectionate; he never came that I was not thankful to see him;

he never went that I was not sorry to have him go. No one can ever fill his place, and I am glad that it is so. The fact that their places remain vacant forever here, is the best proof that our nearest and dearest are waiting for us elsewhere.

CHAPTER IV
LETTERS FROM BRAZIL
1865-1866

THE school days ended, the next important experience in Mrs. Agassiz's life came to her in 1865. In the spring of that year Agassiz recognized that his health demanded a change of scene and climate. He had for years been deeply interested in Brazilian fauna and had already received many tokens of sympathy with his undertakings from the Emperor of Brazil, Don Pedro II, who was a liberal patron of scientific enterprises. Realizing that new scenes alone could supply him with the relaxation that he needed, Agassiz had just decided to go with Mrs. Agassiz to Rio de Janeiro for the summer, when by the generosity of his friend, Mr. Nathaniel Thayer of Boston, his "pleasure trip," as he wrote to his mother, "was transformed into an important scientific expedition for the benefit of the Museum." The expedition sailed on April 1, 1865, for Rio de Janeiro, by invitation of the Pacific Mail Steamship Company on its admirably appointed steamer, the Colorado, which was bound for San Francisco by way of Cape Horn. The party consisted of Agassiz and Mrs. Agassiz, their friends, Dr. and Mrs. Cotting, six assistants, and seven young volunteer aids, among whom were William James and Mr. Thayer's son, Van Rensselaer. The first three months after landing were passed in Rio de Janeiro, the next ten in the Amazon region, the succeeding two in excursions among the mountains along the coast, followed by a brief stay in Rio before the company sailed for home on July 2, 1866.

Mrs. Agassiz was the self-appointed clerk of the expedition, keeping a careful journal of daily events, which she sent as letters to her family, taking complete notes of a course of lectures which Agassiz delivered on shipboard for the benefit of the young men of his party, and recording the less minute results of Agassiz's scientific observations, which he daily gave her, for he knew, as he said, "that she would allow nothing to be lost that was worth preserving." This varied material was later woven together into a narrative in the form of a journal with supplementary notes, combining personal experience and scientific facts; it was essentially the common work of Agassiz and Mrs. Agassiz and was published under their joint names in 1867 with the title, *A Journey in Brazil*. So complete a record of the sixteen months in Brazil is preserved in this book that a full account of them here would be superfluous. A sketch of the manner of life that they led is given by Mrs. Agassiz in a few words in the biography of Agassiz: "Much of the time Agassiz and his companions were living on the great river [the Amazon] itself, and the deck of the steamer was by turns laboratory, dining-room, and dormitory. Often as they passed close under the banks of the river, or between the many islands that break its broad expanse into narrow channels, their improvised working room was overshadowed by the lofty wall of vegetation, which lifted its dense mass of trees and soft drapery of vines on either side. Still more beautiful was it when they left the track of the main river for the water-paths hidden in the forest. Here they were rowed by Indians in 'mont-

arias,' a peculiar kind of boat used by the natives. . . .
When travelling in this manner, they stopped for the night,
and indeed sometimes lingered for days, in Indian settlements, or in the more secluded Indian lodges, which are
to be found settled on the shores of almost every lake or
channel. . . . Sometimes the party were settled, for weeks
at a time, in more civilized fashion, in the towns or villages
on the banks of the main river, or its immediate neighborhood, at Manaos, Ega, Obydos, and elsewhere. Wherever
they sojourned, whether for a longer or a shorter time, the
scientific work went on uninterruptedly. There was not
an idle member in the company."

Mrs. Agassiz's narrative in the *Journey in Brazil* is impersonal, and only in an occasional episode she inadvertently throws a side-light upon her own place in the party;
as, for example, in her description of an evening while she
was staying at the lodge of an Indian, Esperança, in a remote part of the Amazons, when after two of the natives
had danced an Indian dance for her, she executed a waltz
with Mr. Thayer to gratify their request that she show
them a dance "from her country." But in general she successfully avoids drawing attention to herself in her story.
She says also very little, if anything, of the pleasant intercourse with the Imperial family that was accorded her as
well as Agassiz, and that formed an important element in
their visit to Rio de Janeiro. She refrained, too, from publishing statements that might have been interpreted as
criticisms of a country where special favors had so recently
been accorded to Agassiz, yet that now have a certain kind
of historic interest as a description of conditions in the
Brazil of fifty years ago. A few selections from her Bra-

zilian letters to her family, accordingly, are given here which supplement those in the *Journey* and which serve to illustrate her character — her facility in intercourse with people of all stations, her unflagging industry, her affection for the children of her family, her absorption in the pursuits of Agassiz, her unfailingly even temper under conditions that, to say the least, were often sufficiently trying to deserve the name of hardships.

TO MRS. THOMAS G. CARY

Colorado, April 13, 1865

... OUR party is a very compact and pleasant one. As for Agassiz it is a pleasure to see him; he has not had a moment of discomfort since he came on board, and really the courtesy and kindness he receives from the Captain makes the voyage a perfect enchantment to him. He gives a lecture every day at two o'clock to instruct his young men in the kind of work he wants them to do, preparing the ground as he goes along. This lecture is given in the salon and attended not only by all the young men, who seem deeply interested, but by all the passengers, several officers of the ship and the Captain. This hour seems to be looked forward to with pleasure by all, and the lectures are really charming. One reason why I have not written home more regularly is that the recording of these lectures occupies me a good deal, and I want to write them out very carefully because I think it will be very interesting when the work is done to compare it with the plan and see how far the hopes and aims have been accomplished. ...

Our days pass somewhat after this fashion. Breakfast at half-past eight, and we linger over it talking for an hour or so; then I study Portuguese for a couple of hours and then write out the lecture of the previous day. After that comes lunch; then the lecture at two o'clock. After that I indulge myself with a little light reading till dinner at five o'clock. This important matter over (and the table is excellent), we sit on the guards and watch the crimson and golden sunset and the moonlight on the water, and so the evening passes till ten o'clock when we all retire.

I find our party very pleasant. Mrs. Thayer's son is a very amiable boy and always most kind and attentive to me. He is not very fond of study, but he joins me in my Portuguese lesson every day, and I think he is inclined to make the time of our absence profitable as well as pleasant. William James has always been an interesting fellow to me, bright, thoughtful, well informed, and a perfect gentleman; his companionship will always be a pleasure.

Rio de Janeiro, May 1, 1865

I THINK I finished my last letter to you just when Agassiz had gone on shore Sunday, the twenty-third, for his first visit to the Emperor. Agassiz was very much impressed with his intelligence, his very various information and keen discrimination of the men and books and subjects they discussed. When he came home he said, in giving an account of the interview, "To speak of this sovereign in the ordinary terms in which good monarchs are spoken of would be trite and conventional. One should speak of him as a man of high intelligence, of warm affections, of truly *human* character in the highest sense of the word."

On the twenty-eighth we went over in the steamer to meet the Emperor. Agassiz had told him what a magnificent ship she was and how generous the conduct of the Company had been towards the expedition, and the Emperor sent him word on Thursday that he would come out to see the steamer Friday. The whole thing was perfectly informal; no one was invited, and there were present only ten or fifteen persons beside the Emperor and his suite. The Captain received him with a royal salute of twenty-one reports from his Parrott guns, — the first full salute fired from them and delivered with a promptness and accuracy that did credit to the gunners. On arriving he passed directly through the great salon without stopping for presentation; his chamberlain, Viscount of Something (whose name I forget) was introduced to me and remained talking with me till His Majesty returned from making the tour of the steamer. I begged him two or three times to join the others, but he declined, and indeed I rather think the Emperor's inquiring mind makes it tiresome for his attendants to follow him in all his peregrinations, and as the Chamberlain was a remarkably agreeable man, I was glad of his laziness, which induced him to take the less fatiguing duty. The Emperor dragged his puffing, panting staff from top to bottom of the establishment — from the pantries and the butcher's room down into the infernal regions where the firemen live, — indeed, he may be said to have poked his royal nose into every crack and corner of the vessel. Mr. Billings said he heard one of the staff say to the other as His Majesty disappeared into a particularly dark hole, "Is he going in there?" — "Going in there? Yes, he's going everywhere." At last the exploration was over and "them kings" came to the surface. The Emperor returned to the salon, and then we were all presented, your daughter first (excuse the little piece of egotism, but I suppose you want to know), and then he remained talking with me for a little time until lunch was announced. His Majesty sat at the end of the table, my friend the Chamberlain placed me at his right hand, and the Captain's wife sat opposite. I was sorry to be separated from the old Chamberlain, because he would have helped me out; but he was placed on the other side, so I had to get on with royalty as well as I could, for the Captain did not speak a word of French. The Emperor was very gracious and talked with great interest of Agassiz, his expedition and so on. When the wine was passed, the Emperor declined, saying it was a rule of his never to take wine, and a rule he never broke except on extraordinary occasions. "However," he added graciously, "this is an extraordinary occasion. I will take a glass of champagne." We considered the matter a nice compliment. After lunch we went on deck. They remained for a while, the Emperor talking chiefly with Agassiz, and then they went off accompanied by another salvo of guns to the Emperor's pretty little steam yacht which was waiting for them. This is all I have seen of royalty so far, and I do not know whether I am likely to have any more formal presentation. From all I can gather the Emperor receives little except among his Brazilian subjects, has no public levees or drawing-room days.

TO MISS SARAH G. CARY

Rio de Janeiro, May 5, 1865

I HAVE had my first mountain ride, — on a horse instead of a mule, with no guide at his head, left entirely to his own discretion and my own, and I must say I have never enjoyed anything more in my life. But I must begin at the beginning. Mr. Billings [one of the passengers on the Colorado] has been insisting that one day before the Colorado goes we should all go up the Corcovado with him. Various things have interfered with the plan, but today Mr. Billings said that whatever happened he *would* go, and he, Agassiz and I, Dr. and Mrs. Cotting and Captain Coster, one of our fellow-passengers, went. We could drive as far as the foot of the mountain on the Larangeiras road. At this point we left the carriage, and your feeble-minded sister mounted a very tall white horse. It appeared to me a very perilous moment of my existence, and that I might as well make my peace with the world and consider this as the jumping-off place. But Mr. Billings is an excellent horseman; he took me under his especial charge and after a few minutes of hopeless misery I found myself perfectly comfortable, able to keep up an animated conversation and really enjoying myself very much. Well, we reached the top, the last mile of which is very steep, and the road being on this especial occasion very slippery from the fact that the last two days have been very rainy. It is in vain to try to describe a wide view, but certainly very few can combine so many elements of beauty, — the enormous land-locked harbor all hemmed in by mountains with its gateway open to the sea, the broad ocean beyond, the many islands, the nearer peaks with the fleecy afternoon clouds floating about them and a gleam of sunshine over them from time to time. It was most lovely, and the view not so distant that things lost their individuality. Well, my dear, it faintly dawned upon my mind occasionally that we had to get down from this peak, but I did not allow my thoughts to rest upon it for an instant. The awful moment came, however, like the dentist's and all other inevitable facts, and then I found that all the rest of the party intended, with the exception of Mr. Billings and Captain Coster, to walk down the steepest part of the slippery road and take their horses at a lower station. But I said to myself, "I shall never have such a chance to learn again as now when I have Mr. Billings to teach me, and if I'm going to baulk at the first dangerous bit of riding, how shall I get on when there are nobody knows how many miles of muleback before me?" So, as if it were quite my habit to mount horses on the tops of high mountains and slide down to the bottom, I announced my intention of descending as I had come, whatever other members of the party might do. You must remember that all the time I had Mr. Billings to encourage me, so after all I was not so very heroic as I seem; but still the path was too narrow for two, so he could only go before and give me occasional directions about my horse, and then I knew that if he came to any place he thought really dangerous he would help me to dismount, if there was time. However he really did commend me very much, and said for a person quite unaccustomed to riding it was a pretty good feat. You see, my dear, I must brag a little because by nature I am such an awful coward. I confess I was glad when the steepest part of the descent was over. But still I did enjoy almost the whole; the woods were so fragrant and so rich in color and foliage, the glimpse of view as we went along so enchanting and then the culminating view at the summit so impressive that enjoyment overpowered fear.

Rio de Janeiro, May 16, 1865

WE have just returned from an enchanting journey, about which I meant to have written you my freshest impressions, but on our return we are received with such an extraordinary avalanche of public news, good and bad, that it drives everything else out of mind. Richmond and Petersburg taken, Lee defeated at every point, the war virtually over — this was our first news as we neared the city on our return. And then came the terrible close giving an account of this wholesale assassination in Washington, which reads like the last scene in a five-act tragedy and seems utterly incredible. That three members of the Seward family should be left for dead in their own house with all the servants awake and about is most extraordinary. Lincoln's being shot in the theatre seems more possible. I still think we must be the victims of a gigantic street rumor. Here they brought the story with the most singular accessories; it is attributed to the Booths — the brothers Booth, as they call them, and they have got the name of J. Wilkes Booth in full on all the bulletins. This part must be a fabrication. It is in vain I state that Edwin Booth at least is a loyal man — he and Wilkes are in everybody's mouth as rabid secessionists, fanatics, etc. The whole thing seems to me like a bad dream and has a theatrical aspect which makes it the more strange that the Booths should be mixed up in it.

And now let me freshen up your thoughts and my own by an account of what we have been doing. . . . On Tuesday evening (May 9) Agassiz and I went to the Palace together that I might pay my respects to the Empress, which I had not yet done and which seemed to be considered the proper thing to do. The Emperor had appointed this evening for the visit, so we were sure of being received. At the door of the Palace were only one or two men in uniform, and we were shown through a number of long corridors and one or two antechambers where were standing a few groups of gentlemen, — chamberlains, Agassiz said, gentlemen-in-waiting and the like. It looked to me like a dreary kind of business, for there seems to me all the etiquette of a court here and but little of its gaiety or grandeur. One of these gentlemen showed us into a drawing-room where he asked us to take seats.

It opened into a long gallery and presently we heard some one coming down this entry in great haste walking very fast — as I supposed, an official of some kind to show us to the Empress. But it was the Emperor himself, who greeted us with all cordiality and invited us into an anteroom, — a handsome room, very high, with inlaid floor and dark heavy furniture. Here we sat down (I began to think the Empress was a myth) and had a long chat in which my own part, by the way, was that of listener. The Emperor wanted to know what Agassiz had been doing, inquired after the fishes, specimens, projects, etc., and was very genial and pleasant. After about half an hour's chat he asked us to come in and see the Empress and himself, ushered us into a third drawing-room ("veels vithin veels"), where he went to the door and called his wife like any other mortal. In rolled a little lady with the sweetest possible expression, who seemed very kindly and cordial, who invited us to take seats, and, if I may so express myself in the presence of royalty, "make ourselves generally at home." Really if we had gone to make a sociable call on some friendly acquaintance at home, there could hardly have been more ease. This royal pair are so truly well bred that it is impossible to feel any embarrassment. Their simplicity and frankness are quite republican, though I am afraid we must admit that their high breeding partook more, perhaps, of the aristocratic element. There is something peculiarly lovable and lovely about the Empress. She looks so sympathetic and motherly, and she seems to be thought among the people here the very best of women. One thing was quite interesting in the talk we had. The Emperor asking about Agassiz's impressions in Brazil, he answered, "Everything delights me with one exception and perhaps that exception is one which it would be indiscreet to speak of here." "No, no," the Emperor said, "be perfectly frank. I like to have your observations, favorable or unfavorable." "Then," said Agassiz, "I must say it shocks me to see numbers of negroes who are crippled in their limbs in consequence of the numerous burdens they carry on their heads. It is a hideous consequence of slavery here." The Emperor responded at once with the greatest earnestness, "Slavery is a terrible curse upon any nation, but it must and it will disappear from among us." The Empress took up the strain and said she considered it the saddest feature in their social system. They seemed to have no hesitation in expressing their horror and detestation of it and their hope that it would be rooted out. Some measures are being taken toward it, I believe, but it is one thing to theorize and another to practise. However, there is here not at all the feeling of the inferiority of the negro, which exists among us. The free blacks and the slaves live side by side, and the former may rise to wealth and good social position and even to distinguished places in political life. After as long a call as we thought it discreet to make, we paid our parting respects. One thing about the Emperor's way of saying good-bye is very funny, and Agassiz says he supposes it is in order to save strangers the embarrassment of backing out of his presence. He shakes hands and then he rushes out of the room, as if he were going to walk a mile in a minute on some errand of life or death. At first I thought he had gone for something and would be back again; but it was the last we saw of him.

TO MRS. QUINCY A. SHAW

Rio de Janeiro, June 5, 1865

I HAVE enjoyed every moment since I came to Rio. Besides the daily pleasure of the beautiful scenery, I have the delight of seeing Agassiz improve continually in health and spirits, and then time can never hang heavy, for I find plenty to occupy me in doing little odds and ends for him, keeping a record of the journey for his use, writing my home letters, reading, and so on. I have made some very pleasant acquaintances here, and they are all very kind to me. As for your father, he is nearly killed with kindness; he has hardly a moment to himself.

Tell Louis I think about him all the time. I never see a bright bird or a beautiful butterfly or a monkey or a parrot that I don't wish I could show it to him.

July 23

IT's almost like seeing the children to get your letters, though I confess it leaves a slight pang of homesickness. We are sure to find each other almost unchanged when we meet after a year, but every day is precious in a child's life, — their little, lovely ways, their new phrases, their cunning expressions, their wonderful, intuitive wisdom — to enjoy it all you must live with them and watch them constantly.

I enclose a letter for Louis with some bird's feathers and a bird's wing; and the two wings with green and blue feathers are, as I have marked them, one for Girly (I thought perhaps you could fix her up a doll's hat, or with a riband bow, perhaps, it would do even for her own), and the other for Georgie.

TO MRS. THOMAS G. CARY

Rio, [*June* 10, *ca.*]

LAST evening Agassiz gave a lecture in French on the glacial phenomena, at the Emperor's request. The whole affair was so different from such things at home that I must tell you all about it. In the first place, of course, when I heard that Agassiz was to lecture here it never occurred to me that it would not be open to ladies as well as gentlemen, but when I spoke of going, people stared and said that, to begin with, a public lecture was a thing unknown here, and that certainly no ladies would appear. I was very much disappointed and not a little indignant, for I had never heard Agassiz lecture in French, and I knew, too, that he would give his first impression of geological facts here, and I did not want to lose it. We spoke to Dr. Pacheco about it (the director of the affair), and he said that he thought it would be a very good thing, and he knew some ladies who would like to go, but the Emperor must be consulted. So the next time that Agassiz was at the palace he asked the Emperor.

He looked rather doubtful and said his own countrywomen were so ignorant they would not know what the Professor was talking about, but still he had no objection and would think about it, — but how should they be invited? "Not at all," said Agassiz, "let them come with their husbands and fathers, as they do with us, and make part of the audience, and if Brazilian ladies are so ignorant as Your Majesty represents them to be, the sooner you put them in the way of learning something, the better for them and for their children." So after some discussion it was settled that ladies should be allowed to go. Mrs. Davis came here to go with me, and we had the escort of several gentlemen, Agassiz having gone in advance. When we arrived, we were shown into a room where were the Emperor and his suite, and where we were received by the daughter of Dr. Pacheco. By the way the few ladies who did make their appearance were in a kind of demi-toilette; there was evidently great uncertainty as to the proper way in which to appear on so novel an occasion. I had some very pleasant talk with the Emperor, and after standing round for some time we were shown to the hall. Here were several seats reserved for the "strong minded women." In front of them was the Emperor's seat which had been arranged under a canopy as a kind of throne; but Agassiz told me when he first arrived he looked into the hall and seeing the royal arrangement desired them to take it down — said he had enough of that sort of thing and liked to avoid it when he could. So his chair only stood in front of a purple velvet curtain. Before him stood Agassiz with his blackboard. When the Emperor entered we all rose and remained standing until he made a motion for us to sit down. Now you know, my dear friends, that I have a weakness for my dear old philosopher, and I must say that I never saw him appear to better advantage in my life. He spoke with perfect ease, and though I have always thought that he expressed himself well and often eloquently in English, I felt that he would have been a more graceful lecturer in French. The room was crammed and even the entry. I saw ladies standing outside the door the whole time. Altogether it was a great success. There is to be another next week.

June 12

LAST evening was Agassiz's second lecture. The crowd was even greater than before and the Emperor sanctioned the presence of ladies by bringing his wife and daughter with him. These letters are intended only for you all at home, so I put in all sorts of personal details that I know will interest you, but would seem egotistical to any one else. I wish you could hear Agassiz lecture in French. I had not the least idea that English was so like fetters to him. In French the words pour out like a full river without let or hindrance. On the two evenings when he has spoken there has not been one moment's hesitation from the first word to the last. For the first time in my life I feel what a drawback it must have been to him to have to teach in a foreign language. The people here seem enchanted. The room was so hot last night that except [for us] distinguished people, "Emperors and sich," who sat near the door in reserved seats, it was almost impossible to breathe, the people were standing in great part, and yet for an hour and a quarter there was absolute silence; if any one made the least noise they were hissed down at once. After the lecture we went into an adjoining room where we had been received, and where we passed nearly another hour, while the Emperor rehearsed the lecture with Agassiz, questioning him on very many points. The man is greedy of knowledge, and I suppose the fact that he has such rare occasions for intercourse with scientific men makes him the more anxious to profit by the chances that fall in his way. Meantime I talked with his wife and daughter. They asked me a great deal about my travels and seemed to look with envy on any one who was free to go about the world. The Empress cannot leave the province of Rio Janeiro without permission from the government.

Monte Alégre, August 25, 1865

WE arrived here yesterday in the heat of the day, but I waited till nearly evening to go on shore, and then as Agassiz was busy with his fishes I took one of the young men (I have always plenty of beaux) and took a walk. On my return I met Major Coutinho [an officer of the Brazilian engineer corps detailed to the expedition by the Emperor], who had been on shore all day and who told me he had just sent out to the steamer for Agassiz and myself to pass the night at the house of a friend, as by all accounts the mosquitoes might be expected to swarm at the place where our boat was lying. I accordingly returned with him to the house and was already on friendly terms with the Senhoras and the children of the family when Agassiz arrived bringing my bag for the night. At about eight o'clock we were just about to sit down to dinner when we were called to the open door by the sound of angry voices in loud altercation that seemed to threaten blows before long, and were just in time to witness a village comedy that seemed to me more as if it had come off the stage than as if it belonged to real life. The village priest and the village doctor, who was also county judge and administered justice as well as physic, were having a free fight in the square for the entertainment of the neighbors who rushed out to see the fun. The priest's calf had strayed away; he sent his man to catch him; the Doctor of Law and Medicine said nobody should capture live stock in the square without his express consent and permission; and the two physicians of the soul and of the body (who were also, as we found, leaders of the two political parties in this remote little settlement) were shaking their fists in each other's faces and pouring out floods of abuse upon each other. At last some of our party collared the doctor and brought him in by main force to join our dinner and cool down his wrath, which kept exploding in sputtering speeches to the company at intervals for long afterwards. Dinner over, the large sitting-room was prepared for our accommodation, — the preparation consisting of two hammocks and a looking glass, and we presently turned in for the night. Our adventures were not over, however. Agassiz, being restless, rose at about one o'clock and thinking he would take a little stroll to refresh himself, went out in front of the house. There he found a dog entangled in the fence near by. He went to release him, and as he was engaged in his work of charity was saluted by a brickbat, a large stone meant for the side of his head, but which fortunately struck him only in the arm and gave him a severe bruise. The next morning we found that one of the blacks of the house, with his head full of the disappearance of the priest's calf and the last night's quarrel, I suppose, seeing a man at the fence, thought he was a thief after the live stock and flung a great stone at his head as the shortest way of finishing him and his depredations. If his aim had been as good as his arm was strong, Agassiz might never have finished his Amazonian journey. As it was, for a moment, he thought his arm was broken, but with a little arnica it is coming right again and the pain going off. Our good hosts were greatly distressed at this untimely disturbance of their hospitable intentions. However we had a very pleasant and a very amusing time notwithstanding our adventures, and had a good sleep undisturbed by mosquitoes, though I confess to lying awake for some time listening to the rats in the open ceiling above, who every now and then shook a little dust down on my head, suggesting the probability of their coming down themselves; and once I was awakened by the cat drinking out of the bath tub, which the negress had brought in and put down at the side of my hammock just before I went to sleep.

TO MRS. QUINCY A. SHAW

Manaos, September 8, 1865

SOMETIMES when the pictures of home come up so vividly it seems as if nothing one could gain in travelling could make up for the loss of not being with you all and with the children. My darling little Louis, if I could have him only ten minutes! My success in paroquets and parrots has not been good thus far. I have had a number given to me on the voyage up the Amazons; but they have all met with some ill fate, and the last was eaten by the cat in our little garden here. I shall try to bring one home alive to Louis, but I doubt whether I shall be able to. They say that unless you take them home in a very warm season, they are apt to die when they get to our coast. I have not yet seen a monkey in the woods. We hear them constantly, but they are so shy that on the faintest approach they are off.

Our life here is most interesting — full of adventures, full of experiences, which are to be remembered all one's lifetime for their novelty. Our party is a very pleasant one. James, who after his illness in Rio decided to go home, but afterwards changed his mind, is a delightful travelling companion. You know how bright, intelligent, cultivated he is — a fellow of vivid, keen intellect. He works hard and is ready to turn his hand to anything for your father.

Tell Louis if I don't have time to write a little letter today, I shall soon, and that I have his ring on my finger all safe and sound. But tell him the little paroquets I had used to come and sit on my hand, and wanted to nibble my ring with their little sharp beaks. But I had to drive them away and say, "No, no, little Polly, Louis made me that, and I can't have you break it." So then they used to fly away and find something else to nibble. This interesting nursery tale is for him and not for you.

TO MRS. THOMAS G. CARY

Manaos, November 18

I HAVE come to the conclusion that the Brazilians do not know either how to work or play. They have not that activity which makes life a restless force with us and gives it interest, neither have they that love of amusement that gives zest to the life of the Europeans. I have been several times to make calls here with the Barras, and so stately and solemn an occasion you cannot imagine, though they are perfectly familiar with the people we go to see. I feel as if they were all tongue-tied, and stumble about in my poor Portuguese simply because I feel the silence so oppressive that I must break it or get up and run out of the house. One of the habits here is to send word beforehand when you're going to make a call; this is in order that the lady of the house may have time to put up her hair and to put on her gown, which she never does, so far as I can find out except when company comes. If I could only command Portuguese enough, I think I should call all these unconscious sufferers together and tell them what benighted, colorless, crippled lives they are leading, surrounded by beauties which they never see, all nature tempting them to walk, to row, to open their eyes only and look; and they sit speechless and stupefied, putting on their fine things Sundays and festas to show themselves in the streets for a few minutes. They are more to be pitied than blamed, though; the men are to be blamed for it all. A woman is exposed to every sort of scrutiny and scandal who goes out unattended, and her only safety is to stay at home. I believe I am looked upon as a very extraordinary specimen; but everything is forgiven to a stranger, so I go on my way unmolested. When I am walking in the woods here, as I constantly do, I often meet Indian women (whose life is perfectly free and a thousand times pleasanter than the ladies' life), and they always express their wonder at meeting a "senhora" alone and ask me if I am not afraid. To which I always answer, "No, why should I be? The senhoras in my country walk and row and ride and are perfectly safe, and I think it's a great pity that your ladies never go out."

. . . Would Georgie like another feather for her doll's hat? Tell her as the winter was coming on, I thought she might like a change. I cut these from a bird which was beautiful when it was brought to us, but I see that they are losing some of their brilliancy. Give her my best of love and a kiss, and tell her that I hope they will not be spoiled before they reach Cambridge, and that they will be becoming.

December 11 (*on board the "Ibicuhy"*)

JUST as I was getting up from breakfast I was called out to see a Dr. Gustavo, one of the really good and respectable men of Manaos; he was the bearer of a package and a letter, which looked quite like an official document for the "illustrissima Senhora." The package contained a cacoa cup, mounted in silver, the work of the Indians and sent to me by several ladies of Manaos as a parting gift. I was the more touched by this, because the ladies who signed the letter (some half dozen) were not persons whom I had known particularly well here, or from whom I had had any cause to expect such a mark of regard. I send a copy of the letter *especially for you*, though I am almost ashamed to do so on account of its very flattering terms; but you must n't show it to anybody else, and you will see by it that there are some women here who are conscious of the injustice done them and that their feeling for me is rather because I am, as it were, an exponent to them of a freer kind of life than any they have ever known. The same day just before we went on board the steamer Agassiz received from certain gentlemen not exclusively from Manaos but from the province of the Amazons a box of a beautiful dark native wood (like ebony) and containing samples of all the most beautiful woods of the country in small neatly finished blocks. All was the work of the Indians of the Indian school here and bore this inscription: "Louis Agassiz, from his friends of the Amazonas."

These things make me feel as if I have been almost wrong and ungrateful to write you so strongly about the wickedness of Manaos, when we have received such kindness here, and yet what I wrote was strictly true. It is a bad place and the society is the worst I have ever known. These people are the exceptions and the greatest sufferers from their surroundings. The politics of Brazil are the curse of the country — unhappily it's a man's only road to distinction — no other merit (if merit it be) is acknowledged except that of political prominence, and men are ready to sacrifice anything for public office.

In this letter Mrs. Agassiz enclosed the following French translation of the note accompanying the gift from the ladies of Manaos:

Nous autres, les femmes à qui le monde s'obstine à refuser les grandes qualités qui ennoblissent la nature humaine, comme l'intelligence, la fermeté, le courage, l'amour de la gloire et autres, en nous laissant par grace la sensibilité du cœur, nous sommes heureuses de voir reunies dans votre seule personne ces qualités qui rehausées par votre extrême aimabilité et exquise délicatesse nous ont gagné votre amitié; agreez donc recevoir ce faible souvenir de nos sentiments à votre égard. C'est une noix de Coco montée en argent; elle n'a pas d'autre mérite que d'avoir été travaillée par deux artistes indigènes et de vous être offerte par l'amitié.

The following letter gives evidence of Mrs. Agassiz's intense interest in the Museum in Cambridge and its development. The apprehension that she expresses proved needless, for during the absence of Agassiz the Legislature of Massachusetts made a generous appropriation which was doubled by private subscriptions, so that accommodations were provided for the valuable collections that he was making in Brazil.

The book to which Mrs. Agassiz refers in this letter is *Seaside Studies in Natural History*, which she wrote in collaboration with Alexander Agassiz, who contributed the drawings and many of the investigations, while Mrs. Agassiz wrote the text with the assistance of his notes and explanations. It supplies a popular scientific treatment of the Marine Animals of Massachusetts Bay and was published in the hope that it would meet a want often expressed for such a seaside manual.

TO MISS SARAH G. CARY

Manaos, January 8, 1866

PEOPLE think that Agassiz has been working too hard on the Amazons, and so perhaps he has; but work is his life, and I am convinced that the journey would not have done him half the good it has, if he had not had the means of working as he has done. To have seen the means of making such a wonderful collection all about him and not to have been able to do it would have been to him a suffering worse than that of Tantalus of old — it would have been to see the promised land and not to enter it. I anticipate a coming cloud. Alex is alarmed at the size of the collections which he says will be too expensive to take care of, and the Amazons collections which he did not yet know about exceed all the rest. But I am not going to be discouraged. This most valuable and really most extraordinary collection (for with the facilities Agassiz has had from the Brazilian government he has had it in his power to do things on a scale such as no other naturalist has ever been able to attempt) will put the Museum at one stride far in advance of all other Museums in some departments. This is what was contemplated when the Museum was started, though no one could have dreamed of its being done so rapidly; and now if people grumble because it will cost five or six thousand dollars to secure the safety of such a collection, which could not under ordinary circumstances be had for ten times that sum, I must say I think the complaint is unreasonable. With such a spirit the Museum must always remain a third or fourth rate establishment and is not worth the care of a man of first-rate ability. Perhaps I am climbing a hill before I come to it, but I infer these difficulties from Alex's last letter. It never seems to have occurred to the friends of the Museum that it was to be a living thing, — to increase and develop, and therefore to be fed and nourished. If any institution of that kind does not grow and require every year larger means, it is dead, — and what is dead had better be buried forthwith. But you are not the wife of a scientific man ("thanks be to praise," perhaps you say, in Grandma's favorite ejaculation), and so perhaps this will not appeal to your inmost soul.

Pauline writes me that Louis is grown such an obedient little man, and gives up a great deal to the baby, saying, "I can do without it, perf'ly well, Mamma." I can hear him. The next great event is Christmas, of which we long for accounts. I do hope it was just as pleasant as could be, and that the children had a first-rate time. If Christmas is happy for them, it's happy for everybody.

I am anxious to hear how our little book (Alex's and mine) gets on. He has sent me some preliminary notices of it, but these don't mean much. My home letters say it looks well, but so far as I can find out nobody has read it, which makes me quite wrathy. I dreamed about it the other day, and thought it was a most obnoxious looking volume, — a thin book with very small, bad print, and that in order to make it sell, Alex had introduced a number of extraordinary sensation woodcuts, among which was a picture of a city with the plague. I suppose our next letters will have something more about it. After all writing books is rather a perilous business.

Pará, March 8, 1866

. . . As I retreat from my life of the last six months and have it in memory only, I begin to feel more than ever how much I have gained in picturesque images — things that I shall always enjoy as much perhaps in the retrospect as in the actual experience. I find too in talking with the people here that I have seen a great deal which persons who have lived all their lives in the neighborhood of the Amazons have not seen; the fact is that with the exception of the few naturalists who have made the journey people go up and down this great beautiful river for purposes of commerce only and stop only at the regular stations along the main stream; they don't go off into the byways and know little of the life of the "Setios" and the forest population. I was telling Donna Maria and a young friend some of my experiences last evening, and they really seemed as much interested as you would be at home, and said over and over again, "You have seen more and know more about these things than we do, though we've lived all our lives on the Amazons." Next week Agassiz is going on another excursion farther down on the coast. I am not quite sure whether I shall go with him. As I am going to have quite as much of sea voyages in the next three months as I care for (between our journey to Rio and our return to the States), I am rather inclined to stay quietly. Indeed after so many months of travelling, quiet is very grateful and if it were not that I feel bound as the Scribe of the expedition to gather all the material that offers for the journal, I should be rather inclined to be pusillanimous and rest on my oars for a little while. Of my longings for home I say nothing — what's the use? But I must say the idea of next summer at Nahant is a vision of rapture I hardly dare to think about.

Ceará, April 1, 1866

It is just a year today since we sailed from New York. My heart would have sunk if I had thought I should still have been writing to you from Brazil — it seems such a long time to be away. But I know that God is leading us wisely and it is my daily prayer that

He will bring us home to find you all safe and well.

We left Pará last Monday evening on board the Santa Cruz. It seemed quite like leaving a sort of home to come away from Mr. Pimento Bueno's. He has been so good to us and we have been there so long that we quite seemed to ourselves a part of the family. All the day his little girl, who is an interesting child and has something about her that reminds one of Louis, was bringing me little parting gifts, and the last hour before I came away she did nothing but wander from room to room, saying to everybody, "Can't you think of anything else to give to Madame? I can't find anything else to give to Madame."

April 6 (The village of Pacatuba at the foot of the Serra of Aratanha)

... HERE we are thus far on our journey. You know what we are looking for, don't you? This is a hunt after Moraines and Glaciers, and as Agassiz has found all the evidence he hoped for — "evidence of things unseen" I'm sure it is, for who would believe these tropical valleys were ever filled with ice, — the excursion has been a very successful one. But let me begin at the beginning. If you could have had a glimpse of us on Tuesday afternoon, you would have seen our cavalcade consisting of Agassiz and myself, he on a brown horse, I on a white one, armed with umbrellas and waterproofs (for at this season showers may be expected at every minute); Mr. Coutinho and another gentleman, the government engineer of the province; behind us a soldier, one of the President's guard who was to act as a servant; and bringing up the rear two small donkeys almost invisible from the amount of baggage they carried. But if you had seen the amount of worry and vexation of spirit before things could be arranged, you would understand how trying it is to travel in Brazil wherever the old modes of journey still continue. The delay about getting horses and servants, the way people promise and do not perform, the utter impossibility there is for the Brazilian mind to conceive that it's of the least consequence to anybody whether they do a thing tomorrow or a week or a month from tomorrow—of what consequence is it? There's no hurry.

Well, at last we were off. We were only to go a league from the town and sleep at a village called the Rancho. At nightfall we rode into the little cluster of mud houses all more or less surrounded with trees. We stopped at the end of the single street before a low mud house, which I suppose serves as the village hotel. . . . Well, perhaps least said about that night is best. The fleas were rampant, and I must say for my part I was very glad when five o'clock called us all to get up, for it was our plan to start at six. However, it's one thing to intend going anywhere in Brazil and another to get off. When we inquired after the horses they were not to be found; the constant cry in travelling is that the horses go off in the night, but it never seems to occur to anybody to tie them up. Where were the servants? Nobody knew. So there we sat waiting and losing the best hours of the morning till horses and men saw fit to turn up. At last we were off, Agassiz, Coutinho, and I going first, our companion waiting to look after the baggage. If you had seen me, dear Mother, on some parts of that day's ride I think you would not have believed your eyes. You would have said, "either our Lizzie has gone completely out of her senses and is downright crazy, or it's not she at all." What do you think, with my sentiments about horse flesh in general, of my fording streams with the water up to the horse's breast, so that I was in momentary anguish lest he should take to swimming? All I could do was to hold up my habit and tuck up my feet as high as I could, notwithstanding which they got very wet, and then cling for dear life. Luckily there were houses near the two deepest rivers, so I hired a man to come and wade before me to find the best places and take hold of the bridle when the bottom was bad; for often there were logs and deep ruts so that the horses went floundering about in a frightful way. Altogether I think it was the most perilous day's journey I've had yet in all my wanderings. Notwithstanding the anxieties Agassiz was happy for all his prophecies were fulfilled.

We came upon the tracks of moraines and all sorts of glacial débris, to the importance of which I confess I found it difficult to give my mind under the circumstances. We rode in this way a very long four leagues (some twelve miles) and did not reach our next stopping place till two o'clock, having started at half past eight o'clock in the morning. We were going to ask hospitality for the night from some friends of Coutinho and I was, oh, so glad when we turned off the main road into a little wooded path that led to their plantation. As we rode up to the house about a dozen women's heads appeared at the windows, greeting Coutinho in different voices of delight. He is such a favorite everywhere that under his wing we are sure to be greeted with cordiality.

Well, they all came down (and the all means a legion of daughters, some married and some unmarried) and made us most warmly welcome. They took me upstairs, brought me water and towels and a change of clothing, for the baggage had not come and I was thoroughly wet, having waded through all the streams in the country and been rained on into the bargain. They were all very short, little women like the Brazilians generally, and you may imagine I had some difficulty to get into their clothes. However, I finally made my appearance in a purple skirt and a bright blue rowdy, which I had to wear to hide the gaping of the petticoat. Then I went down and had coffee, and we passed the rest of the afternoon till dinner in playing and singing. The girls are very bright and intelligent and two of them very pretty. They really have a great deal of natural gift for music, especially one of them who sings in a very effective way.

The first thing that we heard was that the journey to Baturité was out of the question, that is unless we were prepared to pass an indefinite time. The river was greatly swollen by the rains, and if we passed it we might be caught on the other side and not be able to get back for many days. Agassiz did not care, however, for he had already seen enough to show him that he had all he needed in this immediate neighborhood and that, though it would be interesting to see the higher Serra, the mountains and valleys in the midst of which we were gave him all the phenomena of the ice period. We therefore stayed in the comfortable quarters where we were for two days, being made most warmly welcome. I did not go out except to walk in the garden and bathe in the brook near by, but Agassiz was very busy careering about on horseback (which he says he hates worse and worse every day) and following up the investigations he is so much interested in.

TO MISS SARAH G. CARY

Rio de Janeiro, May 7, 1866

I WISH that I could photograph my life here for you. It would make you understand why I feel that though I long for home with painful intensity, I yet am sure that I shall sometimes have a sort of yearning for my Brazilian life — for the climate where one never thinks of closing door or window, for the liberty of action which such weather gives, for the enchanting scenery which I know I can never forget. So far as personal relations are concerned and indeed everything which regards culture and even civilization, six years with us is worth twenty here; but still for that enjoyment which nature gives I shall always feel that I owe a lasting debt to Brazil and shall always have a lingering affection for it. Then I have formed a few very pleasant friendships here.

Agassiz is giving three or four lectures here, but he

gives only one a week, and as he does this at the request of the Emperor who was very anxious that he should give some account of the journey, he has great pleasure in doing it. The Emperor has been so kind to him and so generous to the expedition that he is only too glad to express his gratitude in some way. The first lecture was last evening and crammed to suffocation. If our party (myself and one or two ladies who were with me) had not entered in the wake of the Imperial family, we should have had a poor chance for even the seats reserved for us. I wish you could see these Imperial people — they are so simple and so gracious in their ways. I had not seen any of them since my return though the Emperor had asked Agassiz to bring me to see the Empress. But we had been out of town and not able to go. When they came into the large room where they stop before going in to the lecture, the Emperor and Empress came across the room and talked to me for some time about my travels, and the younger daughter whom I had known before introduced me to the Imperial Princess, who was in Europe when I was here last spring. I don't tell you this as any special mark of their attention to me, because they would do the same for any one who had any claim on their attention; but only as showing you what frank and affable manners they have. The Emperor had read my article [*An Amazonian Picnic*] in the *Atlantic Monthly* [for March], and was very pleasant about it. This is a strictly private epistle, because I don't tell these little bits of egotism for the benefit of anybody but my own family.

CHAPTER V
CAMBRIDGE — *A JOURNEY IN BRAZIL*
1866–1871

AFTER Mrs. Agassiz's return to Cambridge from Brazil her most important occupation outside of her family cares was the preparation of *A Journey in Brazil*, which, as has been said, was published in 1867. Her record of Agassiz's life in the next four years as during the previous decade is almost the record of her own, so intimately was she connected with every phase of his interests and experience. In less than two years after the expedition to Brazil his health, in spite of the benefit derived from his stay there, broke down again under the pressure of his work for the Museum, and although there were periods when it was once more vigorous, it always remained precarious and a cause of anxiety to Mrs. Agassiz. In 1868 he was able to take an extended journey through the West for scientific purposes on which Mrs. Agassiz did not accompany him; but in the following spring she went with him on a dredging expedition off the coast of Cuba and Florida, of which she wrote an interesting and picturesque account in an article, *A Dredging Excursion in the Gulf Stream*, which appeared in the *Atlantic Monthly* for October and November, 1869. Glimpses of her life during these years — 1866–1871 — so full of occupations, are afforded by the following extracts from her letters, written for the greater part to her mother and sisters while they were in Europe.

TO MRS. THOMAS G. CARY

Cambridge, October 26, 1867

I KNOW that you will be grieved to hear that we have had very sad news of our dear Agassiz's mother this week. She is very feeble and at her age there can be little strength to rally. Had it not been for the hope I have always cherished that we should be allowed to have one more meeting, that perhaps God would let her pass gently away with all her children about her, I should pray that the end might rather be hastened than deferred, for great old age is not a blessing; but it is hard to give up this hope — and if I feel it a disappointment, what must it be for Agassiz. Poor Agassiz! he feels it so bitterly, but he works with the greater intensity the more unhappy he is. It is strange, but it has always seemed to me that intellectual life was to Agassiz what prayer is to others — an act of adoration and the nearest approach to a communion with God. He turns to it in every trouble and always seems to find calm and resignation.

November 18

WE have had a very pleasant week since I wrote you last, — still awfully busy on account of our "literary labors"!! But the guns will soon be fired for the conclusion of the Brazilian book, whether over its untimely grave or for its success remains to be seen. The most absolute failure shall not prevent me from enjoying the rest and freedom of being fairly rid of it. I shall feel as I did when the school was given up;

CAMBRIDGE—*A JOURNEY IN BRAZIL*

and yet I have a kind of fondness for it, too, just as I had for that, because I had worked at it with Agassiz, and we have had so much pleasure with it together. Only we are both tired now and shall be glad when it's fairly done.

November 25

YOU will be sorry to hear that the news we have been expecting, or rather fearing, for several steamers, has come. Agassiz's mother died on the eleventh. The letters are lovely about it, remembering him, thinking of him to the last, sending flowers to be placed before his picture. But still with everything to comfort him, you know this is a terrible parting for Agassiz. Not but that he feels as if in a certain sense she were nearer to him than ever before, but still they are no longer on the same earth together. He works and takes refuge in occupation.

December 17

Do you remember that we are approaching Christmas? What shall we do without you all? Our presents will soon be distributed, but I mean to have some games for the children and make it as gay as I can for them. Our tree is already mounted, and Louis has come to pass the week and help Mary Anne, whom I have got in for the occasion to gild nuts and dress the tree. I mean to take just as little trouble about it as possible and be as fresh as I can for the day when it comes. It is delightful to have Louis, and the little man is as happy and good and busy as he can be.

December 25

WHILE Christmas is fresh in my mind I must write you about it. I dreaded [it] this year, because when you were all away it seemed to me I could not make it pleasant. But I believe because we all feared it might be dull, we "made an effort," like, or rather unlike, poor Mrs. Dombey, and we really were very cheerful. I must say, though I say it that should n't, the tree and the room did look lovely. Ida and Henry who had never seen it upstairs with all the green boughs and garlands and crosses were delighted. Then the children were so enchanted with their presents and so delighted with the tree that it made everybody else gay.

TO MISS SARAH G. AND MISS EMMA F. CARY

Cambridge, January 8, 1868

I HAVE been waiting for a quiet minute to write to you, for you are both so delightfully associated with the Brazil book that now it is finished and the great burden and responsibility is off my mind, I long to talk to you about it and to share with you some of the pleasant results. As to its ultimate success, sale and that sort of thing, I know nothing. It only makes its appearance in the shops today, though it has been bound for a fortnight past. I only wanted you to know, while they are fresh in my mind, the judgment of the few friends who have seen it in its finished form. Knowing all my anxieties about it in matters of taste, style, etc., and knowing too how my highest aim was to show Agassiz — the comprehensiveness of his aims and the way in which he carried them out — you will understand what pleasure these things have given me. Mr. Peirce writes to me, "It is elegant in style, in the most refined good taste, and in all ways worthy of science, our country and our age. But its highest attraction is that it contains such a perfect portrait of our beloved and great-hearted Agassiz. I did not know that you were such an artist." Was n't it lovely that this should come to me the very first thing? It was perfectly spontaneous. I had never talked to the Peirces of the plan of the book, or of my aims in it, and I felt that the picture must be there or he would not have found it. Longfellow's note is longer, but I extract for you part: "The idea of mingling the two Diaries is most felicitous. It is like the intermingling of masculine and feminine rhymes in a French poem. In fact the whole expedition is highly poetical and honorable to all concerned. There is nothing like it since Hipparchus sent his fifty oared galley to bring Anacreon to Athens."

Holmes writes to us together. "United in your book," he says, "you shall not be divided in my note." He writes after having read the whole and says, "It is a new world to most of us, to me certainly, and I am sure we all feel that it is a rare privilege to wander through it, under the guidance of such explorers. So exquisitely are your labors blended that as with the mermaiden of ancient poets, it is hard to say where the woman leaves off and the fish begins. The delicate observation of nature from the picturesque side relieves the grave scientific observations and discussions in a most agreeable manner. If I divide my admiration equally between you, it is because I feel that rare as it is to find a great observer who is also a reasoner and an organizer, it is as rare to find such a mate for him as the lady who keeps side by side with our Professor in all his travels through the realms of space and of thought."

Dr. Peabody, to whom we sent it, writes a very cordial note in which he says, "I have already read enough to know how largely all lovers of good letters are indebted to you and Mrs. Agassiz for a work as charming as it is instructive and as rich in material as it is graceful in execution." He has seen Agassiz since and spoke very warmly about it. I waited with special anxiety for Lizzie [Cabot] Lee's verdict; I trust so much to her exquisite instincts in all matters of taste and culture, and I thought I could judge by her note whether anything had shocked or even displeased her. She writes after having read it and says, "It seems to me you have avoided all the shoals and quicksands that writers of such books are apt to fall into. It has left a charming impression on my mind of having travelled with you, and my dreams are full of blue butterflies, passion flowers, paroquets and rushing torrents."

You see all these notes touch upon the points about which I was most anxious, and whether the book is generally liked or not — is attractive to the public I mean — I feel reassured; I feel as if I had not committed any gross blunders.

The book looks well; there is but one very important misprint which spoils one of my most cherished sentences — and the illustrations are much better than we expected. When I remember, Sallie, the readings with one foot on the fender last winter, the doubts and questionings and anxieties in my mind, and then the proof sheets last summer, dear Emma, I feel profoundly grateful to be so safely through and to have had such help and sympathy from you both. How little we thought that your first tidings of the finished book would be in Rome! What a strange game of consequences this world is! I want very much to send the book to Mother and you all, but Charles Curtis says it would be frightfully expensive. I'm going to see Fields about it today, and we shall manage it if we can. Agassiz longs to have it in Mother's hands; he says of his own dear mother, "If she could only have seen the title page, only have seen our two names together!" It is so different not to have her in the world. How much Father is in my mind at this time I cannot tell you. I, too, feel how I should have enjoyed taking the book to him, showing him all the comments upon it. He would have been happy about it I know. Mother will say he knows all about it, but I don't feel as if where he is now any earthly success would touch him as nearly as it would have done here. Nearest to the kind of sympathy I should have had from him I got from the dear Aunts at Chelsea. One of my greatest rewards has been to see the pleasure and fresh child-like interest they feel in it. It is so great a thing to be able to give enjoyment to your very old friends. . . .

We are going to Washington next Monday, and I hope the change may be refreshing to Agassiz. I must tell you something Louis said yesterday; the scamp, he grows funnier every day. He was wishing that I would n't go to Washington, and I said I must be with Grandfather. "Oh," said he, "can't you let sixty go alone and forty-five stay at home?" He heard me say a day or two before that his Grandfather was sixty and I was forty-five, and we were both growing old. He is a fascinating child to me.

Good-bye. I wanted to pour out my heart to you, and here it is with all the fine things people have said of me, but it would be absurd to make any apologies about egotism to you. Talking to you and Mother is like talking to myself.

TO MISS SARAH G. CARY

Cambridge, February 16, 1868

OUR copper mine is working well — the first edition of the book was disposed of in about three weeks and the second is already before the public. I do wish you had been here to sympathize on the spot with all the pleasant things that have been said and written to us about it. It seems egotistical to repeat them all, but tell this to Emma from Longfellow, who has been delightful about it and always speaks of it as "your beautiful book." He says his present reading of Buffon's old saying, *le style c'est l'homme* is *le style c'est la femme.* "That," he adds, "is my little joke about it." It seems absurd to write all these little things, but if we were together it would be so natural to tell them. We heard yesterday from Vogeli who made the French translation and has just returned to Paris with it. Hachette (the Paris publisher) is going to make an *édition de luxe* with forty illustrations and maps and another cheaper one without illustrations; also to publish extracts with plates in his illustrated journal, the *Tour du Monde*, which is circulated in several languages. This will be nothing to us in a pecuniary point of view, but will give a wider circulation to the book.

Do you see enough of the papers to know how President Johnson is carrying on — as furiously as Mount Vesuvius with all the spit-fire element and none of the grandeur? He really seems insane with passion and does the most unaccountable things, or rather tries to, for he has no power to carry them out; as, for instance, this last act, creating an entirely new and most powerful office for Sherman in order to annoy Grant apparently and separate two good friends. Fortunately Sherman will take no part in this trick and declines to accept the office even were it confirmed by the Senate. You know Grant has given deadly offence to the President by his course about Stanton.

Imagine that I'm going to open a series of teaparties tomorrow evening — that is, it will be a series, if the first turns out to be pleasant; if it's a failure I shall allow it to be the last and consider myself quenched. I came home from Washington, where people receive in a very easy and informal way, fired with the ambition to set up a simmering teakettle and "call my neighbors in." Somehow or other since I returned to Cambridge the frost of New England begins to settle over me, and I am afraid that no amount of tea will make people sociable. However I'm going to begin tomorrow with a judicious selection of Cambridge neighbors and a sprinkling of Boston, and see how I fare.

March 10

I HAVE set up a teakettle and called my neighbors in, as I threatened in my last letter, and greatly to my surprise my neighbors came and seemed to have a good time. I can hear Sallie say that it's another reason for gratitude in being out of Cambridge, if Lizzie is going to undertake to have tea-parties. Sisterly affection would oblige her to come and how she would hate it! Emma would like it and be all ready to help me.

Yesterday we dined at Tom Appleton's [the brother-in-law of Longfellow]. The dinner, by the way, was given to us in honor of the Brazilian book, and one of the ornaments was a very brilliant Brazilian parrot in ice, with a superb crimson sherbet head and every conceivable shade done in various kinds of water ice. It was a very pretty device and made a great deal of fun. Tom Appleton has been very sympathetic about the book — "Such a charming book," he says, "and so ladylike."

Nahant, September 5, 1868

AGASSIZ, I suppose, is now in Denver. It was hard for me to make up my mind to his going without me.

I had thought he could never make another journey of any importance alone, and especially I had thought we should be likely some day or other to go out to the Far West together, perhaps across the Rocky Mountains to California. Apart from the interest and enjoyment of travelling with him, it makes me so much more efficient in writing out his results when I have been on the ground and watched the course of his work. But in this case it was all settled for me. He was invited to go on this journey where no ladies were admitted and there was no question about the importance of his accepting it. He wanted change desperately and perhaps it was better I should not go. I know too much of his anxieties to be the best companion for him when he wants to forget them.

September 11

You know Agassiz is away since the first of August. This strange summer is drawing to a close, and I meant to move up the week after next. I am chiefly occupied now in making the days pass. Thank Heaven, this absence of Agassiz only makes me the more certain that the romance of life does not diminish with time, and so I find the weeks of waiting rather long.

Pauline is coming down tomorrow with the children, of which fact by the way I ought to be profoundly ignorant, for it's a plan of Louis' to surprise me. He made all his arrangements with Miss Lyman, who was to keep me at home "for sure" but by no means to say why, only if I asked, to answer that she knew a gentleman and two ladies who were coming to see me. The scheme was well laid, but I met Ida who told me she was coming to pass the day with them here. Of course I shall feign profound astonishment, but it's perhaps as well that I knew, for I was in town today and put a few appropriate tributes to the occasion into my bag.

Pauline came with the children and they were perfectly satisfied with the effect of the surprise and never dreamed that it was not complete. Even the sponge drops and the plums and the little horn of candy did not enlighten them, and Louis said, "Well, Grandma always does have such good things."

A notable event of the next year, 1869, for Mrs. Agassiz as well as for Agassiz himself was the Humboldt Celebration held in Boston in September under the auspices of the Boston Society of Natural History, at which Agassiz was invited to deliver the address.

TO MRS. QUINCY A. SHAW

If your father delivers the address at all as he has prepared it, it will be really interesting, I think, and from the nature of the subject wholly different from anything you have heard him give before. He means to have it ready for reading in case of necessity. Still I think the whole thing is now so completely in his mind that if he is in good mood he will be able to throw aside his notes and trust memory and impulse. I hope he will, for he speaks with so much passion and power, and he does not read well. For the last week, we have lived Humboldt together night and day. Having collected all the materials, he has given the whole week to arranging them, rejecting all but the salient points and giving himself wholly up to the memory of Humboldt as a man and a companion. I really never felt the sweetness and power of your father's intellect as I have while he has been renewing with me all his recollections of Humboldt; and I think the result of all his contemplation of him has ended in a higher appreciation of his character, so that he comes to the work with a great deal more enthusiasm than he had in the beginning. Everything depends upon his mood. You know how impulsive and emotional he is. If he feels right, I have no doubt he will interest and satisfy people.

Seldom had Agassiz's gifts as a speaker appeared more brilliant than on this occasion. The emotional strain, however, was speedily followed by a more imperative warning than Nature had yet given him that he must make less severe demands upon his strength. An illness followed, and a slow convalescence kept him a prisoner for many months, during which Mrs. Agassiz was his constant attendant. In the spring, on the advice of his physician, they went to Deerfield, a pretty village in the Connecticut valley, where the quiet surroundings and pure air proved so beneficial to him that by the autumn his recovery was complete. The following letter was written by Mrs. Agassiz toward the end of this stay in Deerfield.

TO MISS SARAH G. CARY

Deerfield, September 29 [1870]

THAT music of Mendelssohn's is certainly wonderful, and your letter was a singular answer to my thought.

The night we arrived here I was walking on the piazza with Agassiz; the village street so green and fresh last June was parched and dusty, and the katydids and crickets seemed singing by hundreds their high, sharp, meagre notes. I said to Agassiz, "I wish you knew the *Elijah* of Mendelssohn that you might feel as I do with this drought how wonderful the chorus is by which he describes the sufferings of the thirsty people and earth." Do you remember how all the high, sharp notes of the instruments seem to give that meagre dry character which is in the aspect and all the sounds of nature after a long drought? The next day when the relief came I felt still more how perfectly the music expresses the actual thing, and I only wished I could hear in the midst of the drenching rain for which every living thing seemed giving thanks the "Thanks be to God. He laveth the thirsty land, the waters gather, they rush along, they rush along." If we only had the best music ready for our needs, what a grand thing it would be at the breaking up of a drought from which the whole country has suffered to have those choruses sung in all the churches. But was n't it — I was going to say, curious — but after all only quite natural, considering the truth of the composition, that you and I should both be reminded of it and speak of it at the same time?

Do you know it was a real relief to me to hear that you had been at the Globe Theatre? I thought something serious must be the matter with you when Fechter's Theatre had been open for weeks and you had nothing to say about it. I hope you and I will go together sometimes and decoy Mother in, too, next winter.... It seems as if there might be a kind of revival of the good drama in Boston with this theatre and the interest private people of a good stamp and good dramatics take in it. To be sure, *Monte Cristo* does not look like an effort to elevate the public taste, for I suppose it's pure sensation stuff, but still that may improve with time....

Madame de' Chanal's letter interested us both deeply. I hope she is not wholly right about the republican party. I don't believe she knows anything personally of the people who make the best strength of the republicans, — the respectable merchant class, the wine dealers, the foremen of factories and such people, — among whom there are men of much steadiness and thoughtfulness and honesty of purpose. At least Agassiz thinks so, and yesterday he had a letter from a man with whom he has been in negotiation for an insect collection — a dealer in objects of Natural History in Paris — and he speaks with the greatest hopefulness and says the republic has done more in eight days than the Empire had been able to do in months. I am not sure but that the French will be glad in the end that Prussia did not accept peace on the conditions they offered. The French may yet be able to make peace on their own terms. I must say, if Jules Favre's statement is correct and correctly reported, I think the Prussians were very ungenerous or else they purposely offered what it was impossible for France to accept....

CHAPTER VI
THE VOYAGE OF THE HASSLER
1871-1872

BY the late autumn of 1870 Agassiz's health was in sufficiently good condition to admit of his accepting a proposal from Dr. Benjamin Peirce, the Superintendent of the Coast Survey, to form an expedition for deep-sea dredging, which sailed on December 4 of the next year on the Hassler, a surveying steamer bound for California. With him Agassiz had one of his students from the Museum, two other naturalists — the Count de Pourtalès and Dr. Franz Steindachner, — Dr. Thomas Hill, the ex-president of Harvard University, and Mrs. Agassiz. Captain Johnson, the commander of the vessel, and Mrs. Johnson, as well as the officers, took so keen an interest in the purposes of the expedition that they added greatly to the pleasure of the voyage. The course of the Hassler was directed first to the West Indies, from there to Rio de Janeiro, Monte Video, and the Gulf of Mathias, thence to the Straits of Magellan, where manifold beautiful harbors offered anchorages, and afterward up the Patagonian coast to Concepcion Bay, where she lay at Talcahuana for repairs, while Agassiz and Mrs. Agassiz went by land to Santiago and Valparaiso; here they were met by the Hassler, which proceeded to Callao on the Peruvian coast, then to the Galapagos, and ended her voyage by way of Panama and San Diego at San Francisco, entering the Golden Gate in August, 1872. Under Agassiz's direction Mrs. Agassiz

LOUIS AGASSIZ AND COUNT FRANÇOIS DE POURTALÈS

kept a record of the expedition such as she made for the Brazilian journey. This diary, however, was not fully prepared for the press at the time of Agassiz's death and has never been published as a whole, although portions appeared as three articles — *The Hassler Glacier, In the Straits of Magellan* and *A Cruise through the Galapagos* — in the *Atlantic Monthly* for October, 1872, and January and May, 1873; other parts were also published by Mrs. Agassiz in her biography of Agassiz. Since a fuller record of the voyage, replete as it was with unusual experiences, is worthy of preservation, and since Mrs. Agassiz's part in the company is highly characteristic, extracts from her letters that supplement the published accounts are given here, although some of them have less personal than general interest.

TO MRS. THOMAS G. CARY

December 12, 1871

WE are and have been all day floating along on a summer sea. You can hardly imagine waking in the morning so warm that it is a relief when the cabin boy brings me my bath tub full of fresh sea water. There is little to tell, but I wish you could see us as we sit on deck under our awning, I with my work in my lap and my book at my side, sewing sometimes, reading sometimes, talking, as circumstances favor. Agassiz is busy, of course, and he has begun as before on the Colorado to lecture on the work of the day, only here he lectures on deck. This morning I sat with my back to the little audience, but the Captain told me that nothing interested him more in the scene than to watch the faces of the sailors, some of whom were free and gathered round to listen. He said they looked so earnest and engrossed, and while Agassiz was describing with the help of the blackboard the structure of some of the little animals found on the gulf weed, Dr. Hill went out to them with a microscope and showed them the actual specimen through the lens. It does more than please them. It gives them such an interest in the work [that] they are indeed most ready to help. I am just going to bed having been on deck, with the exception of meals, from half-past seven o'clock this morning till half-past eight this evening. You who know only the North Atlantic voyages have little idea of this tropical sailing.

St. Thomas, December 19

WE are getting rather dissipated at St. Thomas. I began this day by rising at five o'clock and going on shore with Pourtalès. We had planned a walk to a hill-top called "Luisen Height," a pretty house on the very top of the edge of the island. Every native whom I have consulted on the subject looked at me in horror and assured me that it was altogether too rough an undertaking for a lady unless on horseback. It is in fact an easy walk of a mile and a half or two miles, perhaps, and at the hour at which we went not too warm. We were on shore an hour before sunrise; the town was just waking; the negroes just beginning to get their little trays and stands of fruit in order as we climbed the steep street towards the mountain. The streets are so steep here that carriages are out of the question. Some of the ascents are provided with a stair which brings you to a level terraced road cut into the side of the hill; another stair to a road above, and so on. Beyond the town we came into the winding path leading up the hill. The air was heavenly with every kind of delicious fragrance from the earth and trees; almost nothing was stirring. The lizards had not yet come out and even the birds had nothing to say or sing, except some doves that were softly cooing in the wood. We were half way up the hill before the sun had fairly risen, and though you always say the sun spoils everything by his intruding presence upon a sunrise, I must say that this time he came in beauty, gradually filling the great soft clouds on the horizon with light and pouring his radiance through a blue window in the midst of the mass down into the near valley, making it a vivid green while the hill behind remained in shadow. When we looked out we had just reached a point where the harbor with all its shipping and the many islands beyond lay just below us. We kept on, meeting only a negro now and then riding on a donkey between laden panniers in which he was taking milk or vegetables to market, till we came to the house on the summit. There I must say the view is startling. You stand on the edge of the island and look down to the sea on either side. Many beautiful smaller islands break the view on both shores. Just below us we looked down upon a crescent shaped bay where hundreds of pelicans were breakfasting upon shoals of fish. We sat for a long time on the house terrace talking with an old negress who keeps the place, on starvation terms by her account of herself and by her looks, in the absence of the family. Altogether we had a most lovely walk, and Pourtalès enjoyed it as much as I did. We returned to the ship by half-past nine o'clock with an appetite for breakfast.

TO MRS. THOMAS G. CARY

Government House, Barbadoes [December 29]

IT happens we are staying with Governor Rawson, ... at one of the most charming of tropical country houses, a wilderness of enormous rooms with balconies and *jalousies*, and breezes blowing through in every direction. Our host is the most cordial, affectionate man with charming tastes, quite engrossed with his collections, which are arranged in a great central hall of the house with an eye to artistic effect, and with his fernery where one can sit in the shadows and see the ferns kept moist by the play of the fountain on them in a soft mist, and by his gardens where we recognize old Brazilian friends — the crimson Poinsettia (the "Star of the North," as they call it here) and palms and blooming garden shrubs which I have never seen since the first South American journey. All this is very pleasant, and we enjoy it while we may.

At Sea, January 12, 1872

MY letters will be dull enough, for since we left Barbadoes there is nothing to record but an uneventful voyage, very rough during the first part for a week or so, but very pleasant and calm for the last five or six days. What do we do? For my part read, read, read: four volumes of *Froude* are already disposed of and much of my light literature devoured also. I read German every day with Dr. Steindachner, who is most kind in helping me, and then I read aloud a good deal to Mrs. Johnson. I have been reading *Jane Eyre* to her. I felt more than ever in reading it with care that in spite of its faults, and it has great ones, it has wonderful originality and beauty, the true ring of genius, — and it has a high moral aim, too. Then we watch the Portuguese men-of-war on days when they are plenty, and see occasional troops of flying fish and many phosphorescent creatures floating by at night. Still on the whole the sea is a niggard of its treasures — when one thinks how full it is of things, the sight of which, were it only a single one, would make a day rich, and after all how little one sees, it makes you quite discontented. I crave a whale or a dolphin; I would not despise even a shoal of porpoises, and day after day passes and the sea gives us nothing but itself — *ad nauseam,* in the truest sense of the words sometimes.

TO MRS. THOMAS G. CARY

Harbor of Rio de Janeiro, January 23

HERE we are once more in this wonderful country, which seems to me even more beautiful than when I first saw it. We rose early this morning and were on deck before sunrise, for the sail along the mountainous coast and the entrance into the harbor is not to be lost. It impressed me even more than the first time, as everything does when it has the charm of familiarity and association and suggests so much more than itself, — something that is personal to you over and above its own external features. We have been anchored only an hour but have received the visit of the doctor and the washerwoman, always the first comers, and also a messenger from his Imperial Highness, asking the names of the party. The oldest daughter of the Emperor (his only child now, poor man) with her husband, the Conte d'Eu, have the regency in the absence of their father.

Rio de Janeiro, January 25

YESTERDAY, the day after our arrival, the Chamberlain of the Princess came to say she should be in town with the Conte d'Eu in the afternoon and wished we could call if we were in town. We went, of course, and had a very pleasant visit. They were quite alone, having sent word that we should come before the hour of their reception. You know we knew them when we were here before. She has acquired so much gentleness and ease of manner, and she combines the sweetness of her mother's expression now with the decision and intelligence of her father. The Conte d'Eu, since he finished up the war so honorably for the Brazilian people, is their idol. He is what he always was, gay, easy, cordial, and with the self-possession and unconsciousness of perfect good breeding. They bade us good-bye at the hour of their public reception and asked us not to fail to come and see them at Petropolis.

They are not now in Rio de Janeiro, but are living at their summer palace in Petropolis and were in town only for the day.

This morning we took the boat for town at half-past six o'clock; it is so hot all excursions must be made at an early hour. Arrived in town, we took the horse cars which now go to the very gate of the Botanical Garden. You can now do with perfect comfort for twenty-five cents what we used to do in a carriage at a cost of some six or eight dollars each time. I thought the drive more beautiful than in old times — the beautiful bays enclosed like lakes among the mountains; the peaks of Tijuca and Corcovado with the light morning clouds hovering against them; the gardens glowing with flowers and filled with shade trees; and then, at last, the great avenue of palms, symmetrical and impressive as a cathedral aisle. I felt that memory had not exaggerated anything, but that the whole scenery here, all the natural features, are even more striking and unlike what I have seen elsewhere than I supposed. When the Emperor comes back, he will say he has seen nothing since he left Brazil more beautiful than his own home. Coming out from the Garden at about half-past eight o'clock we found at the gate a very pretty little French hotel which I do not remember when I was here before. In the grounds outside under large shade trees were placed tables and chairs, and there we breakfasted, having only taken a cup of coffee when we left the ship early in the morning. I find many flowers which were not in bloom when I was here before, in what they consider their winter. Now there are cactus vines over doors and gateways full of white blossoms which look exactly like the night blooming cereus, as large and lovely, though I suppose they cannot be the same kind or they would not be open in the daylight. Altogether I find myself very happy to be back here again. I did not think it would give me so much pleasure to see it all once more.

Rio de Janeiro, February 10

THE life one falls into on board ship is so strange. You have known it only in the European passages, where in the first place you have so many more companions to choose from, and then you know too that it is only for a fortnight; but to be shut up with some eighteen people for a year in such narrow quarters, seeing them day in and day out, all their little peculiarities brought out by the friction of close contact, is a curious experience; and then you add to it that you yourself are subjected to the same sharp analysis — that they are looking at you through their microscope as well as you at them through yours, and the position is still more singular.

TO MRS. QUINCY A. SHAW

Straits of Magellan, Sandy Point, February 18

HERE we are safe and sound at the threshold of the wonderful region where mountains rise steeply from narrow ocean channels and glaciers plunge sheer down into the sea, — at least, that is what people say. I'll tell you whether it's true the next time we meet. At all events we see superb snow mountains from this point, Mt. Sarmiento, Mt. Darwin, Mt. Buckland; they are beautiful even at this distance of some seventy miles.

In the early part of our voyage I was a little anxious lest the many delays, not only before starting but for the repair of defects in the ship which we did not discover till we were well on our way, would interfere with the success of the enterprise and would make your father so anxious, too, that he would not have any benefit from it either for his health or for science either. But for the last six weeks the real work has begun, and if he had no further successes he would feel more than repaid. He is tolerably cautious, but there are many days when he works as I have not seen him work for years, but he seems to bear it wonderfully well. Tell the children we have four live penguins, a number of wild geese, two cockatoos and two rabbits on board for pets. Many of them are quite tame and will eat from our hands; indeed, the "bunnies" would like to sit in my lap and be fed all day if I would let them.

TO MRS. CHARLES P. CURTIS

Monte Video, February 24

WE started from Rio in fine feather a week ago, expecting nothing in this summer weather but a quick pleasant voyage down to Monte Video. We ran straight into a "stiff gale." I wish you had seen my room, which looked so pretty when we left Boston, about the middle of the second night. All the books had leaped out of the shelves and were rolling round on the floor. My clothes which I had carefully arranged on the big chair had capsized with the chair and formed an indiscriminate heap increased by a number of additional articles which had fallen from the pegs; in the midst of the confusion a port broke open and let in four or five buckets of water which flooded the floor, and there the whole mass went swash, swash,— books, clothes, shoes, up and down, taking a general swim. Such a mess you never saw and is not to be conceived of on land. After this we had a day or two of beautiful weather; then another gale, in the midst of which Mr. Kennedy took me up to the top of the companionway to look out upon the scene. It is more grand than pleasant to see the great waves surging up about the little vessel looking as if they must inevitably pour down upon her. However, they do not, — she rides them like a duck. You need not imagine we have been in any danger from my descriptions, which I flatter myself are very thrilling; on the contrary I believe we've always been quite as safe, though not as comfortable, as if sitting in our parlors at home and that the gales we have met have been bagatelles to a great storm. I'm not ambitious to test the difference and am quite content with what I have already seen of the terrors of the great deep.

TO MRS. THOMAS G. CARY

Off Bahia Blanca, March 3

THE next morning [after leaving Monte Video] we had a dredging which was a delightful chance for Agassiz.

He got a most characteristic and complete collection from the river of great scientific value. Among other things there was the egg of some shell (Agassiz thinks of a large Voluta). It was about the size of a small hen's egg, quite transparent, the egg itself being about the hardness and consistency of isinglass, and contained a number of young, which Agassiz examined. The whole thing was entirely new to him and of great interest. Then, there were quantities of beautiful shells of various kinds of starfishes (some quite rare) and so forth. It is very interesting to see these beautiful living shells, which we only associate with shells in collections, with the animals all expanded and active, walking about. One little shell I saw, a perfect little beauty, had its mantle all spread out, and folding the sides upward it used them just like wings, flapping them with the greatest rapidity and flying through the water like an arrow. How little after all we know of the life and enjoyments of these creatures which we see preserved in Museums.

The next day, March 1, was simply heavenly — like the purest of our September days, without taint or blemish, — one of the days when even I can say that life at sea under such circumstances is delightful. At about two o'clock we had another dredging, now in open sea, if you are particular about localities and depths, to the northeast of Cape Corrientes in about forty-five fathoms. This time we found things that made Agassiz ready to jump overboard with joy. If he had not thought the dredge would do it better, I verily believe he would have gone down himself to see what he could find. Among other things he found a very rare shell, and *two* specimens, the young and the old, one would say, from the relative size, and only known heretofore from the Straits of Magellan where we had had a faint hope he might find it, though even there it's not easy. Then some beautiful sea-urchins and many very young ones, from the size of a pea, and even smaller, upwards, all of which he preserved with great care for Alex, as that is a specialty with him, and the young are not easy to have. Altogether this dredging was more interesting even than the previous one.

On this same day we saw many albatross. It is a beautiful bird on the water, sitting so gracefully with the body half sunk in the wave, the large head with soft glittering white plumage resting above the surface; it looks as much at home and as secure as any bird in its nest on land; when it rises it scuds along on the water for a little way then soars away on wide spread wings, as easy in its motion as in its rest. They say that some of them measure twelve feet from tip to tip of the wings; these did not look to me so large.

Off Port San Antonio, March 6

HERE we are in a land-locked harbor where the ship lies as if she were at the Charlestown wharf, so quiet and motionless. We anchored about five o'clock yesterday afternoon, and immediately after dinner all hands went on shore. The boat with Agassiz, the fishing party and the seine went first; Mrs. Johnson and I followed a little later with the Captain. We landed on a broad dry beach which seemed completely built of loose sea-washed shells. It was a steep slope of shells, making a bank some fifteen feet high, worn down on the summit to a flat surface which made a broad level walk and a nice seat. Wishing to see what was the character of the country behind the beach, I started at once for the sandy slope beyond the shells covered with stubble and low beach cactus, and was running up to get my view before the sun should go down when I heard Agassiz shouting to me to come back. As I did not turn immediately one of the sailors came running full speed to tell me that a very deadly serpent had been killed about five minutes before by Steindachner in those very bushes. I immediately consented to postpone a further investigation of the scenery and returned with remarkable celerity to the shore. Here we sat down on the clean dry shells and watched them draw the seine and enjoyed the sunset over the lonely beach and bay. As the light died out the men built bonfires on the beach, and their fitful blaze succeeded the twilight glow. Then we returned to the ship, and all gathered in the ward room and with the help of a bottle of champagne in honor of somebody's birthday (birthdays are astonishingly frequent on board this ship) we talked over the adventures of the day and laid the plans for tomorrow.

This morning (in a very imperfect state of toilet) I was on deck at five o'clock to see the sun rise. A party went off to explore the southern side of the bay, which is thought to be wooded and somewhat different in character from this. Agassiz stays to superintend the dredging on board; later in the day he will draw the seine once more on the beach, and this afternoon we hope to be on our way again. Had we time to stay here I think we might get some specimens of the larger land animals, for yesterday the gentlemen found tracks of guanacos, wolves, foxes and ostriches, not more than a mile or two from the beach, and as we came up the Gulf we saw the guanacos from the deck. Pourtalès was near being caught "in a tight place," as he said himself, yesterday. When they landed near that steep cliff where the fossils were so thick, you know, he went alone to the top of the cliff which was very abrupt and high, — I believe two or three hundred feet. While on the summit he heard the signal guns for the party to go off to the ship, as the Captain wished to leave the anchorage at a favorable moment for the tide. Pourtalès wanted to reach the boat as quickly as possible and found a gully in which he thought he could descend by a short cut to the beach. It consisted of long steps formed by the successive strata. Down these he found little difficulty in jumping or letting himself down; but after making half the descent he came to a place where the step was a vertical wall, altogether too high for a jump and no crevices for hands or feet. Impossible to return as he came, for though he could jump or let himself *down*, he could neither jump nor drag himself *up*, and the face of the cliff was too steep for climbing. Happily he had with him a hatchet for taking off geological specimens, and with that he cut steps in the wall up the whole height of the cliff; he reached the top utterly exhausted and falling down was obliged to lie there for a little while before he could gather strength enough to return. When a giant like Pourtalès acknowledges such failure as this, he must have had pretty hard work, and you know he always makes light of his own doings.

I cannot tell you how impressive the loneliness of this gulf and shore seems to me. When you reach the top of the bluff behind the beach, you see only a stretch of sandy plains as far as the eye can follow with no growth upon it except dry looking shrubs and coarse grass and low thorny cactus like prickly pear. If it were in civilized regions you would only say it was monotonous and uninteresting; but here where anything human so rarely comes — for I suppose in years no vessel enters this gulf, — it all seems in harmony with the intense solitude. There is nothing to bring men here, neither wood nor water, so that I suppose it will remain deserted for many a year to come.

March 7

WE have said good-bye to our peaceful sheltered bay and are out at sea again. We left our anchorage in faultless weather, so still, that we could hardly say the vessel was moving; the whole gulf was like a mirror and the sun went down without a cloud in burnished gold. We had had such a pleasant visit in the Gulf of San Mathias that we all left it with regret. As long as the shore was in sight we could see our beach fires still burning. We wondered who would light the next fire in this solitary place. The evening was so clear that no one anticipated a change of weather, and everybody being tired we all retired early and were sound asleep, when towards midnight we were wakened by the most brilliant and incessant lightning; the whole sky seemed quivering with it. Presently came pouring rain and then a storm of hail that sounded like a discharge of musketry on the deck. We all came running out of our rooms in the most singular costumes to see what was the matter. Waked so suddenly from sleep one thought the powder magazine was exploding, another, that the vessel was on fire and the sharp clattering was the crackling of wood. I had started with the first rain and fortunately closed all the ports and skylight in our room, or we should have been well pelted. I wondered how the men on deck could stand it. They brought us down many of the stones, but they melted so fast that those I saw were not larger than good-sized marbles or hazel nuts; but they said in falling many were as large as hen's eggs or walnuts. I remember Darwin in his narrative speaks of the hailstones here as very large and says the "guanacos" are sometimes killed by them. I can easily imagine it; an animal would stand a bad chance in these wide shelterless plains under such a fire of ice shot as we had last night. The rest of the night was quiet as possible, and this morning we have fine weather again.

Our next stopping place so far as we know at present is to be the Santa Cruz River shortly before entering the Straits.

THE VOYAGE OF THE HASSLER

March 9

I LEFT you on Thursday, just after we had rounded the point of San Mathias Gulf and river, keeping on our southern course again. We had a fine day and being nearly out of the "Pampiro" region began to flatter ourselves we had escaped, but the sun went down in magnificent clouds which the Captain said were full of wind and looked risky. The whole evening the lightning was superb with chains of electricity from cloud to cloud and down into the ocean. Still the night was still as sleep and the water almost without a ripple. At about ten o'clock with the force of a hurricane and the suddenness of lightning, the land wind struck the ship. After that there was little sleep for any one; everything (in sailor's parlance) that could "fetch away" "fetched away"; among other things my bed, which as Helen and Sallie will remember was clamped with an iron bar to the inner one, worked itself loose and I found myself adrift. I jumped on to the inner bed, and there I remained blockaded calling for help. Finding no one heard in the noise of the storm I climbed over it and called to the carpenter to make all fast. At last I was settled. Towards morning the row abated, and we got a nap. We waked to fine weather though a very rough sea and came out to hear the funny adventures of the night — upsetting of water-pitchers, drenching of beds, smashing of crockery, etc., — but we came through safe and sound, no harm done and have seen the elephant in the shape of a "Pampiro"; once is enough. I don't appreciate the grandeur of storms at sea. However, you must not imagine we have had any alarming ones except to the uninitiated. I only tell you about them to show that our experience is a varied one, and there is always a funny side to these rough times when not only things but people are whacked about without any respect for personal dignity. The sea went down towards evening yesterday, and after the sleepless night before all turned in early. I think the "sleep of the just" must be a restless slumber in comparison to mine last night; from nine o'clock to six this morning I never stirred and when I waked it was a beautiful warm morning and the ship as quiet as our own house in Quincy Street.

We have just been dredging off the Gulf of St. George in about fifty fathoms of water, and beautiful things have come up; a starfish more than a foot in diameter, its ten arms subdivided a hundredfold into countless delicate fibrous-like branches, winding and coiling in an endless variety of curves; another huge starfish, like an immense sunflower, with thirty-seven arms, measuring some fifteen inches from the tip of one arm to the tip of the opposite arm; then beautiful sea-urchins, a skate egg with the living young, etc., etc. As we go south the ship is surrounded with birds, albatross, ducks, gulls and other birds, the names of which we do not know. They are so tame that we pass them quite close without disturbing them.

March 15

YESTERDAY was again very fine, but with a pretty strong wind and sea, and as the beach was difficult to land upon, Mrs. Johnson and I did not have our walk on shore. The two parties started with daylight and at about four o'clock in the afternoon Agassiz and his companions returned. He was on the top wave of life, so happy with the results of his day. You know geologically he is seeking for glacial phenomena, and on their way to a hill between the shore and Mt. Aymond to which Pourtalès and his party had gone, Agassiz had come upon a terminal moraine having all the characteristic features, built of glacier-worn boulders, pebbles and stones of all sorts and sizes packed into a paste of earth. It had been pushed up evidently by a mass of ice advancing from the southward, the southern slope being steep as is always the case with the side of the moraine turned towards the glacier, while the northern slope was more gradual. He also found a salt pond some two hundred feet above the level of the sea with moraine shells living in it. This will please Darwin if he does not already know it, because it illustrates a statement he made many years ago that the geology of this coast was connected with upheaval. The whole party came back in a state of great elation, looking like a company of Nimrods, loaded with game, ducks, snipe, cormorants, a fox and a skunk, the smell of which made me quite homesick, it recalled so vividly certain summer evenings at Nahant. It may be interesting to you as a scientific fact to know that skunks smell in Patagonia exactly as they do in New England. In order that the birds might be prepared we deferred dinner till six o'clock and had it made ready in great style with a centre ornament which we thought could not be matched at any dinner party on Beacon Street or Fifth Avenue. A guanaco skull supported a spreading bunch of ostrich plumes gathered on the Patagonian shore, while the base of our bouquet was finished with green drooping fronds of "kelp" — match that if you can. *First Course:* Mussels roasted on the shell (from the beach of Possession Bay). *Second Course:* Patagonian snipe on toast. *Wines:* Sherry, Sauterne, Claret, Champagne, *Not* native. Our wine cellar is getting low but we thought we would not be niggardly on this first dinner in the Straits. We were quite a snug party, nine instead of eighteen as usual in the mess, for the Mt. Aymond party had not yet returned; but just as we were sitting over our dessert hearing all the details of the day and everybody talking together, a shout on deck announced the return of the second party. We all rushed up and there they were with great trophies. They had shot and skinned a guanaco and brought him bodily, and this morning we have breakfasted sumptuously off guanaco steak (very much like beefsteak and seemed to me as good), but we have been so long without fresh provisions that we are likely to do more than justice to Patagonian fare. They brought also upland goose and other game, but their news was the most interesting of all. Pourtalès had found Mt. Aymond to be the centre of a nest of extinct volcanoes. The mountain itself had two craters very perfectly formed about 200 feet in depth. He gathered fine specimens of lava and volcanic débris all around them. Near the main peak were several lesser hills called the "Asses' Ears" which were all craters and from Mt. Aymond Pourtalès said you could see thirty or forty such craters. All this is very interesting and novel, as none of the explorers seem to have examined these hills though they have been named and entered on the charts, but I suppose their position has been ascertained from a distance. The mountain party with the exception of one or two of the strong ones were "dead beat," for the tramp had been a most fatiguing one, but I never saw Pourtalès look so animated and so excited as he did on his return. They had seen large herds of guanacos, from fifty to a hundred at a time; they say they were so graceful, and when disturbed they hurry close together and stand startled and alert with their pretty heads lifted listening and whinnying to each other like young colts. While they feed on the plain they have a sentinel at watch on high ground to give warning of danger. The skin and fur are very soft and make excellent robes, and the Indians use them also for their tents. The skin and head of the one they shot yesterday are lying on the deck now. It is a beautiful head like that of a young deer.

March 16

LAST evening about four o'clock in the afternoon we anchored off Elizabeth Island and went on shore for the sunset. Dr. Steindachner most amiably dragged my dead weight (which grows daily more imposing on account of much food and little exercise) up a steep cliff, and once landed on the top I took quite a long walk with him to the summit of the central hill of the island. How beautiful it was when we reached it! On one side were Cape Vincent, Martha, and Marguerita Islands, flooded with the sunset light, their yellowish clay cliffs turned to golden, and on the other the quiet waters of Pechet Harbor enclosed in ranges of hills that grew purple and blue in the distance, while on the far horizon were the snow mountains with a broad field of snow looking dim and almost incredible to me. I could not believe that I was getting my first glimpse of glaciers in the Straits of Magellan. I cannot express to you how quiet it seemed on that lonely island. As I sat on the hillside a wild goose walked about within a few feet of me as tranquilly as if no human being were near. Poor fellow, he learned his mistake too soon, for the men from the boat came up and after a little chase captured him alive. Pourtalès found a deserted Fuegian settlement on this island, the places where their huts or tents, or whatever shelter they live under, had been marked by square spots some three feet in diameter dug into the ground to a depth of two feet, and in front of each such place a pile of shells, the débris of their food with stones and flints cut roughly to sharp points and used to open the mussels on which they chiefly live. We returned to dinner at about five o'clock and went to bed early meaning to be up with sunrise. At about six o'clock this morning we left our anchorage and kept on to Marguerita Island where we passed several hours. As we neared the island, which is very picturesque in outline with steep bold cliffs at either end, we could see the sea lions sitting on the beach, and the bold bluffs above were literally studded thick with birds, penguins and cormorants chiefly. Immediately after breakfast we all went on shore, three boats full, for all were anxious to see this famous breeding place of birds and haunt of seals. I despair of describing it to you. The whole face of the cliff and the hillside above are perforated with large openings which are the homes of penguins, cormorants and geese. As our boat neared the shore these throngs of birds (literally hundreds and thousands) broke up and we could see the penguins walking along the edge of the cliff in lines, single file, looking like gaunt little old women with their waddling gait and stubby wings, which they use partly as legs, hanging down like short scant petticoats. When we came to the slope of the hill above the cliff, they had scuttled away or retreated to their nests. I sat down at the front doors of many families and watched them in their houses; for these nests have such large openings that you can see inside perfectly. They have a comical way, when sitting within their holes, of turning their heads constantly from side to side as if in earnest conversation, but without noise, though when disturbed, angry or frightened, they utter a hoarse cry, but in their nests they seem to be carrying on a silent colloquy every now and again, touching and rubbing their bills together. After looking at them for a long while I went to the edge of the hill where I could see the face of the cliff and watched them there. It was curious to see them attracted to the openings of their holes by the disturbance, I suppose, looking out to see what was going on, like people when there is a noise in the street. One in particular attracted me. The opening of his house was just above a narrow ledge of rock, and he sat with his foot resting on the ledge, looking about from side to side with a certain curiosity exactly like a person sitting at the window looking out, with the hand resting on the window-sill. It was sad to see the poor things disturbed in their peaceful home. The gunners had taken their fowling pieces, but there was little need. They were in such numbers that sticks were more in request than guns; they were just knocked down with clubs and killed on the spot, or captured alive. Agassiz selected some fifty good specimens (among which were a variety of species) for alcoholic collection.

March 28

WE left Otter Bay this morning, I am sorry to say without faintly seeing Mt. Burney. It is the first important feature we have missed by fog or clouds, but we could not wait for them to unveil from the morning mists, for we had a long day to our next anchorage, and it is not comfortable to be left out at night in these intricate channels where a "williwaw" [a sudden gust of wind] may come up any minute. So we started at the first peep of day and were prosperously proceeding, when just after breakfast there was a breakdown in the engine, reversing rod broken. It was rather a startling announcement, and we were all a little anxious for a while. Provisions are low; we vibrate between mussel soup, mussel currie, mussels on the shell, and pork and beans; salt beef out, potatoes very nearly so, butter has not been heard of for a long time. Once in a while a very fishy duck or goose varies our fare, but our larder is really not in such a condition that we could be caught here for two or three weeks without being somewhat at a loss even for bread, since flour too is getting very near the bottom of the barrel. However, after an hour's delay the engine was so far repaired that we could proceed, the weather cleared, and we had a beautiful afternoon for the most imposing scenery we have yet seen. My descriptions would be mere repetition. You must imagine a river repeating on its shores mile after mile and hour after hour a panorama of which the foreground is of low hills forest-covered, then a line of very rugged precipitous rocky heights, then a chain of snow mountains behind with very many glaciers in which even with the naked eye you can see the blue color of the ice and the rifts and crevasses that traverse it. Through scenes like these we have come to our harborage tonight, a romantic inlet full of islands and coves and windings, in what is called "Owen's Island." A boat has just returned from a shooting expedition, bringing what Agassiz has exceedingly desired, a "steamer duck," many of which were swimming about when we came in. They shoot through the water with wonderful rapidity, going long distances at a time, and leaving trails behind them like a little boat. They are immense birds, the larger ones measuring three feet and more from the bill to the tail.

March 31, Easter Sunday

AND such a beautiful morning. I was on deck very early between moonlight and sunrise and the sight was a lovely one till the sun came fairly up, as Sallie says, "to spoil it all." I bade you all good-night on the 28th in Mayne's Harbor, or Owen's Island. We passed the 29th there for a more complete repair of our engine, and it was a day well spent for collections and for geology. I took a long tramp up the nearer ridges of the mountains with Pourtalès in search of glacial furrows, and Agassiz dredged on board ship very successfully besides getting a good many new birds from the sportsmen. The next morning we were all right again for proceeding and came on to Puerto Bueno. This is a harbor within a harbor. We anchored in the outer one, and then half a dozen of us took a boat to row to the inner one. I wish I could make you understand what a vagabondish kind of life we lead. For instance, landing at the mouth of a little brook that came brawling down through trees and rocks into the inner harbor, we followed it for about a quarter of a mile and it brought us to a large lake broken by islands. Mrs. Johnson and I found an old log which made an excellent seat. Pourtalès and Steindachner left us to hunt for specimens in the lake and were soon out of sight. Presently Dr. Hill comes prowling along the bank of the brook with his tin box for botany on his shoulder and his hands full of speci-

THE VOYAGE OF THE HASSLER

mens, and he stops for a little talk, and then he too wanders on. Mrs. Johnson and I sit and talk in the afternoon sunshine, and then we stroll back through the woods to the harbor, picking berries as we go and gathering bouquets for the dinner table. Arrived on the shore we encountered Mr. Kennedy who was just coming along in his little dingy, a mite of a boat in which he can run into all the nooks and corners and collect for Agassiz. He lands and makes a fire, and presently Dr. Pitkin arrives upon the scene with some mussels, and we roast them in the cinders, and so the afternoon passes, and the others come back one by one, and we take to the boat again and reach the ship just in time for dinner. This is a specimen of many such little excursions; but this gypsy life will soon be over, I suppose. If things go on all right, we shall be out at sea again in a few days.

Talcahuana, April 12

I LEFT you on the third of April putting out to sea about sunset and taking our last look at the snow mountains of the Straits in all their rosy moonlight beauty. We met head winds outside and had two very rough days and nights. How easy to write it, how hateful to experience! On Saturday, April 6, the weather was again delightful, and we entered Corcovado Gulf (now you must look on the map and see where that is, because I'm confident you don't know). Here we had beautiful snow mountains in sight all day, the peak of Corcovado and a wonderfully beautiful volcanic mountain called Melimoya, white as the purest marble to the summit, and the crater clearly defined against the sky. We anchored in the Port San Pedro, no port in the sense of settlement, only a harbor surrounded by forest-covered hills, the silence unbroken except for the cry of the birds which whiten the rocks and now and then the rush of a steamer duck through the water. We went on shore at a lovely little beach and collected animals and plants. The flowers on the bank of this beach were beautiful, among others a superb specimen of the wild pineapple kind with very large crimson leaves and lilac centre. We enjoyed our ramble on this beach very much, and we saw from there a sunset I shall never forget. The opening of the harbor gave us a full view of the snow mountains, and Agassiz said he had not often in his life seen the Alps in such beauty at that hour.

We put to sea again and made the upper end of the island [of Chiloe] and anchored at the little town of Ancud, or San Carlos, on Monday, the eighth. I see that the book speaks of this generally as a squalid little place and of the climate as dreary, rainy and foggy to the last degree. Everything depends upon the circumstances under which things are presented to you. All I can say is that the little town of Ancud on one of the most brilliantly beautiful days we have had seemed to me a cosy, cheerful, picturesque little place. Her great volcano, Osorno, was quite uncovered, without a cloud, and so was the whole snowy Cordillera, the southern spurs, I suppose, of the Andes. We only intended to stay a few hours, and while

Agassiz and his corps went at once to their scientific researches, Mrs. Johnson and I devoted ourselves to the social investigation of the little town.

First, we went to the market, a central square surrounded by booths where were lying and sitting, grouped about in all sorts of attitudes, some asleep, some nursing their children, Indian and Chilian women, with their bright shawls thrown mantilla-like over their heads and shoulders, men lounging about in their characteristic poncho and slouched hat. We met in the market a gentleman, whose name we did not know, but he joined us, offered to be our escort and took us all over the village, up on the hill where stands the Catholic church commanding a superb view of mountains and harbor and hillsides with little farms scattered about. Then we wandered through the streets under his escort, looked in at the school, were invited into one or two houses where we saw the linen lace work made, were presented with flowers, and altogether treated with much cordiality. We saw the fuchsias growing wild in tall bushes in the poorest gardens; we saw the groups of Indians who come in across the river in the morning from their outlying farms to sell milk and eggs, now resting and sitting about on the street corners with empty milk bottles and egg baskets. We saw the country people driving out their double teams of strong powerful oxen drawing shallow wooden troughs filled with manure for their fields. We saw the ladies of Ancud, always with the half shawl, half mantle, drawn over head and shoulders, sitting in their porticos around the braseiro where simmered the little kettle for the preparation of their maté tea; altogether it looked to me very cheerful and vastly entertaining, perhaps because we had been for three weeks so out of reach of people. When we returned to the landing place to embark, we were met by a most gratifying spectacle. Now I have already mentioned that our larder was low and the truth is we had had nothing but beans and bread for a number of days, and not too much of that. Our caterer and steward were on the wharf with chickens, beef and mutton, with potatoes, eggs, cheese and butter, with fresh rolls and loaves from the baker's, with cabbages, cauliflowers, beets and carrots. I dare say that sounds very commonplace and uninteresting, but it is utterly impossible for you people living on the fat of the land to conceive of the emotions awakened in the company of the Hassler by the sight of these provisions. I shall never to my last hour forget the soup we had for dinner that day. We left that afternoon and had a good run to Lota, our next port, where we were to take in coal. We reached there toward evening on the tenth. Lota has left a strange impression on my mind. We went on shore that night and visited the great copper foundries which lie just along the beach and are fed by the coal mines on the shore, the discovery of which has made or is making the fortune of this little place, which hardly existed fifteen years ago. A foundry has always a kind of weird, uncanny element to me with its fierce unceasing fires, and this was especially impressive at night with the roar of the surf on one side and the roar of the huge furnaces at white heat on the other, and the figures of the workmen moving about between in the intense Rembrandt lights and shadows. This is the only picture I brought away from Lota, for we left early the next day, and I did not therefore go on shore by broad sunlight to dispel my fantastic vision of the night.

TO MRS. QUINCY A. SHAW

Talcahuana, April 15

WE are really having such a delightful let-up from sea life here. I wish you could see this place and some of the wonderful flowers. There is a vine here growing wild in the woods; no description can give you an idea of its beauty — a deep crimson bell two or three inches in length, of a perfect shape and clustering all along a graceful vine. I have never in all my life seen a more beautiful flower. It is shy of cultivation and even here in its native climate does not grow well in gardens.

We have a plan (I think if we carry it out, it will be a pleasant one) of taking a carriage and driving from here to Santiago — a four days' journey — and then from there to Valparaiso by the cars, where we shall meet the Hassler, which meanwhile goes on a deep sea sounding and dredging expedition to Juan Fernandez and from there to Valparaiso. I am of course glad of the exchange from sea to land for a little while.

TO MISS SARAH G. CARY

Talcahuana, April 25

THE other day we drove out to a true country ranch where we passed the day; if you have not seen a ranch you could hardly imagine one exactly as it is. They seem to vary from mere thatched huts and sheds of the poor people to those of the better class, which are a picturesque mixture of roughness and comfort. This one was a gentleman's ranch. Its dark wood walls were hung with guns and bows and bugles and musical instruments; a skin or a mat here and there was thrown down before a lounge or an easy chair; it was ill lighted, for the windows are few and the verandahs deep, but there was a fireplace and one could imagine when the logs, ready laid in the chimney, were ablaze in the evening, how cosily the sombre interior would light up. Sitting-room led to chambers, these to dining-room, this to all sorts of offices and storerooms where produce of all sorts — beef, fruit, vegetables, but especially beef (for this is a great cattle ranch), are prepared for the market. They seemed to wander on endlessly, all on one floor (upstairs seems to be a thing unknown here), and all opened upon the inner court, where were all sorts of picturesque sheds serving as kitchens, servants' and shepherds' rooms and so on.

We lunched on delicious fruit, grapes, pears, etc. with fresh butter and excellent bread, and then took the carriages again to drive through the woods to the shore. The drive was rough; we had often to get down and walk where the carriage could not go, but it was lovely with bits of wood and groups of trees dotted all over it as if they had been arranged by a landscape gardener to produce picturesque effects. It reminded me of park scenery in England and would need little training to make it as beautiful. This brings us to the shore where a large river (the Rio-Rio) pours into the sea; on one side of the beach the quiet waters of the river make a gentle ripple, on the other a furious ocean surf drives in on very broken masses of rock. At one end of the beach is a superb cliff pierced by a cave. Altogether the scenery is very wild and picturesque. Here in the river side of the bay we drew the seine and Agassiz got many valuable specimens. Afterwards we went up to the fishermen's tents on the bank. Certainly poverty is a great deal more picturesque in Southern countries than in Northern ones. Any one of these huts with their deep porches, on the walls of which are hanging the fishing nets, the oars, the saddle, perhaps, and working tools of all sorts, while a pussy cat sits on a cross beam and looks out through the thatch, and cocks and hens and dogs and children group about a handful of fire in the mud floors, would make a picture; I know it's no less squalid and miserable than poverty in one of our Irish tenements, but it's ever so much prettier. It attracts instead of repelling you.

We returned to the ranch for dinner with Chileno country dishes, a *casuela*, a sort of half stew, half soup made of chicken, *puchero*, a dish which reminds me of Meg Merrilies' famous stew in the gypsy cave, because it has everything in it that happens to come to hand and is relishing and savory in proportion to the variety of condiments.

We drove home by moonlight after a delightful day. Since then we have had one or two such excursions and a day at the City of Concepcion, some ten miles from here. It has only been completely destroyed three or four times by earthquake in the last two centuries. There has n't been one for some time, and it occurred to me that we might be swallowed up or buried in ruins any minute; but no one seems to think much about it.

The houses are fascinating; very inconvenient according to our notions, you know, but the wide doors stand ever open in this mild climate and give you a view of the central court planted with bright flowers and trees and looking so pretty.

TO MRS. THOMAS G. CARY

Curicu, Chili, May 4

WE have had a most fascinating land journey from Talcahuana here, travelling post, five horses abreast and an outrider, after the fashion of the country. But I must tell you all about it in detail from beginning to end if you will have patience.

Sunday morning we started off, Agassiz, Steindachner and myself in a big coach we had chartered for the week. Our first day's journey was to a little seacoast town called Tomé. The road was most picturesque, and I fancied it might be something like the Cornice road, winding steeply zigzag over very steep hills gullied into deep wooded valleys and following the shore and giving beautiful views of the open sea and of the bay of Concepcion, until at last we came to a high cliff along the edge of which we descended corkscrew fashion with turns and windings as sharp as the Swiss mountain roads, and looking sheer down upon the surf breaking on the rocks below and the little fishing town bordering the beach. At Tomé we passed the night in a tolerable inn, though to be sure we shared our quarters with the permanent residents, the fleas; but then these abound everywhere in Chili, and of course travelling in the country you do not expect very good accommodations. Our second day's journey was to be to the hacienda of a Senhor Martinez situated on a river from which Agassiz wanted to get fish. He had met Agassiz at Concepcion and invited him to remain at his farm for as long as he liked though he was not there himself. The second day we came into the agricultural country where the culture of corn, wheat and grapevines is the business of every one. It was so strange to see all the work of the autumn going on in May, the gathering in and carrying to and fro of the harvest and vintage. We would meet hundreds of mules laden with sacks of corn which they were carrying down to Tomé, and carts, the queer primitive carts of the country, with huge red wine jars in which was the fresh new juice of the vintage, large enough for the jars in the "Forty Thieves." The road was full of life and animation and of the most picturesque sights.

Every poor hut would have made a pretty sketch. The houses of the poor are simply a rough trellis of tree stems interwoven with boughs, and green as an arbor while the boughs are fresh. As they dry, these boughs form a rough thatch made closer by a coarse rushlike grass put on in bundles. There is always an open house place, a sort of porch in front shaded by a roof of thatch supported on posts. This is the living place of the family in the daytime, usually a rough little table and perhaps a bench. Here you see them sitting in the sun or sometimes grouped around a bit of fire on the ground where simmers their pot of soup or beans.

Well, about five o'clock in the afternoon we reached the hacienda of our hospitable friend, but I could not find that any one expected our coming. The people said the "Major Domo" of the farm, Senhor Morro, to whom we had a letter, had gone away and might not be back till the next day. I felt discouraged, for I had taken cold at Tomé, had a bad headache and really wanted rest, as we all did indeed, for we had come over a very rough road. As we stood debating in the yard, [there] rode in a gentleman on horseback; every moving thing here is on a horse. This man looked thoroughly a gentleman; we explained our situation. He said he was a great friend of Monsieur Morro's and would undertake to do the honors of the house in his absence. We were shown upstairs; a door was opened on to a verandah which was full of the afternoon sunshine and looked directly over a beautiful river and a pretty country bordered by a range of hills. My spirits began to rise. Had we dined anywhere on the road? No. Directly then we could perceive that great preparations began in the yard below; the fatted calf, in other words, sundry chickens were about to be killed and other preparations made for our entertainment. In about two hours (which this friendly neighbor employed in showing Agassiz about the banks of the river where he was interested in the geology) dinner was served; the tablecloth was perfectly clean, the service nice; the dinner consisted of half a dozen courses of meat preceded by soup; the wines were excellent, the fruit abundant, that is delicious grapes heaped up without stint. Now I began to see preparations for the night, and after a casual glimpse of the chambers, I was inexpressibly relieved to find two beds made up not only neatly but with the finest linen, embroidered and marked and fresh and neat as it could be. The comfort of the bed I shall never forget; I was so tired and wanted a good sleep so much.

The next morning I sat on the piazza and watched the scenes on the river, and fascinating they were. Teams of fifty or one hundred mules would come winding down from the opposite hillsides and ford the river, guided by a mounted horseman here and there, perhaps two or three to a troop. The river was wide and deep; the animals were up to the breasts in water, and the whole scene, the neighing, and cries of the men, the struggles of the mules, was exciting and interesting to me. Then there were many carts crossing dragged by oxen and rafts full of people, the country people in their bright dresses, the men in ponchos, the women in gay shawls worn like a kind of mantle. Oh, if I could only make effective sketches, what pretty ones I could bring home!

At ten o'clock they served us an excellent breakfast (I forgot, by the way, to say that early in the morning Monsieur Morro arrived and expressed the greatest cordiality, regretting only that he had not been there to receive us the day before); breakfast over we started again, crossing the river on a raft, a *lancha* as they call them here. Our ride today was only of four or five hours to the town of Chilian, quite a large old Spanish town. Our road lay through the valley of Chilian, a broad flat plain bordered by the Cordillera of the Andes to the East. Again the same fascinating scenes along the roadside. I never failed, when we stopped to change horses, to get down from the coach and go into some of the wayside huts. In one porch I found an old woman sitting in the sun and spinning wool, but after a laborious primitive fashion. She had no wheel, only a rough spindle on which she threaded out the wool to the necessary fineness by the hand, stretching it and smoothing out the inequalities till she had filled the spindle, then beginning it again and thinning it out more and more. She showed me the cloth that was made from it. In another, the family was sitting around their dinner on the mud floor. Here were many grapes hanging up in the thatch, of which they offered us a number of bunches, declining pay, but not refusing a little present of money.

Arrived in Chilian we were in a decent hotel enough, indeed much more comfortable in many respects than you would find travelling in out-of-the-way places at home. The picturesque repays me for a great deal of discomfort, and here the general aspect is effective. For instance, the hotels and indeed all the houses are built around *patios* — open square courts with a gallery all around on which the chambers open. The street side of the *patio* has a large hall through which you pass into the *patio* and on either side of which are usually the drawing-rooms or salons fronting on the street. Our hotel in Chilian was such a house, and there we dined very cosily, we three around a little table, our funny, frisky, fat landlord, Gascon French by birth, as he told us, dashing in and out *au désespoir* because we were dining ill, or *réjoui* because we expressed ourselves satisfied. He seemed exactly like excitable surly landlords on the stage. Steindachner is a great comfort to me as a travelling companion. He's just like a woman in some respects, enjoys going prowling about in strange places, into the churches or into the private gardens. We see a house door standing open (they all do stand open here), giving a fascinating view into a *patio* within planted with flowers and trees, sometimes with grape trellises. We walk in; the Senhora appears. *Steindachner:* "Pardon, Senhorita, but we are strangers walking, and your garden looks so charming, so inviting, we ventured in," etc., etc.

Of course the Senhora asks us to come in, often gives us flowers and is full of an amiable curiosity as to who we are and the strange countries we have come from.

The next day we left Chilian very early, having our long day's ride before us. This journey seems to make real for me what I have read of the mode of travelling a century and a half ago in England, — posting with five or six horses and an outrider, fording streams in the absence of all bridges; then the number of horsemen on the road, looking to be sure like Spaniards and not like Englishmen, in the broad hat and brilliant poncho, and with the enormous heavy stirrups; then women riding on pillions behind the men, sometimes countrymen with their mates, sometimes the better class of horsemen with a lady behind in flounced dress and crinoline. The life of a Spanish American on his horse is truly a double life; it is fascinating to see them, the man is absolutely one with his horse. One day we passed a troop of laden horses, and a man was trying to catch one that had strayed. He tore along at full speed, horse and man swaying together and sometimes swooping sideways at such an angle that it seemed as if the man must fall off. The next instant he had thrown his lasso and was upright in his saddle as quiet as you please, the horse trotting quietly.

This night, the fourth of our journey (Wednesday, May 1) we reached Sinarez. This is a small town and we should have fared badly at the little country inn but that a polite Chileno hearing a Senhora was in the case gave up to me the crack room of the house, the only nice one I fancy, so we fared very comfortably.

The next day, May 2, Thursday, we had a beautiful journey. To be sure part of it was through a sandy plain not fertile, but broken by a thorny mimosa scattered all over it; but it was bordered by Cordillera of the Andes on one hand and by the mountains of the coast range on the other. Then we came into a more fertile soil watered by many rivers, and we were constantly fording small streams. Here the houses were frequent (that is, the wayside cabins), and as our driver changes horses frequently and was long about it, I had a chance to make acquaintance with many of these little houses, so poor and so pretty. In one a young girl was sitting by a fire on the floor on which was simmering a *casuela*, a national dish between a stew and a soup, and a pot of beans; from the thatch hung a shallow cradle made out of coarse woven straw with a baby asleep; another lay on the floor kicking and crowing. They were twins. Over the porch of a neighboring hut was a grapevine and we bought excellent grapes there. Many of the better class of these thatched cabins serve as a kind of country hostelries for the drivers and poorer travellers. You see the table in the porch covered with a white cloth, a plate of *tortillas*, the bread rolls of the country baked in the ashes, a bottle or two of wine (such as may be had here for ten cents) set out for any chance comer. Sometimes we passed a village market in the open air full of picturesque groups. In the middle of the day we crossed a deep river, of course in a raft. You must add to all the rest of the enjoyment the perfect beauty of the weather, the soft haze of Indian summer with a cloudless sky and the mountains so beautiful on the horizon.

We got into Talca, our next stopping place, early, and I had my usual prowl with Steindachner. We met such a pretty dark-eyed boy like an Italian with a basket of the finest grapes on his head I ever saw, — a transparent amber in color, enormous bunches and very large berries, of the richest Frontenac flavor. I have never seen such grapes, and Agassiz who knows the European grapes so well said he had never seen finer. They are peculiar to Talca and do not bear transplanting even to a neighboring soil. There is one very pretty feature of these old Spanish towns, which I am told is a direct inheritance from Spain, — the *Alameida*, that is long alleys of poplars planted close together so as to form thick walls, very straight and erect; as they grow to a great height here, the vista they form is often very fine. In the evening Steindachner and I went out into the public square to hear the music; there was to our surprise a very good military band playing with taste and in excellent time and tune.

The last few days we had begun for the first time to see more real poverty than before. Dreadful beggars deformed with dirt and disease, such as are described in Italy, hung around the inn doors and implored alms. Till then I had never seen any begging in Chili, at least only the Indian children in Talcahuana, who after I had given some beads to a few of them whose photographs Agassiz wanted, would come outside the windows half a dozen at a time, "Senhorita, pretty, kind, much appreciated, give me a *collarcita* " (little necklace), but they had pleasant, sweet entreating voices and nothing of the street beggar about them.

Yesterday, Friday, May 3, was the last day of a journey I shall never forget. Being the last day I indulged myself in a bit of romance and lunched under one of the thatched sheds where I have told you the poorer travellers take their meals. We had the new wine brewed yesterday and the *tortillas* on our cosy little table in the open air. I felt about eighteen and brimful of sentiment and poetry. Early in the day we reached Curicu, the small town where the railroad begins and romance ought to end. We did not expect much comfort here knowing it was a little place, but to my great surprise we were welcomed like friends by the host of a most respectable looking inn. He was a German, a political refugee, having taken part as a student in the revolution of '48, was condemned to ten years' imprisonment, escaped, and here he was. He was quite a gentleman, a man of education, knew all about Agassiz, had heard that he was on the road, had our rooms all ready for us, and gave us a hearty welcome.

Steindachner and I took our usual stroll after we had brushed off our dust and taken a cup of coffee (we always dine late to make the most of the daylight). We wandered through the *Alameida* and came to the foot of an excessively steep hill up which a winding path had been cut. As we went up we met many women and children either descending or ascending; there were very poor women among them and some quite aged ones, and at first we could not understand it for it was quite a toilsome climb; but presently we saw that there was a cross on the top and these were devout people going up to pray. When we reached the summit we found groups of kneeling women and children around the monument of a Jesuit Mission surmounted by a cross, and as we approached we heard the low murmurs of their "Aves" and "Credos." We wandered on to the farther brow of the hill and waited for sunset. The whole panorama of the Andes, magnificent from this point, grew purple and rosy in the glow, and all the outlines of the peaks of the abrupt jagged walls and volcano-like summits were clearly defined against the eastern sky. It was beautiful, but the Andes have none of the loveliness of the Alps; none of the lower green slopes and soft pasturage grounds that lead you gently up to the rocky summits. The Andes rise arid, rugged, stern from base to crest; there is nothing to break a something in their character which seems to me forbidding, terrible almost. We stood watching till the last rays of the sun died upon them, lighting up the cross too and the kneeling people on the hillside, gathered now in numbers. As we went down we saw the candles glimmering at the foot of the cross, and here and there a single lamp burning at some of the intermediate stations where they kneel to rest and pray on their way up.

We returned at six o'clock and dined in our room (it was not much the habit for senhoras to go to the table d'hote and there are no hotel parlors), waited on by our attentive host, who would superintend everything himself, though there were plenty of servants, and who talked politics and science and literature between all the dishes.

TO MRS. QUINCY A. SHAW

Panama, July 13

WE have had a quiet fortnight in Panama, for the most part staying on board the ship in harbor, though we went once for a day or two to a station house belonging to the railroad about half across the isthmus. It was lovely to be again in the midst of a tropical vegetation, — the last time I shall ever see it, I suppose, and indeed I hope, for I've no desire to roam any more. Still it was a pleasure to see the same brilliant flowers, and to see the same rich vines and massive forest, and even to hear the same woodland sounds that used to surround us at Esperança's cottage on the Amazons. Ask Louis if he remembers that he had a peculiar whistle and that I used to make him repeat it for me, because it reminded me of a bird that had a wailing note, which I used often to hear deep in the forest when I was staying in the Indians' houses on the Amazons. I heard it the other evening here in the same way, as if it came from some deep recess of the woods, — a long falling note with a certain sadness in it. It carried me strangely back to the life we led there with all its wild picturesqueness.

Good-bye, may God bless you and yours, and keep us all in His love together.

TO MISS MARY FELTON

San Francisco (on board the Hassler), August 31

I WALK up and down the deck and say to myself, "Is it true? You are here, the voyage so dreaded is over; that day, when you waved your handkerchief from the port to the tug in Boston Harbor is ever so far away in the distance, and you are anchored before the wharves of the San Francisco Company." I really cannot believe it. It seems impossible. The voyage was so long when we looked forward, and then all the doubts as to the results! I have not been on shore yet. I feel too excited and happy, and it is enough to know that we are here. I want to pause and take it all in. We will stay on board tomorrow and rest and get our traps ready. Ah, how strange it has seemed to me to take down Mrs. Sargent's "Bon Voyage" and dear Sallie Whitman's picture, "His blessing like a line of light Is on the water day and night" (how often I have taken comfort from it), and the picture of the Nahant house hanging beneath it, and the shoe bags and the comb cases. Many of the things I hope to put up in my room at home, for it will be a pleasure to recall my cosy little chamber here. I thought I could never become attached to the Hassler, but your prophecy was a true one, — I feel as I sit writing to you in the little cabin that, though I would not sail another mile in her for a fortune, I shall leave her with a kind of affectionate feeling.

CHAPTER VII
PENIKESE ISLAND — THE DEATH OF AGASSIZ
1872–1873

WHEN Agassiz returned to Cambridge in October, 1872, he at once became involved in a project long dear to his heart and matured by friends in his absence. This was a plan for establishing a summer school of natural history on the Massachusetts coast. When the Legislature of Massachusetts made its annual visit to the Museum in the following March, Agassiz presented a special plea for an appropriation for the endowment of the projected school. "Never did he plead more eloquently for the cause of education," Mrs. Agassiz writes. "His gift as a speaker cannot easily be described. It was born of conviction and was as simple as it was impassioned." It should be said in passing that these words of Mrs. Agassiz have an additional interest if read in connection with the scene in the State House twenty years later, described below in Chapter X, when she appeared before the Legislature and pleaded successfully for the charter of Radcliffe College with an eloquence that rested as truly as that of her more impassioned husband on "conviction and simplicity." The report of Agassiz's appeal that was published in the newspapers aroused the interest of Mr. John Anderson of New York and led him to make a gift of Penikese Island in Buzzard's Bay on the coast of Massachusetts as a site for the proposed school, together with an endowment fund of $50,000. The school was organized in April, 1873, under the name of "The Anderson School of Natural History," and its opening was announced for July 8, in spite of the fact that this date allowed only two months for constructing the entire establishment and equipping it with all its apparatus and appointments. What took place when, on July 4, Agassiz and Mrs. Agassiz arrived on the scene, and the part that Mrs. Agassiz played in saving the situation is best described by herself in the following letter.

TO MISS SARAH G. CARY

Penikese Island, July 7, 1873

I HAVE had a good many odd experiences in my life, but I think never one more original than this. When we arrived in New Bedford the first greeting was that the building on the island was utterly unfinished — no floors — no shingling — etc., etc., etc., — a tale of the most discouraging character. Agassiz took it all with a calmness perfectly amazing to me; he said the eighth of July was his date; this was the Fourth; by the eighth he dared say everything would be ready, and he should believe in no failure till he had seen it. My heart sank to my shoes, for I could not help asking myself what we should do with the fifty-eight people to be lodged, clothed and comforted. We passed the night at the hotel, listening to the little boys firing crackers under our windows and making night hideous; the next morning we started with the steamer at nine o'clock. We brought with us Professor Wilder, his wife and child, and invited a stray lady teacher, whom we found at the hotel,

ELIZABETH CARY AGASSIZ
1872

having come by some mistake three days in advance. She lived at a distance and had not received the last circular. We told her she might not have where to lay her head, but should share what we had. The two hours' voyage was rough and rainy, and we were glad to land at the little wharf. Con [Felton] and Mr. Tilden were there to meet us. They looked like shipwrecked mariners and I rather think no two mortals were ever more glad to see their rescuers than they were to see the "Helen Augusta," which was to restore them to the bosom of society. They had worked like beavers the evening before and had got all the furniture under cover and well sheltered, which was a great matter.

They had done all they could, but for want of boats and money had not had much means at their disposal; then the Fourth of July intervened, and the men could not be kept by any seductions whatever. They left by the boat which brought us, and I suppose have returned to Nahant by this. As soon as they had gone and we had had some ham and fried eggs, I went to work with Flanders (the man in charge here — a capital man as Con will tell you, — intelligent, active, hopeful, — he's a great help). Together we got the greater part of the old Anderson house, in which the carpenters had been living, cleaned and arranged for our habitation and were really, all of us, very comfortably settled for the night with a bed or two for a friend. This house in which we are, is, you know, the old farmhouse occupied by Mr. Anderson.

Now let me tell you about the new ones. There were (or are to be eventually) two big and very nice looking barracks — each to have four laboratories on the lower floor and twenty-five sleeping-rooms on the upper. Of these one building is up, but when we arrived had no floors — the other is represented only by the foundation. The wonder is that they are there in any shape, considering that the lumber was landed on the island hardly five weeks ago. At first the aspect of things was discouraging, but the architect does not accept failure any more than Agassiz, and he told us his plan was to complete the floor of the first story, put up a partition, and divide it into great camps, one for the ladies and one for the gentlemen, — then the furniture could all be put out and arranged, and gradually as the rooms were completed above, each could move to their own quarters. The next day was Sunday, but Flanders made a thrilling address to the carpenters — told them the object of the building — not for business, not for money, but for instruction, and he thought that on this occasion, considering the emergency and the motive, their duty was to make the day one of work, not of rest. They agreed, and before night the floors above and below were nearly completed. With the help of one or two boys and Dr. Wilder, Mrs. Burns, Mrs. Wilder, and I unpacked and washed all the glass and china for dormitories and dining-room, — no light task, I can tell you, for it consisted of twenty-four dozen plates, six dozen cups and saucers, vegetable and meat dishes without end, many dozens of glasses and fifty-six chamber sets containing all the ordinary pieces. In the midst of our work Sunday afternoon we had a visit from a fashionable New York yacht and Robert Minturn and Mr. Holyoke came up to see us. It was a lovely afternoon, we were all on the piazza washing glass and china, and they seemed to think it quite a delightful picnic. We were able to muster a cup of coffee and tried to be as hospitable as circumstances would admit. Here then, we stand — today we are to unpack the furniture and we intend to place the little belongings of every person together so that it shall represent a room, though not of course partitioned off. I will write you tonight the result of our chamber work.

In the biographies of Agassiz and Alexander Agassiz accounts may be found of the school and its future fate, which there is no need of repeating here. The following letter from Miss Emma Cary, however, adds an animated description of the life on the island, as it had been depicted to her by Mrs. Agassiz.

FROM MISS EMMA F. CARY TO MISS SARAH G. CARY

Nahant, July 17, 1873

LIZZIE is very pleasant telling about the island life. Do you remember a genial element in *Charles Auchester* in spite of its nonsense — as if they were on a perpetual artistic picnic? There is the same feeling at Penikese; enthusiasm, romance, open air, discomforts, very good food, science, colonies of gulls, hard work and amusement, all mixed together. The servants hurry to finish their work to come and hear the lectures, but they work well and quietly, separated from the lecture part of the big barn by the diagram board, which shuts off the pantry from the audience. Agassiz has given the three finest lectures on glaciers that Lizzie ever heard from him. Wilder is an admirable teacher and speaks without notes. Hawkins, the wonderful draughtsman, draws fishes on the blackboard developing them by degrees from the tail upwards till the spectators are wild with excitement. Then the fifty tired, faded teachers are sent out to learn from nature and put in practice methods of study given by Agassiz and Wilder. They come home to a nice dinner, — chowder, beef and lamb and an excellent pudding, and at night there are the nice little rooms emerging one by one from the big dormitory.

The Penikese school was the first of our marine laboratories and involved Agassiz in the difficulties of a pioneer enterprise as well as in the labor of lecturing. The strain proved far beyond his already uncertain strength, although he remained at his post until the season closed. With untiring zeal he resumed his work at the Museum in October; yet the watchful eyes of Mrs. Agassiz could not fail to observe his waning vitality as the autumn passed into winter. She was not required, however, to bear the pain of seeing him endure a long period of suffering and weakness. The end was heralded by less than a fortnight's illness, and the parting came swiftly and peacefully on December 14, 1873.

CHAPTER VIII
CHANGED CONDITIONS — THE BIOGRAPHY OF AGASSIZ
1873-1879

THE life of Agassiz, though characterized by remarkable unity, falls into two distinct periods, and with only a little less precision the same may be said of that of Mrs. Agassiz. In fact she might almost have been describing her own experience in 1873, when in her biography of Agassiz she wrote of his departure from Europe for America in 1846, which formed the dividing line between the two portions of his career, — "So closed this period of Agassiz's life. The next was to open under wholly different conditions." For with his death Mrs. Agassiz entered upon an essentially new existence. The end had come to the days of wide travel, of engrossing and stimulating scientific interests, and of absorption in the welfare and pursuits of her husband. The character of this absorption has appeared again and again in fragments of letters in the preceding chapters, which, although they convey a mere passing breath from years of devotion, serve to show how completely when companionship with him ceased, she was deprived of the controlling motive of her daily life. Moreover the inexorable changes that follow such a loss did not come unattended. Eight days after she had parted from Agassiz, she saw the happiness of her dearly loved stepson shattered by the death of his young wife, who left him with three little sons, the youngest only two years old. In his bereavement he turned to Mrs. Agassiz for the perfect understanding that he had received from her ever since she had first entered his own boyhood and for the care that he desired for his children. Some few months earlier he had come with his family temporarily to his father's house, expecting to pass the winter in Nassau. On the death of his wife he at once took the house in Quincy Street for his own residence, and there Mrs. Agassiz had her home for the rest of her life, his companion, the presiding genius of his household, and the mother of his three boys, George, Maximilian, and Rodolphe. To the youngest, Rodolphe, she literally took the place of a mother, and she brought him up as if he had been her own child. A year later Alexander Agassiz began to build a house at Newport, Rhode Island, and after 1875, the family used to separate for the summer, Mrs. Agassiz going as usual to Nahant and the rest of the household to Newport. Thus while the outer setting of her days remained unaltered, with the close of 1873 a wholly new epoch in her occupations, her cares, and her habits began.

Under these conditions her exceptional qualities did not fail her. "She was so constructed," Mrs. Curtis writes, "that she could really accept her own sorrow with more fortitude than that which came to her children; and I remember a sentence in a letter that I received from Sallie when we went abroad two years after all this, in which she says, 'I do so miss Lizzie's happiness.'" There is a noticeable entry in Mrs. Agassiz's diary thirty years later: — "December 14, 1903. The anniversary of Agassiz's death — and Annie's the week after. How that month, December, 1873, changed life for us all! Mimi sent me wonderful roses and mignonette; she is always so kind and thoughtful. — Today (this afternoon) the College Club gives a tea for Mr. and Mrs. Briggs. I will go." There is no other reference in Mrs. Agassiz's diaries to her sorrow of 1873. Her natural serenity and freedom from the least tinge of morbidness steadied her, and the words that she wrote a few years later to a friend in great grief give a clue to the spirit in which she took up her altered life: — "I dare not face the future for you, — but we will not talk of that. Each day has its own burden and is enough in itself." "We know," she wrote to still another friend, "how the character ripens in suffering and grows as it were out of this world into the next. And yet happiness seems such a natural atmosphere — like light and sunshine for a plant — one must believe that somewhere and somehow we shall find it without fear of loss or change." With self-forgetfulness and self-control she accepted the passing of the old and the coming of the new duties, and from watching the ship freighted with her treasure sail away from her to the unknown sea, she turned to welcome the three little craft that floated into the ample harbor of her care and affection — affection that followed them and theirs to the end of her days.

During the next few years Mrs. Agassiz naturally lived in retirement, occupied with the care of the boys and supplying so far as might be the void in her son's life. The sympathy between them was strengthened by the tie of a common sorrow and by her ardent and intelligent interest in his professional aims, projects and pursuits. He was in the habit of submitting to her his scientific papers in manuscript and found in her his most valued critic. Many of the letters that he wrote to her during the separations occasioned by his scientific expeditions have been published in his biography and in a small degree reveal their intimacy, but hers to him, which would have given an outline of her daily life at this time, have been destroyed. A few letters, however, which she wrote to Mrs. Curtis, who was abroad in 1875 and 1876, convey an impression of her interests and of the cheerfulness that the current of sadness running through her wonted occupations did not sweep away.

TO MRS. CHARLES P. CURTIS

Cambridge, October 31, 1875

WELL, my dear, there's one thing you can't do in Europe. You can't hear Von Bülow play, because he's playing for us. I have never enjoyed piano concerts so much; he plays so much good music, his programmes are so dignified, so well distributed, so that each piece tells by what precedes and by what follows as well as by its own beauty. I suppose Rubinstein has greater genius, but Von Bülow respects his art and his audience and is incapable of lowering the one and insulting the other, as Rubinstein certainly did in Boston. In Paris where he *must* do his best, Pauline said he played divinely. So he did sometimes here, but by no means always.

Cambridge, November, 1875

WHY am I not gifted like you for letter writing, and I would make you laugh till you cry as I have just done in reading your last letters to Sallie and Mother. They all sound as if you were leading a

CHANGED CONDITIONS

pleasant life. It is delightful to hear and to think of happy people. . . . I have to remind myself how intensely happy I have been, and then the hope comes that what has been will be. I am glad of one thing, — I knew how happy I was — every day and hour had its full value, and looking back I have a sense of possession that nothing can take from me. What I have had is mine. Alex keeps pretty well thus far but will go off somewhere in February, I think. I miss him desperately when he goes, for Alex is to me a very companionable man. He tells me a great deal of his scientific life and work, of his plans for the Museum, etc., and that keeps me still a little in the same intellectual atmosphere to which I am accustomed. We dine at six — coffee after; then I read to the boys for an hour or more; before nine they are in bed, and then Alex and I have a cup of tea — destructive and dangerous to the nerves, but very pleasant, — and then is our time for talk, and if Alex is writing anything, he often reads it to me, and we discuss it together. All this is a real source of happiness, and you must not think I do not appreciate it. I do, and constantly think how blessed I am in my children and grandchildren. But with all his activity — and Alex's life is crowded with work from morning to night — it is such a broken life. You see it in his look whenever his face is quiet and thoughtful — at least, I do, knowing his expression so well. The children are all well — Rodolphe enchanting and developing in intelligence wonderfully.

Cambridge, January 9, 1876

... Oh, won't it be nice ever to be where anxiety does not come! I wonder how far off it is, for I've an idea that to leave this earth is not at once to enter Heaven. The Catholic idea of purgatory (not in a material sense) seems to me to be founded on a reasonable idea. There seems no reason why the fact of death should absolve you at once from all your faults and errors and their consequences. But I think somewhere in the far future there must be a time when all is made right for us, and the happiness of which we have such lovely glimpses here becomes a safe and permanent possession.

Cambridge, April 9, 1876

... I MUST tell you about our baby. My delight is to go in and take my place in the room adjoining [his mother's], where the baby lies, and watch my chances. Sometimes if he is awake I have him for a long time, and I think there is nothing like the peace that creeps in upon you with a baby in your arms. There's something in the little soft roll of warm flannel, something in the quiet shaded room from which all the bustle of the world outside is excluded, that takes away all the pain and sting of life by some subtle power.

The following letter was written after a visit of the Emperor and Empress of Brazil to Cambridge.

CHANGED CONDITIONS

TO MRS. CHARLES P. CURTIS

Nahant, July 23, 1876

... MOTHER and Sallie upbraided me with not writing you about our Imperial experiences, but the truth is that the visit was such a trying one to me — so full of what might have been and was not, that I found it difficult to write or talk about it, — to do anything but live through it in the best way I could. In the old time I should have found much to amuse you with, for there was a very funny side to it. Do all you can to set aside etiquette and ignore everything but the purely human relation, there are little hitches when you have Emperors and Empresses to entertain that complicate the matter and bring about the most ludicrous situations. However, the Emperor made it as easy for us as he could. I wrote them a word of welcome on their arrival in this country and said that though the time was past when we might perhaps have done something for their pleasure, yet my children and I would be glad to render any service we could, and that Alex especially might facilitate the Emperor's plans in Boston and Cambridge. The Emperor answered most warmly — said he accepted without any fear of being a burden, "for," he added, "I know you feel as affectionately for me as I do for all of you." Arriving in Boston he wrote me at once and asked Alex to come in, for he would make no plans till he had seen him. He gave him a warm welcome, hugged and kissed him French fashion, and while he was in Boston did nothing without him. As he is an active party Alex found his place no sinecure; but, of course, he was glad to do all in his power, and Alex never appeared more charmingly. The same day I passed a long time with them both; I am really with them, when there are no outside ceremonies to be observed, as old friends, and the Empress is so sweet and sympathetic. The Emperor proposed to come to breakfast the next morning, — as he took the initiative in everything it made the arrangements easier, — and we had a few guests to meet him. The one of honor was Longfellow, and it was a pleasure to me that they met under our roof. The Emperor has long been an affectionate admirer of him. The whole occasion was pleasant, the weather lovely — a beautiful June morning, — every one was sociable, and I think there was as little awkwardness as possible. Then he went all over the college, the Museum, etc., then to Mt. Auburn, then closed the day by dining with Longfellow — only he and Alex, Holmes, Emerson and the family. . . .

The next day in the afternoon the Emperor and Empress went to drive with us, but the weather was gloomy, and if he had n't been very funny and she very cordial and sweet and ready to take everything in the pleasantest way, I should have felt it rather a failure; however, they *would* go and insisted it was all right. I saw them every day afterward, and the Emperor came out to bid me good-bye the last hour before leaving. He seemed delighted with his visit in Boston. He said he thought Boston

CHANGED CONDITIONS

had a kindly star for him, because everything had fallen out just as he wished. Just the last day Whittier arrived in town; when I told him of it, he said that was the crowning pleasure, for he had had a special desire to see him and did not know how to manage it, asked me where he was staying, and said he should go and call, which he did the next day, though he was to leave in the afternoon, and one would have said you could not get a thread paper in between his engagements. You may remember that one of Whittier's early poems is called *Ama Perdita*, a bird of the Amazonian woods, so called because it goes through the forest with a sad, wailing note, that has given it the name and connected with it the superstition that some *ama perdita* really goes wandering and lost in that wilderness of trees and water. It seems the Emperor translated this poem and sent the translation to Whittier *with* the veritable bird. So you see there was an old relation between them which made it very pleasant for them to meet.

Well, I have just given you the skeleton; the many lovely things this good friend said to me of the past, of the memories and regrets, I have not told you — they are so difficult to tell. Now it is over I am glad it has been, and feel that it was a satisfaction though so full of sad associations. Parting from me he said, "I shall write to you, and you will answer me." There is always a kind of simple force in his language. When we left him in Brazil, and I spoke of Agassiz's never seeing him again (as indeed he never did), he answered quietly, "My affections are steadfast; I shall never be parted from him any more." I think his character is noble and ardent. His intellect is of the encyclopedic kind, though it is true that his steady purpose (that of applying all he can learn to the welfare and enlightenment of his people) gives coherence and unity to what would otherwise seem a rather fragmentary accumulation of disconnected facts. His capacity for receiving and retaining that kind of knowledge is wonderful; how far he digests it I do not know, but he acquires a certain familiarity with means and processes which makes it more easy for him to introduce them afterward in his own country.

The following note from Longfellow is in harmony with the foregoing letters. It was written in acknowledgment of a basket of flowers which Mrs. Agassiz had sent to him on the same day with a birthday greeting, although his birthday had occurred a fortnight earlier. The "three friends," with whom Longfellow recorded his friendship in the well-known series of sonnets, *Three Friends of Mine*, were President Felton, Agassiz, and Charles Sumner.

TO MRS. LOUIS AGASSIZ

Cambridge, March 12, 1877

DEAR MRS. AGASSIZ: I thank you very much for these lovely roses and lilies that are filling my room with perfume, and still more for your kind remembrance of me and my birthday. Coming a little late they are all the more welcome, and friendly remembrance is never too late.

The three friends of mine never seem to me dead, but only absent for a while, and hardly so much as that, so living and present are their forms and faces. And yet not really to see them and speak with them is always a great sorrow to me, and I constantly think and feel how much greater it must be to you.

Pardon me for laying my hand on such a wound, and believe me,
>Ever yours very truly,
>HENRY W. LONGFELLOW

During these years of which we are speaking Mrs. Agassiz was engaged in preparing a biography of Agassiz. There is no record of the exact date when she began the task of collecting and arranging her material, but by March, 1877, the work had advanced so far that she was finishing the second chapter, which contains the account of Agassiz's student days in Munich. How she came to undertake the book, and her aim in doing so she has explained in the Preface: "My chief object was to prevent the dispersion and final loss of scattered papers which had an unquestionable family value. But, as my work grew upon my hands, I began to feel that the story of an intellectual life, which was marked by such rare coherence and unity of aim, might have a wider interest and usefulness; might, perhaps, serve as a stimulus and an encouragement to others. For this reason, and also because I am inclined to believe that the European portion of the life of Louis Agassiz is little known in his adopted country, while its American period must be unfamiliar to many in his native land, I have determined to publish the material here collected." In the earlier stages of the work Mrs. Agassiz was assisted by her stepson, but eventually, owing to the pressure of his other pursuits he was obliged to leave it entirely in her hands, except for the final revision, which he undertook. A greater amount of labor was entailed than might be inferred even from the two volumes that were the outcome. The larger part of the correspondence was in French or in German script and often very illegible. Therefore the normal difficulties of the selection, arrangement and presentation of a mass of material were vastly increased by the necessity of deciphering the originals and then of preparing satisfactory translations as preliminaries to the composition of the whole. To this labor it was impossible for Mrs. Agassiz to give uninterrupted time. The nursery perpetually called her. Mere oversight of the grandchildren did not satisfy her; she nursed them in their illnesses and shared in their amusements. For example, her diaries tell us on one day that she had herself taken Rodolphe to school "to try his new sled"; on another, that she was "practising" with Max on his new stereopticon; again, during an absence of the boys' father, when the woes of Rodolphe first with a diphtheritic throat and then with earache were making complications, "Max accidentally fired off his father's pistol. No harm done, but rather startling." To complete the story it should be added that the next day a friend by request discharged the remaining cartridges in the pistol amid the violent protests of George that his rights as eldest son and natural guardian of the household were being invaded. It is no wonder that Mrs. Agassiz's days were, as she said, "broken to inch bits."

Moreover, at this time she had many family cares outside of her own roof, was taking German lessons, and before the biography was completed had formed her connection with the "Harvard Annex." The book was therefore only incidental to a life of many claims. At one time she hired a room in a house in Felton Street, not far from her own, in order to have a place where she might write in absolute privacy. Her habits of early rising and of working before breakfast gave her an advantage; in fact, not requiring much sleep she used often on waking in the night to read or write as she was disposed, and she habitually kept by her bedside the appliances for making tea, so that whenever she woke she might have a cup of tea before proceeding to her work, without regard to the time. Upon these hours before the rest of the household was stirring she relied for the accomplishment of her task. In the summer of 1877, for instance, she made the following entries in her diary at Nahant: — "*July 10*. Worked from six to eight A.M." — "*July 11*. Worked before breakfast." — "*July 12*. No work after eight o'clock." — "*July 23*. Up at five; worked till half-past seven o'clock. Took eight o'clock boat; various errands in town. Returned at ten by narrow gauge railroad. Settled at work by twelve o'clock. Pauline and Quin came down in the afternoon." "My work is again at a stand-still," she wrote to a friend, "but I am ready to thank God that life is so full of close and tender ties that we are constantly drawn aside to minister to each other." It is not strange that at least eight years elapsed between the commencement of the book and its publication, although, as is seen from a letter quoted below, there was additional reason in Mrs. Agassiz's judgment for a certain degree of delay. The work was executed with characteristic care, and the manuscript submitted to such competent critics as Professor Arnold Guyot, Longfellow, and Horace E. Scudder, as well as to Agassiz's cousin, Auguste Mayor, who lived at Neuchâtel. The following letters written at intervals while the book was preparing are of interest here.

TO FRAU CECILE METTENIUS

Cambridge, May 15, 1876

... I THINK you would be disappointed in [a "Biography," should I write one]. I should be especially careful not to give it a controversial character. I should let facts, dates, and the completeness and coherence of the man's whole intellectual life tell its own story. Time would do the rest, and claim and assertion only awaken counter-claims and counter-assertions. Another thing will disappoint you, I think. I believe we should not be in haste about this biography; as a general thing I believe biographies are written too soon and have a certain crudeness in consequence. . . . I think it will be better to wait till things take their true proportions. Do not think that this conviction will delay my work in the least. I give to it every day and hour I have at my command; but to tell the truth it is my earnest hope, my prayer before all other prayers almost, that I may leave it for some one else to publish. . . . There has been a great deal of preliminary work — thousands of letters to look over, throw away, sort and arrange, for Agassiz's correspondence had long since become too voluminous for his management, and he had taken the habit of putting away his papers without examination. They filled many trunks. From this mass I have preserved all that I thought of the least biographical interest — much that I probably shall not use. Beside the arranging of this manuscript it has been necessary for me to make a careful review of his early works. Of course [for] the technical scientific work I am entirely incompetent. I cannot even understand it. I try to grasp the larger generalizations, the ideas underlying the whole, and to see when these thoughts first dawned upon him — how early in life the outline of his intellectual work was sketched out and how it was gradually filled in. This I strive to do. He himself helped me to understand it — indeed he gave into my hand the key to his intellectual history. The technical work — I mean the critical revision of his investigations in detail — I should, of course, leave to Alex. However, as far as possible I shall let the letters write the biography; we have many, and they make in themselves, if judiciously put together, a coherent narrative. But you will easily understand, knowing as you do and following with such sympathy our domestic life, how difficult it has been for me to go on connectedly and rapidly with my work. Of course the care of my three boys (Alex's children) occupies me very much.

TO AUGUSTE MAYOR

Nahant, September 17, 1877

THE number of the *Révue Suisse* containing the Memoir of M. Ernest Favre upon Agassiz only reached me yesterday. . . . All these short biographies of Louis (especially if they come from any one familiar with the whole field of scientific investigation in his department) help me in my work. They serve to bind together in a compact form the salient points of his life for which the materials in my hands afford such ample and varied illustration. I think I wrote you that I had now completed what I consider as the first period — including boyhood and youth, closing with his return to Switzerland from Munich in 1830-1831. . . . On my return to Cambridge in October I hope to begin the critical reading of it with Mr. Longfellow. You know how warmly he was attached to Louis, and I could have no better adviser or guide in the matter of literary criticism or in the final selection and sorting of material. But while I go on very steadily with my work and consider it fairly advanced (since much of the material belonging to later periods is also partially prepared), I hope his friends and especially his nearest family — his sisters — will not feel disappointed if I defer all thought of publication for the present. Were the work completed, I am daily more convinced that some years had better pass before its appearance. It seems to me much better that time should mellow the crude and often prejudiced appreciations of a distinguished man's life and work, before the final word is spoken about it. My feeling about this does not diminish my industry, but I should like when the book is done to put it away and let it ripen in the dark for a while — not without hope that when

THE BIOGRAPHY OF AGASSIZ

the fitting time for publication comes I might be out of hearing of discussion or criticism.

The following letter was written not long after the death of Alexander Braun.

TO FRAU CECILE METTENIUS

Cambridge, November 17 [1877]

... I FEEL an ease and pleasure in writing to you that seems to me like the growth of an old and intimate relation rather than the correspondence of people who have never met. Is it perhaps that I have been, as it were, educated to love and revere your father? Uncle Louis talked to me so often both of his character and his intellect with such affectionate respect. I seem to hear him still, for only two or three days ago in reading over one of his early letters to his mother (1832) from Paris I came upon this passage: '*Tu ne saurais te faire une juste idée de la puissance et de la consolation que me procurent mes relations avec Alexandre, — il est si bon et en même temps si instruit et si élevé dans ses idées que c'est pour moi un vrai bonheur qu'il soit mon ami.*" So he felt it to be to the end. I only wish he could have had the happiness of being more constantly with him. That spiritual elevation of which you speak in your sister seems to me so like him. It is lovely to be with people who seem to have by instinct as the pure gift of God what the rest of us are fighting for and winning only by the hard experience and discipline of life. Such a nature is a benediction to every one. You don't know our Pauline very well, but her presence is like your sister Mary's, a blessing for us all. Do you know Wordsworth's two lines:

> "Glad hearts without reproach or blot,
> Who do Thy work and *know it not*."

That expresses what I mean about these unconscious pure natures, who seem to live very near to God. . . .

I did find, as you said I should, great support and encouragement from Mr. Longfellow. He came every day for a week and passed two hours with me, while I read aloud to him my work as far as it has gone. He was intensely interested in the material, letters, etc., and cheered me very much about it all. The manuscript has now gone to Mr. Guyot, — the only survivor of that circle of young men who sympathized so affectionately in each other's intellectual work. I know that his criticism will be of great service to me. He also has written me very warmly about it, but has not yet finished it.

Cambridge, January, 1879

... I HAD it in my mind to write a month ago, but I have been delayed because I wanted to send you these two or three letters of your father's, which it seemed to me you would all be glad to read now, or if you have seen them before, to re-read. They are so full of elevating and noble thoughts, especially the one of January, 1833, where he speaks of self-sacrifice in love, — the being able to bear and to suffer together as the closest tie. I think he says

THE BIOGRAPHY OF AGASSIZ 189

rightly that it is sometimes a mistake to hide what pains and troubles us from those we love — they have a right to share it, — except, of course, in certain circumstances where it may be necessary and right.

The biography appeared in 1885, in two volumes, under the title, *Louis Agassiz. His Life and Correspondence.* "Just now I am so anxious about my work that I find it best not to speak of it. I hardly have the courage," Mrs. Agassiz reports to Frau Mettenius in March of that year, when it was almost completed. Upon it, however, perhaps, her most permanent individual reputation rests. It is essentially the history of Agassiz's career as a naturalist — a history that she was peculiarly fitted to write by her technical acquaintance with his scientific investigations and their relative importance. More notable, however, than this familiarity is the discrimination with which she emphasized essentials and disregarded non-essentials for a just comprehension of Agassiz's contributions to science. Such an episode, for example, as the well-known controversy between Agassiz and Darwin which loomed large in the lives of both, although it never disturbed their friendly personal relations, she passed by in silence evidently recognizing that it was merely secondary to Agassiz's important aims. But more fundamental for the understanding of Mrs. Agassiz's own nature than these characteristics of the book is the degree to which she excluded herself from the narrative. It is literally as if we saw the brilliant life and personality of Agassiz reflected in a mirror held by an invisible hand without a suspicion that the same hand had ministered to him constantly for twenty-three years.

Shortly after its publication the book was translated into French by Monsieur Auguste Mayor and into German by Frau Mettenius. That this labor was performed by friends, who were also members of the family, was a source of gratification to Mrs. Agassiz. The following letters are the best comment on her attitude toward the biography.

TO MRS. WILLIAM B. ROGERS

Cambridge

DEAR MRS. ROGERS: It touched me very much that you should have taken the pains to write me about the memoirs of Agassiz, and it gives me the greatest pleasure to find that your judgment of it is favorable. I knew that the material left to me was interesting in itself, but I was beset by many doubts as to whether it would bring to my readers the impression it had made upon me, — whether I could so put it together as to show the enthusiasm controlled by patience and industry which seemed to me so characteristic of the life.

Thank you with all my heart; I feel both your sympathy and your appreciation — all the more to me because your own life has brought you into contact with pursuits of the same nature, followed with a like ardor and devotion.

With affectionate remembrances (dating back to our Temple Place days), believe me,

Most cordially yours,

ELIZABETH C. AGASSIZ

TO AUGUSTE MAYOR

Germantown, Pa., June 10, 1887

I HAVE constantly intended to thank you for your letter giving me an account of the fête given by the Société de Belles Lettres on the occasion of placing Louis's bust in the new Academic Building.

It is most touching to me to see the ever increasing affection and respect for Louis's memory in his own country. Even in this last letter you give me most remarkable instances of it; not the least striking is of the person at Nice who was steadied in the long hours of waiting in danger and doubt by the story of his life.

I received the Italian notice of the book and was much pleased with it, as you were. It had a different character from any of the other reviews, but it was very graceful and gracious in tone. I was glad also to hear of the old friend at Porrentruy, who had made the book his companion in the long winter months.

Many of the currents in Mrs. Agassiz's life spoken of above continued long after 1879. In that year she began to share a new interest destined to become important to her, although always standing apart from her other occupations. This interest was the "Harvard Annex," to which the next chapter is devoted.

CHAPTER IX
THE SOCIETY FOR THE COLLEGIATE INSTRUCTION OF WOMEN: THE HARVARD ANNEX
1879–1893

IN Mrs. Agassiz's diary for 1879 the note for February 11 reads: "At home, morning. Meeting about Harvard Education for Women, afternoon." This, the first record of her connection with a work of which she became a large part and of which Radcliffe College is the outcome, is supplemented by a slender sheaf of papers in the possession of the college, consisting of the copies of notes made in the form of a diary by Mr. Arthur Gilman, a well-known literary man and author, deeply interested in education, and a familiar figure in Cambridge from 1870 to his death in 1909. In this diary he jotted down day by day from November, 1879, to June, 1882, the activities of the little group of earnest enthusiasts, a self-constituted committee, with whom Mrs. Agassiz first met on that February afternoon in 1879. These papers containing information that only Mr. Gilman, as secretary of the committee, could supply, he gave to the Library of Radcliffe College in 1904, saying in his letter of presentation, "I thought that if some one in 1636 or thereabouts, had made such notes and had preserved such printed and written matter about the College now called Harvard, he would have been a benefactor. Perhaps somebody will thank me, even in 2172." Appreciation of his labors, however, has tarried till no such distant date, for his little collection of documents is in fact our

THE HARVARD ANNEX 193

only source for some of the data that are of consequence in a memoir of Mrs. Agassiz, whose relation to the institution cannot be understood without a clear conception of its unique aims and the gradual process of its growth.

The history of the beginnings of Radcliffe College has been told by Mr. Gilman himself in an article on Mrs. Agassiz that appeared in the *Harvard Graduates' Magazine* for September, 1907, in a chapter contributed by him to a book of which he was the editor, *The Cambridge of Eighteen Hundred and Ninety-Six*, in a short paper, *The Society for the Collegiate Instruction of Women*, published in 1891, and in a pleasant sketch written for the *Radcliffe Magazine* for June, 1905; an excellent article on the college by Mr. Joseph B. Warner, its first treasurer, may also be found in the *Harvard Graduates' Magazine* for March, 1894. But although the somewhat unusual story of the institution has not lacked narrators, it acquires a fresh interest when looked at from the angle of Mrs. Agassiz's part in the plot, and when it unfolds itself chapter by chapter as the principal characters in it record the events that they were themselves shaping. How Mrs. Agassiz entered on the scene we learn from the following items at the beginning of Mr. Gilman's *Notes*.

1878, November 25. My wife has for two years urged upon me the need that exists in Cambridge for an institution for the higher education of women. Lately we have considered the matter more thoroughly. ... A plan has occurred to me. Suppose I find a number of ladies wanting to get the same education that men have and I will tell them, "I will arrange a course exactly the same that Harvard offers men and get the Harvard professors to give the instruction." I therefore arranged a list of teachers based on the present year.

November 26. Yesterday I asked Professor [James B.] Greenough to spend the evening in my library. He came with his wife. We discussed the plan. He approved and made out a list of teachers. We ... separated, promising to consider the subject of its practicability.

Within a month Mr. Gilman sent the following letter to President Eliot of Harvard University.

TO PRESIDENT CHARLES W. ELIOT

Cambridge, December 23, 1878

DEAR SIR: I am engaged in perfecting a plan which shall afford to women opportunities for carrying their studies systematically forward further than it is possible for them to do it in this country (except possibly at Smith College).

My plan obliges me to obtain the services of some of the professors, and I address you before approaching them, in order to assure myself that I am correct in supposing that their relations to the University are such as to permit of their giving instruction to those who are not connected with it.

I propose to bring here such women as are able to pass an examination not less rigid than that now established for the admission of young men and to offer them a course of instruction which shall be a counterpart of that pursued by the men. It is probable that a very small number of women will be found at first, but it may grow.

I am aware that some of the professors now give instruction to private pupils and teach elsewhere. If my plan prove a success, it will relieve them from such irregular labor and give them a regular addition to their income.

It is, however, needless that I enlarge or trouble you at greater length. I desire only to be assured that if I make approaches to any of the faculty, I shall be asking them for services that they can render or not, without in any way interfering with their first obligations to the University.

   I am
     Very truly yours,
         ARTHUR GILMAN

The *Notes* continue:

1878, December 24. President Eliot replied in person that I was at liberty to arrange with professors. He suggests that the young women would need a home.

1879, January 14. Conferred with Professor Greenough. He has spoken to Professor William James, N. S. Shaler, and others who are favorable. We discussed funds and plans at length, Mrs. Greenough and Mrs. Gilman being present. Proposed forming a committee of ladies to manage the matter, I being secretary.

Ten days later, as we learn from the *Notes*, a meeting was held at which Miss Alice Longfellow, who had been mentioned on January 14 as a possible member of the committee, was present in addition to the four other conspirators, Mr. and Mrs. Gilman, and Professor and Mrs. Greenough. They made further nominations for the committee of ladies and proposed among other names those of Mrs. Louis Agassiz, Miss Lilian Horsford (Mrs. William G. Farlow), and Mrs. Josiah B. Cooke, the wife of the eminent professor of chemistry in Harvard University. "The grade of instruction to be given was discussed, and it was agreed that it should be equivalent to that of a Harvard course; a certificate to be given at its end. Professor Greenough and Mr. Gilman were appointed to frame a circular announcing the formation of the committee and its plan."

The next item of interest here is dated February 4, and records a meeting at which "Mrs. Louis Agassiz was again discussed and Mrs. Cooke appointed to invite her to join the Committee." Two days later Mr. Gilman notes that Mrs. Agassiz had accepted the place on the committee, and that he had sent the following letter to President Eliot, which speaks for itself.

TO PRESIDENT CHARLES W. ELIOT

February 6, 1879

DEAR SIR: I hand you herewith a copy of a circular that is to be put into the hands of those interested, in accordance with the plan that I laid before you in my note of December 23rd.

The circular has been worded with care to avoid two possible misconceptions: (1) that the plan in any way savors or tends to coeducation, and (2) that Harvard College is in any way responsible for it.

The ladies are all opposed to coeducation and are earnestly in favor of the present movement.

All are very glad to make the experiment without involving Harvard, but when success has been achieved we shall be glad to give the glory to her.

Very truly yours,

ARTHUR GILMAN

The events that are recorded so succinctly above were narrated with greater detail by Mr. Gilman many years later in the two following letters, which are quoted here because they serve to set forth the exact nature of the enterprise with which Mrs. Agassiz became identified. Miss Leach, mentioned in the letter, who later became professor of Greek in Vassar College, had been distinguishing herself by her excellent work as a private pupil of Professors Greenough, Goodwin, and Child.

TO MRS. LOUIS AGASSIZ

Cambridge, February 1, 1883

MY DEAR MRS. AGASSIZ, . . . The first discussion of the subject of obtaining the services of the college for women grew out of the fact that my daughter Grace, having been at school in Cambridge for some years, was ready to go further in her studies, and Mrs. Gilman and I were reluctant to send her daily to Boston or to send her away from home. This was in the autumn or winter of 1876. During our consultations it occurred to Mrs. Gilman that some plan might be arranged by which women could be instructed by the instructors of the college. We studied the subject for months, and at last came to the conclusion that we could not get such instruction for our daughters without forming classes in some way, so that the expense would be divided among several. Time passed on, and we did not effect any arrangement.... We did not give up our study of the higher education of women here. I looked over the field, found out what had been done and then tried to learn if there was any general demand for such instruction as the Harvard professors gave. This led me to conclude that there were a good many women who wished to get exactly the same course of study that was given in college.... In the meantime Mrs. Gilman and I studied plans to accomplish our desire. We thought of hiring a building, placing it under the care of a matron and arranging with the professors to give repetitions of the college courses in it. Other plans suggested themselves to us, before we decided upon the one since adopted. When we had reached this stage, the matter was held in abeyance for months, because I feared to present it to any of the professors lest it should be received with disapproval. At last ... I concluded to approach Professor Greenough and ... I laid out the scheme [before him], as it has since been carried out. I told him that I had made out a list of instructors in the different departments, and wished that he could do the same, and that then we would compare them. He expressed much interest in the plan and entered into it with warmth. He made out a list of professors, and it proved very much like mine. He told me of Miss Leach, whose presence, he thought, would lead the instructors to look favorably on the plan.... He said he would speak to some of the professors

THE HARVARD ANNEX

about it, and from time to time reported that one and another had given approval.

Meanwhile I had laid the plan before President Eliot, asking if there was any objection to carrying it out. He called on me and told me there was no objection. In January, 1879, we began to form the committee of ladies, taking pains to choose such as did not represent any "cause," or who would be looked upon as "advanced," or in favor of coeducation. . . . On the sixth of February you were kind enough to agree to coöperate with us, and from that time you know the history of the movement.

TO MRS. ANNIE NATHAN MEYER

Cambridge, December 3, 1887

. . . Our movement here was of the simplest nature, and it seemed strange that no one had made it before. My object was to get the collegiate instruction for women, and at the same time conciliate both those who wished women to be immediately admitted to the classes with the young men and those who wished them never to be so admitted.

In order to accomplish these desirable ends, without which all former attempts had failed, I determined not to mention the subject of "coeducation," as it was then called, or the admission of women to the classes of men. This subject has no relevancy to the present movement. Our sole and simple purpose is to give to women the same instruction that men have here — that is, instruction of the same grade, in the same subjects and by the same professors. The instruction was to be systematic, — that is, it was to be the same which leads to the first collegiate degree. It was necessary for our purpose that a body of ladies should be formed to give the public confidence that if young women were sent to Cambridge they would be cared for. In seeking for these we confined ourselves to such as had no reputation as being opposed to or in favor of the admission of women to Harvard College.

Turning back to Mr. Gilman's *Notes* for 1879 we find that the next important step was the issuing of a circular by the ladies of the committee with the assent of President Eliot.

PRIVATE COLLEGIATE INSTRUCTION FOR WOMEN

THE ladies whose names are appended below are authorized to say that a number of Professors and other Instructors in Harvard College have consented to give private tuition to properly qualified young women who desire to pursue advanced studies in Cambridge. Other Professors whose occupations prevent them from giving such tuition are willing to assist young women by advice and by lectures. No instruction will be provided of a lower grade than that given in Harvard College.

The expense of instruction in as many branches as a student can profitably pursue at once will depend upon the numbers in the several courses, but it will probably not exceed four hundred dollars a year, and may be as low as two hundred and fifty. It is hoped, however, that endowments may hereafter be procured which will materially reduce this expense.

Pupils who show upon examination that they have satisfactorily pursued any courses of study under this scheme will receive certificates to that effect, signed by their instructors. It is hoped, nevertheless, that the greater number will pursue a four years' course of study, in which case the certificates for the different branches will be merged in one, which will be signed by all the Instructors and will certify to the whole course.

The ladies will see that the students secure suitable lodgings, and will assist them with advice and other friendly offices.

Information as to the qualifications required, with the names of the Instructors in any branch, may be obtained upon application to any one of the ladies, or to their Secretary, Mr. Arthur Gilman, 5 Phillips Place.

> Mrs. Louis Agassiz
> Mrs. E. W. Gurney
> Mrs. J. P. Cooke
> Mrs. J. B. Greenough
> Mrs. Arthur Gilman
> Miss Alice M. Longfellow
> Miss Lilian Horsford

Cambridge, Mass., February 22, 1879

This circular was previously sent to a large proportion of the members of the Harvard faculty with the request that if they were willing to coöperate with the Committee, they would notify Mr. Gilman, and on February 20, the devoted committee met at the house of Mr. Gilman in a heavy snowstorm to hear his report on the replies. Fifty-three had been received, the first in the affirmative from Professor William E. Byerly; forty-four more were favorable, some of the instructors saying that they were ready to give their services without remuneration rather than allow the plan to fail. At this meeting "Mr. Greenough was requested to attend all meetings as advisor," and thus formed a nucleus for the future Academic Board of Radcliffe College. On March 7, it was decided to "ask the professors or a representative body of them to meet the ladies for consultation" at the house of Mr. Gilman. At this meeting four applications from prospective students were read, three of which had been received by Mrs. Agassiz. On March 12, Mr. Gilman was chosen secretary for the committee of ladies, an office which he held virtually until 1894. A few days later an advisory board of five professors was appointed to act with the ladies, and in the following August, the committee having by that time received nearly $16,000 in subscriptions, they appointed Mr. Joseph B. Warner, a well-known lawyer of Boston, as their treasurer.

On September 24, entrance examinations began, and Mrs. Agassiz's diary has the noteworthy record for that day, written at Nahant: "To Cambridge. Meeting for the Harvard girls." The "Harvard girls" who began to attend the courses offered were twenty-seven in number, two of whom left early in the year, one to study abroad, the other, who lived in a neighboring town, because of the difficulty of regular communication with Cambridge. The remaining twenty-five continued throughout the year, three

THE HARVARD ANNEX

of them taking the regular course, and the remainder ranking as special students. Quarters, beginning with two and speedily extending to four rooms, were rented in the house of Mr. and Mrs. J. F. Carret, 6 Appian Way, near the present site of Radcliffe College, and here hospitality was given in good measure, literally pressed down and running over, to the expanding but modest enterprise. The proud memory of Mrs. Agassiz making and hanging the muslin curtains for their windows, which some of the first students retain, is characteristic of the simplicity and economy that marked the scanty equipment. Yet the departments of study and the instructors were not to be despised: Greek, L. B. R. Briggs, W. W. Goodwin, J. W. White; Latin, W. W. Gould, J. B. Greenough, G. M. Lane; Sanskrit, J. B. Greenough; English, A. S. Hill; German, G. A. Bartlett, E. S. Sheldon; French, F. Bôcher, A Jacquinot; Philosophy, G. H. Palmer; Political Economy, J. L. Laughlin; History, G. Bendelari, E. Emerton; Music, J. K. Paine; Mathematics, G. R. Briggs, W. E. Byerly, B. O. Peirce, J. M. Peirce; Physics, R. W. Willson; Natural History, G. L. Goodale.

Thus September, 1879, saw private collegiate instruction for women established in Cambridge under the direction of seven ladies as managers, of whom Mrs. Agassiz was one, a secretary, a treasurer and an advisory board of five professors, which had developed from a single advisor, Professor Greenough, as a nucleus. A more informal or less "organized" committee has rarely existed that has accomplished such far-reaching results. It was even nameless, but its offspring was almost at birth promptly christened the "Harvard Annex," by (as tradition goes) a Harvard student, who might thus have immortalized himself but missed a chance for distinction by failing to claim as his invention the name that had no rival for fifteen years in spite of more official designations.

Mrs. Agassiz had been sought as one of the managers, apart from her own personality, because of the aims in education with which she had been identified in the Agassiz School, one of the objectives in which had been, like that of the Committee, to provide instruction for young girls from members of the faculty of Harvard College. There can be no doubt that it was principally because she regarded this movement almost as a continuation of the aims of the school that Mrs. Agassiz was ready to take part in it. "But for the school," she wrote toward the end of her life to Miss Cary, "the college (so far as I am concerned) would never have existed." Yet in February, 1879, she did not in the least foresee the proportions in her life that this new undertaking was to assume. The mere fact that in her diary she made no record of her invitation to serve on the Committee is an indication of how entirely informal the arrangement was and how far from important the matter seemed to her. At the time of the first meetings she was occupied with the revision of her *First Lesson in Natural History*, of which a second edition was about to be issued, and her daily entries chronicle the stages of her work on this little book, but pass by in silence or barely mention many of the meetings which Mr. Gilman's *Notes* show that she attended. In fact, Mrs. Agassiz later admitted that only a conversation with President Eliot led her to realize that by putting her signature to the first circular she had brought definite responsibilities upon herself in regard to the care of the prospective

THE HARVARD ANNEX

students. But both in her diaries and in Mr. Gilman's *Notes* enough is said to make it clear that she immediately became an effective member of the Committee, conferring at once with Mr. Gilman, making visits upon friends in Boston who might become interested in the scheme, and writing letters in its behalf. On May 30, 1881, for example, Mr. Gilman writes: "Mrs. Agassiz was appointed a committee to see Mr. Eliot to learn if any arrangement can be made for the young ladies to use books in the Library and more particularly the feeling about our future"; and considering her later success in many similar delicate missions, it is not surprising to learn that she reported a "satisfactory interview." Unfortunately the series of Mrs. Agassiz's journals is interrupted from February 14, 1880, to January 1, 1892, and for these intervening years, highly important for the collegiate instruction of women in Cambridge, we have scarcely a word from her outside of her published addresses and reports.

The following letter written in 1882 shows Mrs. Agassiz's excellent practical judgment in matters affecting the policy of the Annex, and her steady adherence to the original plan of the committee of providing Harvard instruction for women, not of establishing a new college for women.

TO MR. ARTHUR GILMAN

Cambridge, March 24, 1882

My dear Mr. Gilman: Will you kindly allow me to see you again before you take further steps about raising money? Of course, if we are to live, we must have the material means of living. But with reference to the final form which our scheme is to take I think it is important to state clearly and to be agreed among ourselves upon some definite plan with reference to the college. It has been partly my own suggestion, I believe, that for the present we should raise a small sum and take care of our own affairs for another term of years, supplementing the college instruction, if necessary, with officers of our own. But the more I think of this, the more I fear that we shall drift into the building up of another female college, distinct from the University. I believe that this would be a great mistake; it would be repeating the error already made about men's colleges, — namely, multiplying them and so weakening all, instead of strengthening those which already exist. We must be careful to avoid this rock.

The next important entries in Mr. Gilman's *Notes* are the following:

1882, April 25. Meeting of the Managers and Advisory Board. The Secretary stated that he had received a note asking how money could be left to the cause by will and that upon consulting the Treasurer had been advised that the simplest method would be for the body to become a legal corporation. . . . It was

Voted: that it is the opinion of the meeting that the body should be incorporated. The name to be adopted for the Corporation was then discussed at length, and it was

Voted: that the name be "The Society for the Collegiate Instruction of Women."

THE HARVARD ANNEX

Voted: that the Corporation be the present Managers, the members of the Advisory Board, the Treasurer and Secretary, and that Professors Charles E. Norton and Francis J. Child be added.

With this entry the *Notes* of Mr. Gilman end. The period of informal organization was over and gone, and the remaining records of the society are kept as formal minutes. On May 22, 1882, Articles of Association were signed by which the Committee agreed to constitute itself a corporation to be known as The Society for the Collegiate Instruction of Women, whose purpose was to promote the education of women with the assistance of the instructors in Harvard University. The signers of the agreement, besides Mrs. Agassiz, were Mrs. E. W. Gurney, Mr. and Mrs. Arthur Gilman, Professor and Mrs. J. B. Greenough, Miss Lilian Horsford, Professor Charles Eliot Norton, Professor W. W. Goodwin, Professor C. L. Smith, Professor F. J. Child, Miss Alice Longfellow, Professor J. M. Peirce, Professor W. E. Byerly, Miss Ellen F. Mason, Major H. L. Higginson, Mr. Joseph B. Warner. At the first meeting held after the Articles were signed, on July 6, 1882, it was decided that the officers should be a president, treasurer, secretary, an Executive Committee, and an Academic Board. Mrs. Agassiz was elected president; Mr. Gilman, secretary, Mr. Warner, treasurer, Mr. Greenough, chairman of the Academic Board. On August 16 this association became incorporated under the laws of the Commonwealth of Massachusetts as The Society for the Collegiate Instruction of Women — a title that was used only on state occasions, and not always then, so much simpler it was to cling to the less formidable and less dignified " Harvard Annex."

Mrs. Agassiz's position as president of the Society is the better appreciated by an understanding of her relation to her colleagues. All those who had signed the Articles of Association were in varying degrees influential members of the community, and some had a wide and enduring reputation, as the mention of their names sufficiently shows. Many of them were already warm personal friends of Mrs. Agassiz, one, indeed, was her son-in-law, Major Higginson, who from these early beginnings throughout a long connection with Radcliffe College never failed in rendering it affectionate and incalculable service. Professor and Mrs. Gurney were also zealous fellow-workers of Mrs. Agassiz and always welcomed the students to their house, not only for Professor Gurney's classes but for social occasions as well. "Few who shared the privilege," Mrs. Agassiz said in one of her addresses, "will forget the hours in Mr. Gurney's library, where all the surroundings heightened the pleasure of the lesson." Mrs. Gurney was herself a constant student of language and literature, versed in the classics and modern letters, heartily interested in the education of women, and a valued adviser of Mrs. Agassiz. To Mrs. Arthur Gilman, too, Mrs. Agassiz was in the habit of turning for counsel in all matters connected with the students and found her support, as she said, "an unfailing source of satisfaction." Among the other members of the group, who stood in especially close relations to the enterprise and consequently to Mrs. Agassiz were Professor Greenough, "one of the most hopeful of the professors," as she characterized him, whose presence was always a blessing to the college; Professor Goodwin, who opened his study to his classes, shared with them his books and photo-

THE HARVARD ANNEX

graphs, and usually brought his lecture hour to a close around Mrs. Goodwin's tea-table by the fireside; Professor Norton, for whom Mrs. Agassiz's great regard, as well as his for her, is apparent in letters quoted later, and with whose view that the tendency of instruction at that time was too exclusively toward the less imaginative studies, she completely sympathized in spite of her strong bias toward scientific pursuits; and Professor Child, for whom her warm affection is expressed in the following letter written many years later on hearing of his death.

TO MISS GRACE NORTON

Nahant, September 13, 1896

... For myself this great break (for such it is even for those who rarely met him) brings the strangest revival of my youth, when I knew Child first or rather when I saw him most frequently. I was often at my sister Mary's for long visits, and then a day rarely passed without my seeing him. It was a very interesting time in my own life when I was just beginning to know Cambridge, and Felton's house was a sort of centre for the older professors; into that pleasant circle Child brought such a bright young spirit. He cannot have been much over twenty, for he was several years younger than I. After his marriage and mine we did not see so much of each other, and it is perhaps on account of that interruption that my memory bridges over the intervening time and makes these early days stand out to me more vividly than the present. But this cessation of frequent intercourse never lessened our affection for each other. I can say that for myself, and this very summer I had a note from him which I shall always keep — a last word as it proves, and so affectionate — full of a kind sympathy which I can never forget.

What a gentle, genial nature — sensitive and shy, but always cordial, and quickly responsive to any friendly expression!

Among the signers of the Articles of Association no one stands out as more important to the daily life of the Annex than Mr. Gilman. Professor Byerly, who was actively associated with the institution from the time when, as we have seen, he outstripped his fellow-instructors at Harvard in accepting the invitation to teach at the Annex, until 1913, was said to be the most indispensable person connected with the college, but Mr. Byerly himself pointed out in 1910 in the *Harvard Graduates' Magazine* that for the greater part of fifteen years Mr. Gilman was practically the one executive officer of the Annex. "Of the numerous friends and workers who made the college a success he was the one with whom it held the first place. The professors who labored so faithfully and effectively for the new institution were busy Harvard teachers who devoted to the 'Annex' the precious time they could spare from their exacting Harvard work. Mrs. Agassiz's many duties, social and philanthropic, were not laid aside when she became interested in the 'Annex,' nor were those of the other ladies who served the college so efficiently.... Mr. Gilman lived for it, and served and fostered it for years unweariedly and ungrudgingly."

Such was the group with whom Mrs. Agassiz was closely associated in her official position, and since most of them continued to share her responsibilities even after the Annex was merged into Radcliffe College, their opinions and their friendship may be counted as important factors in her daily life.

The paramount object accomplished by the managers when they obtained their charter from the Commonwealth was that the Society was thereby placed in a position where it could legally hold and administer funds for its purposes, and could properly attempt to raise a sufficient endowment to establish its work on a permanent basis. In the late winter of 1883 the Executive Committee determined to solicit money for an endowment fund to be transferred to the President and Fellows of Harvard College whenever this could be done to advance the purposes of the Society. Later in the spring, in accordance with a suggestion made by Mrs. Agassiz, parlor-meetings were held in Boston attended by friends who were interested in the experiment, at which Mrs. Agassiz read a report of the previous work of the Society. This at once brought not only the Society but Mrs. Agassiz herself into greater prominence and identified her with the education of women in the mind of the public as she had never been before. There is no better way of telling the history of the years from 1879 to 1883, with the varying phases of which Mrs. Agassiz's thoughts had been daily occupied, than by republishing selections from this address, the first of any consequence that she made on behalf of the Annex. It was adopted by the ladies of the Executive Committee as their report and printed with a slightly different introduction in 1884.

We propose this afternoon (I speak for all the ladies of our Committee and at their request) to tell you the story of the so-called "Annex" and interest you if we can in its future fortunes.

The name is often heard in Boston, but we doubt whether much is known of its character or of the work it has thus far accomplished. This is not strange, for it came into life so quietly, and has had so natural and healthy a growth out of existing circumstances, that it has attracted but little attention . . .

Our enterprise, undertaken with many doubts and with a perfect readiness to abandon it, should it prove wise and right to do so, is now in its fourth year. Instead of presenting special difficulties and complications, it has worked simply and well. Whether considered as a test of the genuineness of the desire for university education among women, and especially among women desiring to teach, or of their ability as students, the result has been most satisfactory. The standard of work has been high, — exceptionally so in a number of instances, — and the interest of the Harvard instructors has kept pace with the zeal of their students.

Since the first year, when we opened with twenty-seven pupils, our number has averaged from thirty-five to forty. . . . We have to confess in reference to our numbers, that the Annex is, for the class of women to whom it especially appeals, very expensive. The charge per year for a full college course is $200 — $50 more than is paid by Harvard students. It therefore costs those who enter for the whole four years $800, beside the expense of living in Cambridge. The single courses are $75 a year. This puts our instruction out of the reach of many who covet it, and some of those who come even for one year only do so at a great sacrifice, though not, we think, without finding the investment a profitable one. Were every facility offered them, however, we hardly suppose that women would ever look upon a college course of study subsequent to their school life as an inevitable or even necessary part of their education; nor do we think it would seem to any of us desirable that they should do so. But this being granted, there still remain quite enough for whom such a completion of their earlier training is important in view of their occupation as teachers, and if there are others who ask it purely for its own sake, we surely should not deny them. . . .

Thus far our Annex students have belonged to the classes of woman named above. They have been young women fitting as teachers, or older women who are already teachers, but who allow themselves, out of their small earnings, the rare luxury of a little change from teaching to learning, that they may go back to their work refreshed and better prepared; or women of scholarly tastes, with means to gratify them, who come, as we have said, to study under higher auspices simply because they enjoy it. We have had as yet no flighty students, brought by the novelty of the thing, and very little fragmentary, half-digested work. Our instruction has of course been limited by the lack of laboratories, apparatus, books, etc. We have, however, with the help of friends, collected a working library of some 800 volumes. For the first time this year, we have also, through the generosity of Mr. Harold Whiting, our instructor in Physics, the command of a small physical laboratory, fitted up by him with all the necessary apparatus.

One thing it may be well to state here. Certain anxieties respecting the presence of young women in a university town, without constant oversight of their daily lives, have vanished on nearer approach. Our students are scattered by twos and threes in Cambridge families, their lodgings being chosen for them by their friends, or by the ladies of our Executive Committee. In Cambridge such arrangements are easily made, and we have had no difficulty in finding safe and pleasant homes for them. They quietly pursue their occupations as unnoticed as the daughters of any Cambridge residents; nor has any objection or obstacle arisen on that score. It should be added that the health of our students has been excellent thus far, — we have had but two cases of serious illness in our four years' experience, and many of the students have gained rather than lost in the general look of vigor.

But while difficulties are thus dispersing, and educationally our scheme is growing apace, our means are dwindling even more rapidly, and we are fast approaching the end of the sum we had provided. The Annex has, on the whole, been more nearly self-supporting than we had expected, and we have still funds enough remaining to carry it on for a year or two longer. Unless, in that interval, we can raise a large endowment fund, by which means we also hope to

THE HARVARD ANNEX

commend ourselves to Harvard College and establish a definite relation with the University, we must renounce our attempt for this time. And yet that would seem a pity, for we believe there was never a better opportunity for securing what is by so many so greatly desired, — a share for women of the educational advantages to be had at Harvard.

Nor was there ever a moment when the University could so safely grant us this boon. In the form in which this effort in behalf of women's education has been started and is likely to be continued, it stirs no prejudices, excites no opposition, involves no change of policy for the University. Our students themselves manifest no desire for coeducation. The element of competition with men does not enter into their aims. They simply want the best education they can get, and they seek it at Harvard because the means to that end exist there. We only ask the College, therefore, in case we can provide for our own expenses, to continue a work which has thus far been conducted so quietly and inoffensively that it has hardly attracted observation.

It may, and no doubt will, be asked, why we desire to establish a college for women in Cambridge when several successful ones exist elsewhere; when we have Vassar, the Boston University, Smith, and Wellesley. We readily admit that such a college would be both undesirable and superfluous, unless we can connect it directly with Harvard College. Failing this, we should miss the distinctive thing for which we have aimed.

... In the presence of our old University at Cambridge, with all its traditions of learning and experience, possessing ample means of higher instruction, officered by teachers of well-known ability, among whom are always to be found men of real eminence in their departments, we find the only good reason for presenting our scheme to you and asking your help and sympathy in carrying it on. It may not be easy to define why the older University has the advantage. But we must all admit that its relation to the intellectual world outside, its maturity of thought and methods, its claim on cultivated minds everywhere, give it a hold on our respect and affection which women share with men. We must not wonder if some of them long also for a share in the gracious gifts it has garnered up in years gone by, and which perhaps may have in years to come, a still wider use and beneficence. ...

There is a general impression that Harvard College is very rich, — that what she *will* do, she *can* do, so far as her means are concerned. Her large deficits for several years past tell us that this is not true. Harvard needs all that she has and more, for the institution as it now exists, — to fulfil the objects for which it was originally founded. We ask her to enlarge her borders, to assume new responsibilities, involving new expenses, and we must come not as charity scholars, but with full hands, to strengthen rather than impoverish her. To this end we appeal to the public, feeling that we are justified in doing so, now that our enterprise has passed out of the stage of doubtful experi-

THE HARVARD ANNEX

ment into that of ascertained use and value. We need many subscribers, for less than $100,000 would surely make us, financially speaking, an unsafe acquisition for the University. Of this $100,000, something more than $36,000 have been subscribed in the last three or four weeks.

Even if we should succeed in raising the whole of this sum, it could not put the education of women on a par with that of men at Harvard. Indeed we are advised that, considered as a permanent foundation for so large a scheme, it would be quite insufficient. But it might give the College the means of continuing, on a somewhat broader basis, the work already begun, and would be a nucleus around which additional resources would gather as soon as the character of the undertaking was fully understood. Good work wins good will, and we cannot but hope that if the College accepts us, we too shall have, when we have secured the recognition of the community, our occasional gifts, our bequests and legacies, like other departments of the University.

We learn what the further fortunes of the enterprise were from passages in Mrs. Agassiz's informal address in June, 1884, when she had invited the second class that had completed the regular four years' course of study to her house in Quincy Street for their "Commencement exercises." The response to her appeal in March which she reports here demonstrates her possession of one of the prime requisites for the president of a budding institution — an unusual power of persuasion. This power rested not at all upon either eloquence or art, but chiefly upon her utter unconsciousness of self, which made her as it were a translucent medium for all that was worthy in the interest that she was representing, and established the confidence of her hearers in it by her own complete sincerity. Added to this her native grace of manner and expression gave her a distinction that never failed to attract attention.

I believe we have disarmed enemies and made friends. For this happy result we have in great measure to thank our students themselves. By the sincerity and efficiency of their work and the modest and unobtrusive spirit in which they have carried it on, they have unconsciously overcome much prejudice of which they hardly knew themselves. Better than any argument of ours in favor of allowing young women a share in University education is the fact that a considerable number, from forty to fifty annually, have actually pursued their university studies here for five years as undisturbed by comment or criticism as the daughters of resident families in Cambridge.

I am sure I need not remind you all that for the intellectual success of the Annex thus far we have to thank the professors and teachers of the University who have worked with us in such a sympathetic spirit. But for them the Annex would indeed have been shortlived. I should find it difficult, I know, to express your gratitude or my own for all they have done for us. With their help and a continuance of the spirit in our students which they have shown thus far, I hope the Annex has a long life before it

THE HARVARD ANNEX

Still if we do not live by bread alone, neither can we live without it, and that brings me to the financial question. You all know probably that some eighteen months ago, feeling assured after a trial of four years that our experiment deserved support, we appealed to the public in its behalf and started a subscription for an endowment fund of $100,000 with the purpose of asking the Corporation of Harvard to take us under its protection. This fund is not completed but considering the great difficulty of the times we have no reason to be discouraged. About $70,000 has been already subscribed; of this $62,000 and a balance are already in the hands of our banker drawing good interest. This is not a bad nest egg as it stands; and had times been better, we had intended to come before the public again, to remind them that the last stage of a journey is the longest and ask their further help. I have little doubt that in ordinary times the remaining $30,000 would have been forthcoming, but just now one might as well cry for the moon as ask for $30,000, and we are content to bide our time till fortune's wheel makes another turn.

Meanwhile the moderate sum which we raised at first in order to try our experiment for four years has carried us bravely through the fifth, and we have a balance left with which to begin the work of next year.

By the next spring — that of 1885 — it had become evident that the elasticity of even 6 Appian Way could be stretched no further, and that the Annex must seek less cramped quarters. Before the classes for women had been formed at all, Mr. and Mrs. Gilman had looked with longing eyes at one of the older residences of Cambridge, which seemed peculiarly suited to the needs of their contemplated experiment. This was a brick house at the corner of Garden and Mason Streets, standing somewhat back from Garden Street on which it fronted, and just at the point where the road divides to encircle the historic elm under which Washington first took command of the American army. It was a house pleasant in its associations, for among its long line of occupants, since it was built in 1806 by Nathaniel Ireland, a well-to-do iron-worker of Boston, there had been many of personal eminence. Its history has been told by Mr. Gilman in the *Harvard Graduates' Magazine* for June, 1896, and need not be repeated here. Half a century before it assumed consequence for our story, it had been bought by Samuel P. Fay, judge of the Probate Court of Massachusetts, at whose death in 1856 it became the property of his daughter, Miss Maria Fay. During the occupancy of Judge Fay's family the house had been distinguished for its hospitality, and its doors had opened familiarly to many figures whose names became known in far wider fields — Story and Lowell, for example, Longfellow and Holmes, whose father's house had been separated from it by only the width of the Cambridge Common. In 1885 Miss Fay, left alone, and unwilling that another family should occupy the rooms that her own had lived in for fifty years, offered the house for sale to the Society for the Collegiate Instruction of Women for $20,000, and on May 23 of that year the purchase was approved by the Corporation. The ladies

THE HARVARD ANNEX

of the Executive Committee again made an appeal which met with a sufficient response to enable the Annex by the following September to leave Appian Way and begin the year in the Fay House.

It would have been difficult to find in Cambridge at the time more suitable quarters for an institution of which Mrs. Agassiz was the president. Associated with the traditions of such a life as she herself represented, it made an admirable setting for the young college that she was fostering. No Radcliffe building of later days can have the indescribable charm that the Fay House possessed when the Annex was first domiciled there. As had been intended its character as a private dwelling remained so far as possible unaltered and stimulated those qualities in the students that were most desired for them by the wise administrators of the simple arrangements. For a time before Judge Fay had bought the house, it had been somewhat romantically called "Castle Corner," but the Annex preserved the name of Fay, which has been retained throughout the history of the college.

The investment in this piece of property inaugurated a distinctly new phase in the development of the Annex. Its importance is explained in Mrs. Agassiz's address at Commencement in 1886:

I cannot meet you on this first commencement in the new house which has given us all such a sense of security without feeling that this has been an eventful and happy year in our little community. There are some few of the students here who remember with me the poverty of our earlier years. And it was perhaps well that our experiment began under such bare and meagre surroundings. We had nothing to offer you except the education which Harvard provides and which by the liberality of her professors was in great degree opened to us. There were absolutely no temptations outside of this, — no social attractions, no amusements, few facilities even for intercourse with one another for the reason that we had no room, no space. The common ground was simply that of study, recitations, lectures. It must be confessed that it was a somewhat austere beginning. But I do not regret this. It was a crucial test of the sincerity and genuineness of your demand for something more full and far-reaching in education.

I rather looked myself to see the Annex dwindle under these circumstances — it was so much less attractive than many other institutions for women. But it grew quietly, steadily: we heard no complaint — on the contrary its members were very grateful, very appreciative of what was done for them. But though they made no complaint, the Committee felt that this state of things could not be permanent. After six years of patient waiting this pleasant home, the pleasanter because it is an old home, mellowed by many associations and to Cambridge people connected with the hospitalities of past years, came within their reach. It was, to be sure, a little too much for our purse, and we were loth to cut in upon the Endowment Fund which we had been husbanding so carefully. But friends were generous — about half the purchase money was subscribed, — the other half we took from our treasury. It seemed a little extravagant,

THE FAŸ HOUSE IN 1887

THE HARVARD ANNEX

but a daring expenditure is sometimes a wise economy and so I think it will prove in this case.

And so it seems to me a memorable fact that we meet here today, — that for the first time our certificates for graduation and for honors are given under our own roof.

Within the next four years such had been the growth of the Annex that the limits of the Fay House had become all too restricted, and in February, 1890, the Executive Committee began to consider ways and means for enlarging its walls. The ways presented less of a problem than the means. In the late spring a meeting was held in Boston for such good Bostonians as might be interested, at which Mrs. Agassiz reported on the success of the Society and the disadvantages of its narrow habitat. The following portions of her address describe the conditions of the four years after the purchase of the Fay House and again illustrate her powers of persuasion. Her only references to the subscriptions for which she hoped are quoted below:

... In order to state the object of this meeting fairly from the beginning I would add that if we succeed in winning your sympathy for the work in which we are engaged and which we hope to carry on hereafter, we will ask you to help us in raising a certain sum toward the enlargement of our building which has been insufficient for our increased numbers and beside want of room lacks many conveniences for the work carried on there.

I have often been told that as President of our Society I should call attention from time to time in a more public way to its existence, its progress and its needs. The moment seems a fitting one, for we are now at the end of our first ten years of life, and the close of a decade always suggests a pause, a retrospective consideration of the road over which we have come, a thoughtful glance along that which lies before us — in short, a review of the past and a provision for the future.... In the autumn of 1885 the opening term found us in our permanent home. Since that time we have spent another portion of our patrimony in land adjoining the Fay House estate in order to make a well-proportioned, spacious piece of ground and give room for such additional buildings as may be needed hereafter. On this ground we have already put up two small laboratories — very inexpensive buildings in wood but quite pretty and convenient for our classes in chemistry and physics.... The material side is, however, but a small part of the story. We have to show not only that we have administered our funds carefully, but that the work is worth all and more than all that has been spent....

Our first aim was simply to give to young women intending to be teachers the best intellectual outfit at our command, in order that they might enter upon their work well prepared. We wished also to enable young women who loved study for its own sake to continue their education on a wider basis after leaving school....

A third class has been added of which we had not thought in the beginning. This consists of teachers — often women who have had a good deal of experi-

THE HARVARD ANNEX

ence in teaching and who come partly because they value the contact with the broader methods of University instruction and wish to strengthen themselves in their own special departments of work, perhaps also because the change of attitude from that of teacher to that of pupil is a rest and refreshment....

... To sum up the work of the Annex in the last ten years. Having hardly a recognized existence during the first two or three years and with a capital never exceeding $75,000 it has become known during this period as one of the prominent educational institutions for women in the country, its pupils have risen in numbers from some twenty-five to about one hundred and fifty and are yearly increasing, its graduates are scattered over the country as teachers and excellent reports of their work come back to us, it has given to a number of already well-established teachers the opportunity which they greatly value of studying under Harvard methods of instruction and under scholars of known distinction in their different departments of work, and it has enabled many young women who have studious tastes to pursue them under especially helpful conditions. I would add that we have no instruction outside of Harvard and that we have between fifty and sixty Harvard professors and instructors on our lists of instructors. Of course this is our best guarantee. With this preface I will now bring forward the special object of our meeting. A woman's postscript is, as you well know, the most important part of her communication.

We have tried to husband our means and to carry

on our work with as close economy as was consistent with a liberal fulfilment of our educational programme. But our very success compels us now to make a new appeal. We have wholly outgrown our pleasant home and we find our recitation rooms, halls and reading rooms so overcrowded that an enlargement of the building is absolutely required. The house is a delightful one, — known to some of us for nearly half a century, and in reality much older than that — one of the old-fashioned, comfortable and dignified houses of New England. We value this character and have endeavored to preserve it in our plans for enlargement, to retain the character of a home while giving it a greater fitness for the work within its walls. For this we shall need from $20,000 to $25,000. We have already received in recent subscriptions $3500, and a friend has proposed to take upon herself the cost of the Library which is to be one of the most charming features of the establishment — a room fifty feet by twenty-seven, lighted from above, but having charming windows beside — among them a deep oriel window, — a large fireplace, excellent arrangements not only for the books themselves, but for their easy use.

I would add that subscriptions may be sent to the office of Lee, Higginson and Company, State Street. ... It only remains for me to thank you for your kindness in coming and your attention in listening. I hope I have not tired you too much with my long story.

As a result of this meeting a sum of money was speedily raised sufficient to justify the commencement of the work

THE HARVARD ANNEX

by which the building was enlarged to twice its original size. During the summer of 1892 a still further addition was made which provided an auditorium large enough for all the general meetings held under the direction of the Society. Here the Commencement exercises took place in 1893 and 1894.

With what satisfaction Mrs. Agassiz regarded these improvements and how hopefully she looked into the future we may see from the following paragraphs of her address at Commencement in 1892:

I look back upon our opening life in the Annex as having a certain charm notwithstanding its difficulties, — the charm of a new and interesting undertaking. The whole subject of collegiate education for women has advanced with amazing strides in the last ten years, and our present students may wonder that I should speak of our first attempt as if it had been a kind of exciting adventure. But I assure them that it had something of this character, for it was surrounded by obstacles and prejudices. Remonstrance and expostulation came to me from some of my nearest friends, who felt that the dignity and reserve of Harvard were threatened and the whole tone of the College to be lowered. However, the nine days' wonder was soon over. The Annex kept on its quiet way so unobtrusively that when at the end of our first four years, we felt its success to be so secured that we might make some appeal to the public in its behalf, we had almost to recall its existence to them; it had grown into a college unawares as it were, unheralded and almost unheeded outside its own precincts. That

I address you here today in this cheerful, well-appointed building is evidence enough of our progress from those days to these, and I have to congratulate you especially on the improvements of the past year, on our new lecture and recitation rooms, our well-lighted studio for our art classes, and lastly on the hall, where we now meet, — which has contributed so much during the last winter, not only to your means of instruction, but also to your pleasure and amusements.

This review of the past is very cheering and may well give us hope for the future. I must add in no spirit of egotism but in one of very sincere thankfulness that this hope is strengthened by the ever-increasing confidence of the public in the Annex, of which we have frequent evidence. And in this connection, let me say that in addition to many former acts of kindness and sympathy from the Women's Educational Association in Boston we owe to them a new debt of gratitude for their efforts in our behalf this winter. They have always known that we looked toward a closer affiliation with the University as our final goal, and this winter their committee, appointed by them for the purpose, has striven with untiring energy and zeal to raise a large sum in order to help us in this direction.

I ought perhaps in the present uncertain state of our affairs, to refrain from even a distant allusion to our hopes with reference to the University. But to part from you today without some reference to what is I know uppermost in your minds as well as in mine, would seem like a want of that frank sympathy in all matters concerning your interests here which has always existed between us. If I have nothing definite to say upon this point I can at least share with you my own belief that with the approval of the public, the support of friends of education in Boston, and with the confidence expressed by the Faculty of Harvard in the Annex and in the right she has won to what is best in education, we can hardly fail of a steady advance. But let me say in closing that whatever strength we may derive from without, the students more than any one else hold the fate of the Annex in their hands, and I believe they feel and accept the responsibility. Whatever be its attitude in the future, — whatever its relation to the University, — whatever name it may bear, — I hope it will always be respected for the genuineness of its work, for the quiet dignity of its bearing, for its adherence to the noblest ends of scholarship.

So I commend our young institution to the keeping of our students with a strong belief that they will be faithful to the trust.

CHAPTER X

THE PASSING OF THE HARVARD ANNEX
1893-1894

IN the few words of Mrs. Agassiz with which the preceding chapter closes the foreshadowings of events that followed in the next year may be seen. Already in the course of 1893 it had become evident that enthusiasts on the subject of women's education, restless under the somewhat anomalous position of the Annex, where women received collegiate instruction but no academic degrees, were eager to see an official relation established between it and the University. The situation was set forth by Mr. Warner in the article in the *Harvard Graduates' Magazine* referred to above: "It had become plain to every one that the institution had passed its phase of private experiment, and was entitled to some formal recognition by the University. What shape this should take was a question with many difficulties, for the university scheme had no place ready for the newcomer.... Of course, no one wanted to incorporate the Annex bodily into the University and mingle its students with the young men. It was plain that the young women must be separately cared for, and that their household concerns and domestic economy must be in the hands of a board composed, at least in part, of women. Furthermore, the President and Fellows of Harvard College were unwilling to add to their administrative work, already excessively heavy, by taking charge of the property, or attending to the executive details, of another

THE PASSING OF THE ANNEX 231

enterprise, and they preferred, for general convenience, to commit to a distinct body the management of an undertaking which was to be detached, in many respects, from the present organization of the University."

Beginning with March 14, 1893, Mrs. Agassiz's diary reports almost daily interviews with President Eliot or other friends of the Annex in regard to the advisability of making advances to the University looking toward a closer union. The time seemed ripe for a direct appeal for adoption by Harvard, and on March 21 the Society voted that it was expedient to transfer to the President and Fellows of Harvard College its entire property, whenever the College would assume the management of its affairs and undertake to carry on the work and to offer to women academic degrees in arts. On March 27 Mrs. Agassiz addressed to President Eliot the following statement of the situation, which exists in her rough draft:

TO PRESIDENT CHARLES W. ELIOT

Cambridge, March 24, 1893

DEAR MR. ELIOT: I hear that you may bring forward our hopes and fears to the Corporation on Monday next — not perhaps as an official communication, but as an informal opening of the subject. I am most anxious that we should appear in our true light, as reasonable and not aggressive, and therefore I repeat in writing what I have often said in our recent conversations. We are well aware that the Annex owes all its success to the support received from the professors and instructors of Harvard, and also that in silently endorsing the part they have taken in its gradual development the Corporation has already done us a great service. But we now stand, as you know, in need of their more direct intervention, without which the farther progress of the Annex is likely to be checked, and indeed I hardly believe it could be long maintained were its present conditions understood by the public to be permanent. For this instability there are two causes, — first the uncertainty of our instruction as long as it depends upon the courtesy of the Professors and the consideration of the Corporation, — second, the lack of any College degree. With reference to the first we ask that our present instruction should be continued to us as an educational department of the College, with the authority of the governing boards, and second that under this provision should be included the granting to our students of the academic degrees. In asking for the latter it should be understood that we think of them only as credentials of scholarship, eliminating everything that may concern rights and privileges of graduates in the business affairs of the College, — as votes for various offices, etc., etc. Within the last few months, we have been made to feel more than ever our want of a secure foundation. Our efforts to raise money in order to come to the Corporation with a fitting endowment have been met everywhere with the objection that we have no direct relation to the College, and no one is willing to give us any considerable sum without any assurance that the University will take us under its protection. That doubt removed we are

THE PASSING OF THE ANNEX   233

confident that the money will follow. Should the Corporation accept us under the conditions above stated, we should pass over all our present property, — an invested capital of $150,000 with landed estate, buildings, etc., to the Corporation. Within our present limits we are fully self-supporting, and we should look for farther educational opportunities from the College only as we can bring means for our increased expenses. We know that the funds of the College are all appropriated and cannot be diverted from the purposes for which they were given. We recognize therefore the necessity of producing the means for our own support and for our future development. But we believe that whatever means may accrue to us in the future will be spent for the Annex to greater advantage by the Corporation than by ourselves. To them we should confidently entrust the administration of our affairs both financial and educational. Forgive this long letter, my dear Mr. Eliot, and believe me always

    Most cordially yours,
      ELIZABETH C. AGASSIZ

On March 29, Mrs. Agassiz records in her diary, "I think our aim will be accomplished, but it will be slow work." Meetings, discussions, conferences, one or the other, followed almost daily. An idea of some of the difficulties in the way and Mrs. Agassiz's method of encountering them may be formed by the following note from Edward W. Hooper, the treasurer of Harvard College, with the draft of Mrs. Agassiz's reply. Her letter which called forth the note from Mr. Hooper is not available:

TO MRS. LOUIS AGASSIZ

Cambridge, April 10, 1893

DEAR MRS. AGASSIZ: Owing to my absence in New York, I did not get your note until midnight on Sunday, and could not therefore talk with you before the meeting as I should gladly have done. It is, of course, quite natural that we should have serious doubts about more permanent relations with the Annex, and think of the dangers to the College which we have inherited as a trust for life only. My talk with Mr. Warner showed me quite clearly that there was really no reasonable limit to what the Annex might fairly ask of us. The Annex really wants all that the College has, and does not expect to get it except through the College. If we give our degrees we must give the instruction necessary to fit women for those degrees, and that means either a duplication of our instruction, or to some extent coeducation. I have no prejudice in the matter of education of women and am quite willing to see Yale or Columbia take any risks they like, but I feel bound to protect Harvard College from what seems to me to be a risky experiment. . . .

Yours very sincerely,
E. W. HOOPER

TO EDWARD W. HOOPER

DEAR MR. HOOPER: I have been away from home a day or two and so did not answer your letter promptly, but so far as I am concerned a great deal less than "all the College has" would content me. I believe that much might follow, not because the Annex would desire it, but because in the natural phenomenon the College would be likely to give it. When you say that the Annex does not expect to get what it wants "except through the College," to that I agree, because we have aimed at academic education from the very start, and to accept outside instruction including that from women teachers (without any intention to depreciate it) would place us on an exact level with all the women's colleges, and we really do not need one in Cambridge, nor is there any reason for establishing one here. In the early days of the Annex we have said this over and over again, — nothing but the proximity to Harvard justifies the establishment of a woman's college here. As to coeducation except in the most limited sense, it would be desired neither by them nor us.

While affairs were in this condition a little incident occurred that had great importance in its consequences. This incident was related in an address delivered at the Radcliffe College Commencement exercises in 1902 by John C. Gray, Royall Professor of Law in the Harvard Law School, who later became a member of the Council of Radcliffe College. It is peculiarly interesting because it illustrates the fact that the Annex owed the important advance that it was about to make to the personal regard that Mrs. Agassiz's friends had for her. The story is best told in Professor Gray's own words, which were published in the *Harvard Graduates' Magazine* for September, 1902:

... Here was an institution, to use a neutral term, so strong that it could boast with justice of giving an education equal to any in the country, and yet so feeble that it could not give its students the recognition which every other collegiate institution, good or bad, gave, a degree.

The solution of the difficulty which it was easiest to propose was that Harvard University should give the degrees. But this solution, easy to propose, was difficult, nay, impossible to carry out.... Many wise men, and by no means unfriendly to Radcliffe, felt that a great trust had come into the hands of the University rulers, that its organization and resources were already greatly strained, and that the strain ought not to be increased.

Then came a time of depression and anxiety. Some of the sincerest friends of Radcliffe, who in the days of small things had not spared time or money thought that the College should sit still and wait. But the authorities of the College felt that this state of things could not continue indefinitely; that the College could not drag along in this maimed and humiliating condition, unable to grant what every other college of men or women was granting: it must assert its competence to confer degrees; yet how to insure that the degree should have the weight and character that a degree granted to students trained as hers were, ought to have? How to be independent of Harvard University and yet have her degrees as valuable as those of the University? That was the problem.

And now you must pardon me if I give a bit of per-

THE PASSING OF THE ANNEX

sonal history. One evening my wife told me that she had seen Mrs. Agassiz that day, that Mrs. Agassiz looked troubled, and was much distressed and perplexed about Radcliffe College and its degrees. At that time, to my shame be it said, I knew little and cared less about Radcliffe College, but I was sorry that Mrs. Agassiz should be harassed, and I began wondering whether anything could be done to relieve the difficulty. Shortly before, I had happened to be counsel for a famous school of learning in a case in which the functions of *visitors* had been much considered. And the idea came into my head: "Why should not Harvard University be the Visitor of Radcliffe College?"

What is a visitor? Under the English law all collegiate institutions have visitors. If there is no other visitor provided for by the statutes of the college, then the Crown is the visitor. . . . The Board of Overseers are the visitors of [Harvard] University, and I need not say how important and controlling are the functions of that Board. No one can be chosen a member of the Corporation or a professor in the University without the Overseers' consent.

It was determined that the Corporation of Harvard University should be asked to become the Visitor of Radcliffe College.

The last sentence anticipates our narrative somewhat. The chapter in the story that follows Professor Gray's happy thought of "visitors" to the Annex is told in a letter to him from Mrs. Agassiz, in reply to one in which he had outlined his scheme to her, but which unfortunately has not been preserved.

TO PROFESSOR JOHN C. GRAY

MY DEAR MR. GRAY: I am truly grateful for your letter. The acceptance of such a scheme by the Corporation would seem to me all we can reasonably ask for the present. If later they should feel ready for a closer affiliation they can themselves define the terms. The Annex will plead its own cause, and I think some of the lions will disappear as the Corporation becomes more familiar with its work and its ways.

We have always needed a name, and I hope something distinctive and appropriate will be found, — something if possible which would indicate a relation to the College rather than a separation from it. Mr. Norton once suggested Emmanuel College, as being the one from which John Harvard came?

2d. It would simplify matters much to retain the present organization, leaving to us the financial responsibility with matters concerning the life of the students, etc., etc. We offered to give all that, only because we thought the College might prefer a complete surrender.

3d. Your idea of "visitors" had never occurred to me, but if the Corporation would accept such a duty, that in itself would be a tacit recognition of our relation to the University.

4th seems to me still more important — that the appointment of instructors or examiners should rest with the visitors.

5th. To me personally it would be perfectly satisfactory that our diplomas should bear the seal and

THE PASSING OF THE ANNEX

signature of the College. I would rather have a foothold in the College on such terms as the Corporation may be willing to grant than any sum of money — much as we should like the latter, — I think, however, the form of our diploma should be carefully considered, — that it should not be differentiated from the "A.B." of the College as a "ladies' degree." Work is work, and must be judged without fear or favor by its own value.

6th. Here again is a most important point in our favor, — a place in the Catalogue.

Your seventh point would be for us our culminating point, — taken with what precedes it seems to me all we can reasonably ask at present. This is much more than half a loaf and promises more than it grants. I am so glad you have taken the pains to set it before me with such clearness. It was very good of you, and very kind in Mrs. Gray to suggest it. Please thank her for me.

The fruits of this plan are seen in the following letter from President Eliot, which Mrs. Agassiz read at a meeting of the Society on June 6, 1893. It makes the foregoing letter more intelligible, since the numbered items in both are evidently the same.

TO MRS. LOUIS AGASSIZ

May 29, 1893

DEAR MRS. AGASSIZ: At the Corporation meeting today I was authorized to say to you — the President of the Society for the Collegiate Instruction of

Women, that the President and Fellows of Harvard College are now pleased to consider carefully any proposition for close union between the University and the Society for the Collegiate Instruction of Women, which the Society may hereafter make to them in general conformity with the following memorandum.

Memorandum of an agreement or contract between the President and Fellows of Harvard College and the Society for the Collegiate Instruction of Women.

1. The Institute established by the Society to have a name — "X College."
2. X College to be self governing in all respects, — in organization, business management and discipline.
3. The President and Fellows of Harvard College to be the visitors of X College.
4. No instructor or examiner to be appointed or retained by X College without the approval of the Visitors.
5. The diplomas of X College to be counter-signed by the President of Harvard University and to bear its seal.
6. Graduates of X College to be given a place in the Catalogues and official publications of the University.
7. This agreement may be cancelled by either party on four years' notice.

Very truly yours,
CHARLES W. ELIOT

The memorandum contained in this letter was at once accepted by the Corporation of the Annex as a basis of

THE PASSING OF THE ANNEX 241

agreement with the Corporation of Harvard University, and in less than a fortnight later Mrs. Agassiz is found in correspondence with President Eliot, consulting him in regard to a name for "X College."

TO MRS. LOUIS AGASSIZ

Cambridge, June 19, 1893

DEAR MRS. AGASSIZ: I send you herewith some information about the first woman who ever gave anything to Harvard College, namely Lady Mowlson, who founded a scholarship here which has just been revived by the Corporation on evidence procured by Mr. A. McF. Davis. She seems to have been a patriotic person, and she has left no children. To revive her memory would be analogous to the act of the Corporation in naming Holworthy Hall after Sir Matthew Holworthy, who gave the College a thousand pounds in the seventeenth century.

Very truly yours,
CHARLES W. ELIOT

Mr. Davis embodied the results of the researches which President Eliot mentions here in an article, "Anne Radcliffe — Lady Mowlson," in the *New England Magazine* for February, 1894. Briefly the story is that in 1641 Thomas Weld, pastor of the church in Roxbury, was sent to England by the colony in Massachusetts to arrange certain matters of importance to the country. While in England he received for Harvard College the gift of £100 from the Lady Mowlson "for a scholarship, the revenue of it to be employed that way forever." According to arrangement this money, instead of being paid to the college, was "given in on account to the state," apparently in 1643, and the treasurer of the college thus being relieved of all responsibility in accounting for the fund, and other confusing circumstances having also arisen, in the course of time it was forgotten, until by the investigations of Mr. Davis the Corporation became apprised of the facts, when they promptly set aside $5000 for the purpose of reëstablishing the Lady Mowlson Scholarship. This took place just at the time when the name for "X College" was under discussion, and the discovery that the first scholarship at Harvard was given by a woman suggested the idea of christening the new college for women after her. The maiden name of Lady Mowlson was Anne Radcliffe. In 1600 she was married to Sir Thomas Mowlson, later Lord Mayor of London, in the church of St. Christopher le Stocks in London, which occupied the site of the present Bank of England. Their only child was a daughter, who died in infancy. Lady Mowlson died in 1661, after a widowhood of twenty-three years, and was buried beside her husband in the vault beneath the church where they had been married. Practically all that is known of her beyond these facts is that in May, 1644, she made a contribution toward a fund to be sent to the Scottish army in the north, which not long after won the battle of Marston Moor. From this donation and that to the college in Massachusetts we may see in what way her sympathies turned, and may infer that she was alive to the religious and political interests of her country. The suggestion that her name be given to the Annex was made by Mrs. Agassiz at a meeting of the Council. "It seems appropriate," she said, "to name the first woman's

THE PASSING OF THE ANNEX 243

college ever connected with Harvard for this lady who two centuries ago gave our University the first money it ever received from a woman.... The name is also a good one — Radcliffe College, — dignified and convenient, and the association with this lady of the olden time and her generosity to Harvard has a certain picturesqueness." But when the name was publicly announced an old friend of Mrs. Agassiz wrote to her: "I should prefer to have it the 'Agassiz College,' and I must think it ought to have been, for what are £100 [of money], when compared with more than that number of flesh, blood and brains given cheerfully for so many years!"

Further friendly negotiations were carried on between the President and Fellows of Harvard College and the Society until on October 31, 1893, at the annual meeting of the Society it was voted that proper legal steps should be taken to change the name of the Corporation to that of Radcliffe College; that the Corporation should give degrees in Arts and Sciences, and that a Committee should be appointed by the President to obtain from the Legislature the necessary power; that the President and Fellows of Harvard College should be appointed the Visitors of the Corporation; that no instructor or examiner of the Corporation should be appointed without the approval of the Visitors; that in case the President and Fellows of Harvard College should accept the powers thus conferred upon them, they should be requested to empower the President of Harvard University to countersign the diplomas of the Corporation and to affix the seal of Harvard University to them. Consent was given to the arrangement embodied in these votes by the Board of Overseers of Harvard University on December 6. The entries in Mrs. Agassiz's diary record some of the details of these days so eventful to her:

1893, December 6. To Annex tea. Heard the good news from the Harvard Overseers — great enthusiasm among the students. Evening, M. and C., Quin and Pauline. It was very pleasant and all full of sympathy about the Annex. Closed the evening with a note from Miss [Anna] Lowell, enclosing check of $1000 for the Annex, and we have also received the $90,000 from Mrs. Perkins's [estate]. It has been a bright day for that young institution.

December 7. Concert, evening. Many congratulations on all sides about the Annex. Mr. and Mrs. Palmer walked home with me. They are very glad.

December 8. To Annex for Idler Club. All excited about the new name and attitude of the Annex. The students already begin to call themselves "of Radcliffe College."

When the action of the Board of Overseers became known to the public, loud objection was raised to it by some of the zealous advocates of "higher education." The principal ground of criticism lay in the informal nature of the contract, which was regarded as too elastic in conditions and in duration to guarantee the standard that should be demanded of an institution chartered to confer degrees in the Commonwealth of Massachusetts. So strong were the objections felt by certain remonstrants that two petitions on the subject were addressed in January, 1894, to the Board of Overseers of Harvard University. One of these, from various residents of New York, petitioned that Har-

THE PASSING OF THE ANNEX

vard University grant the ordinary degrees to properly qualified women; the other, from certain members of the Association of Collegiate Alumnae, asked that women students be admitted to such graduate courses in the University as could be opened to them without involving the University in further expense. The former was refused by the Board of Overseers on the ground that women were not permitted to qualify for the degree of Bachelor of Arts in Harvard University, and this form of qualification was implied by the degree; the latter was in effect granted, for the Overseers agreed, with the concurrence of the President and Fellows, to admit any students of Radcliffe College to any courses of instruction designed primarily for graduates, subject to such limitations as the Faculty and the corresponding governing board of Radcliffe might set, it being understood that such students were not to be deemed students of Harvard University.

But, in spite of the friendly attitude and deeds of the Harvard Corporation, "the howl grew louder against Radcliffe," according to Mrs. Agassiz's diary, and the criticisms from outsiders directed against the new plans involved her in a mass of correspondence and many perplexing experiences. An extract from a letter written in reply to one from a group of graduates of the Annex who had expressed regret at the proposed change, exemplifies the manner in which Mrs. Agassiz met criticism and also sets forth her own policy toward Harvard University, the wisdom of which events proved:

MY DEAR GIRLS: ... A year has been spent in the most careful deliberation and earnest discussion between the Harvard Corporation, the College faculty, and our own Society as to the means of bringing about a closer relation between the Annex and the University.

. . . We began the Annex as an experiment. We did it in the hope that Harvard would finally take us in some way under her protection. She has now made the first step in that direction. She has assumed the whole responsibility of our education, and I confess it has never occurred to me that a degree given under her signature and seal would not be equivalent to a Harvard degree. It seems to me a distinction without a difference. What can any institution give more sacred than its signature and its seal? A pledge so guaranteed cannot be broken by any honorable body. To make this guarantee valid Harvard must keep our education up to the level of that of the Harvard student. She cannot set her hand and seal to an inferior degree. But I do her injustice in even hinting at such a possibility — the offer is made in perfect good faith and with the purpose of enlarging our education as fast and as fully as possible.

It seems to me unreasonable to expect the Corporation of Harvard to declare to the public between today and tomorrow everything they intend to do in a new departure which must be experimental for them as it has been for us. You may say that our experiment should suffice for them; on the contrary theirs is far more complicated, and has intricacies upon which ours did not touch. In saying this I allude to the governing boards, not to the professors. It would have delighted you to see the enthusiasm and earnest-

THE PASSING OF THE ANNEX 247

ness with which the professors pursued the discussion in the faculty meetings, the confidence they showed in us, their readiness to do all and more than they have done for us. The fact that this body of teachers acquiesced in the final arrangement should satisfy you that it was one which was not intended to limit or retard our development.

But there are technical difficulties in the way of the governing boards which do not belong to the Faculty, and which touch upon a trust which they (the governing boards) have held for two hundred and fifty years and more. They must in loyalty to that older trust move cautiously and smooth over these difficulties gradually.

I do not believe in forcing the hand of the Harvard Corporation either by the weight of outside opinion or of individual remonstrances. I do not believe in an aggressive policy. I do believe in making the governing boards of Harvard our allies, — in showing them that all we ask can be granted without incurring any change of policy in the general government of the University or trenching in any way upon its original rights.

We have doubted (I mean we of the Annex) what part we should take in the sudden and startling protest against Radcliffe, which has taken us by surprise, because at first the air seemed full of congratulations. We decided not to enter into the newspaper lists. Patience and silence after all seemed best. We must go on with our work, keep our standard as high as possible, and let the results prove that we have not been mistaken in trusting ourselves to the guardianship of the University. This is always supposing that our act passes the Legislature, and that we really become Radcliffe College. Otherwise I am afraid there would be great depression in our ranks and we should find it hard to keep up our courage.

Believe me always
>Your old and affectionate friend,
>ELIZABETH C. AGASSIZ

As may be expected from the concluding paragraph of the above letter, remonstrances did not avail to check the efforts of the Society to obtain an act of legislature for its incorporation as a college with the right to confer degrees and to change its name to that of Radcliffe College. A hearing before the Committee of Education was held at the State House in Boston on February 28, 1894. The Committee on Endowment of Colleges of the Association of Collegiate Alumnae, who were the principal opponents of the act, were represented by Mr. G. W. Anderson and Mr. G. S. Hale. Their objections were, first, that the petitioners brought "no adequate guarantee that the new college is able to maintain the high character which it is the duty of the State to require of all institutions which it charters to grant degrees," inasmuch as "the essential basis of such guarantee is an adequate endowment fund"; second, that "it is expressly provided that Harvard University may at any time withdraw its visitatorial power and decline to countersign the degrees," and, third, that "the fact that it is proposed that the degrees of the new college shall be countersigned by the President of Harvard University is in itself a confession that alone the new college

THE PASSING OF THE ANNEX 249

may not be a competent degree conferring institution."
Mr. J. B. Warner appeared for the Society, and was supported by Professors Norton, Byerly, Goodwin and Goodale, and Mrs. Agassiz. After the presentation of the subject, the remonstrants withdrew their opposition, on condition that the clause, "provided, however, that no degree shall be conferred by the said Radcliffe College except with the approval of the President and Fellows of Harvard College," be inserted into the act — a clause, which, as was pointed out at the time, merely gave emphasis to the original intention of the Society.

An account of the hearing was written by Mr. Gilman in 1904, selections from his manuscript copy of which are published here.

The room appointed for the hearing was all too small for the number of women who wished to attend. The audience was mainly composed of our opponents. . . . The chairman of the legislation committee wished us to present our views, and a member of our corporation made a plain statement of what had been done and what it was intended to do — namely, to give to women the same instruction that men had so long enjoyed, and said that the charter was asked in order that the Annex might be permanently established, and be authoritatively carried on with the aid of the President and Fellows of Harvard College. Mrs. Agassiz was called upon to tell of the past work, and of the plans for the future. Her words made an evident impression. Professor Goodwin, who had taught classes of girls from the beginning, told the committee how he had found the woman mind, and as a member of the management, he emphasized the economical merits of the Annex plan. President Eliot surprised *me*, at least. He had been friendly to the Annex from the beginning. In fact, it could not have taken its first step if he had not been. Now he took a step in advance. We were asking the legislature to permit *us* to do something; but Mr. Eliot took the ground that Harvard was the active agent. He outlined the history of the advance of the college, showing how, established to insure a godly ministry, its scope of activity had been widened by taking up instruction in law, in medicine, in whatever else, and he asked emphatically, if Harvard College takes up the education of women is there any reason to suppose that it will ever renounce it? This remark appealed to the committee, and it overthrew at once the argument of the opposition that Radcliffe College might not be permanent.

The greatest surprise was now to come. When our presentation was closed, one of the opposing attorneys . . . rose, and announced that his client withdrew all opposition! The senior attorney remarked that this was a little too sudden, and stated a few unimportant points that he wished guarded. We at once gave our consent, and all opposition was withdrawn. The hearing was closed. The chairman of the committee told me that he had never attended a hearing at which he had learned so much, nor one at which both sides seemed so completely satisfied.

The committee reported to the legislature, favor-

THE PASSING OF THE ANNEX

ably of course, and Radcliffe College received its most generous charter.

The address of Mrs. Agassiz, which was the most important that she ever made, is given here in full:

I am asked to say something on the subject which is before you today, concerning the Society for the Collegiate Instruction of Women, better known by its more familiar (its household name, as it were) of the Harvard Annex, — names which we now petition you to change. Not because the more familiar name is not dear to us; on the contrary it belongs to the very initiation of our Society. It has the value of things which are associated with difficulties and sacrifices, with strenuous effort, with small means and high aims. There are such times in the lives of institutions as well as of individuals, — times when the ideal side bravely takes the ascendency and seems to declare its independence of material means. At such a time, the name of the Annex was given to us, half in jest, half in earnest, wholly in good feeling by the students of the University. We were, perhaps, as impecunious a body as ever started on an important enterprise. Without any of the ordinary accessories for collegiate work (as buildings, books, apparatus and the like), with only enough money to cover the bare expenses of every day, we ventured to believe that we could build up an institution of learning for women which would eventually give them all the educational advantages which college gives to men.

And why did we have this faith? Because of the

proximity of our old University, honored and beloved throughout the land. Under its shadow we stood, — into its gates we hoped to enter; — and when in later years, as the scope of our undertaking became better understood, the prefix of Harvard was added by common consent to our friendly designation of the Annex, the name so lightly given became to us very significant and very precious as an earnest of success, — a good omen as it were. We have indeed been led through these fifteen years by the hope that we should finally come under the acknowledged and permanent protection of Harvard. And now the President and Fellows have taken the first step toward that end. Overburdened by the care of the University which represents a trust stretching over a period of nearly three hundred years and has grown in that time into an immense organization, they decline to assume in the same comprehensive sense the additional care of our society, — of its property, its internal economy, its discipline, etc., but they consent to take the whole responsibility of our education, and to guarantee the worth and validity of our degrees by the signature and seal of the University. In order to facilitate this arrangement, they ask us to take a name as a college proper under their educational supervision. As our own name of the Annex, pleasant as are its associations, did not seem quite appropriate, we have chosen from the many names suggested one which connects itself directly with the early history of the University. Anne Radcliffe founded, as you know, the first scholarship ever given

THE PASSING OF THE ANNEX 253

by a woman to the University. It seemed fitting that she, who thus showed her sympathy with liberal learning and with the principles of freedom embodied in the first New England college, should be commemorated in the first college for women ever associated with Harvard. This adjustment between the Annex and Harvard has been reached after a year of the most careful deliberation between the Corporation of Harvard, the Corporation of our Society, and the Harvard Faculty. Surely the combination of three such bodies in full knowledge of the facts and in perfect accord with each other, — the Annex Society representing fifteen years of experience in the intellectual training of women under Harvard instruction, — the Harvard Corporation ready to accept at the hands of the Annex the whole direction of the future education of their students, — and lastly all the professors supporting this transfer — surely such a triple Alliance may be trusted as having all the elements of safety and permanence.

I am aware that our small means have been made a reproach to us, and that our opponents and your petitioners say that we are not rich and well-endowed enough to be trusted with the giving of degrees. It is true that our means are small as compared with certain of the colleges for women. But such as they are, they have been well husbanded; and the fact that we never have been in debt and that we have now pleasant buildings with accommodations for the instruction of three hundred students, with ample recitation rooms and lecture halls, with an excellent working library containing several thousand volumes, and beside this a fair spending income and a moderate surplus for emergencies, — all this will perhaps reassure you as to the practical management of our affairs. Neither must it be forgotten that if our endowment is small, the active and cordial coöperation of the professors and teachers of Harvard is better than money for us, — it would be so for any young and growing college. Without that support the $280,000 which now represents our whole property (inclusive of certain legacies) would perhaps be an insufficient capital for the maintenance on a high standard of a new college without other support. But the true builders of the Annex have been and are the Harvard professors. They have brought it to its present prominent position. They represent its true wealth and its strength, — not a bad substitute for endowment funds though measured by other standards.

I must not take your time with details about the instruction given or the work done at the Annex. The friends who are here with us from the college will do that better than I can. Still I should be sorry to close without a word of our students. My own relation with them is one of affectionate personal intercourse rather than any immediate direction of their studies, — a duty which belongs to our academic board, made up of officers of the college, and to the professors and teachers themselves. But I have constant evidence of their deep gratitude for the opportunities offered them at Cambridge. They are fully sensible of the liberal and comprehensive quality of the instruction

THE PASSING OF THE ANNEX 255

they receive there and of the generous spirit in which it is given. Of course our students belong largely to the class of teachers, — young girls who are fitting for that career, or older women, many of whom are experienced teachers, but who come to make themselves familiar with the larger methods of university instruction, and carry back to their schoolrooms what is freshest and most interesting in their own department of work. No one can be blind to the advantage for our public education of thus bringing our public schools into more direct and vital contact with our oldest University, with its large and varied means of instruction, its great outfit in all departments, its learning and its old associations. I know there are those who look upon Radcliffe College as likely to limit rather than enlarge these privileges. But we have to remember that it is not the habit of Harvard to make itself responsible for inferior work, — all her traditions, all her standards, all her principles of action are opposed to such a course. The governing boards of Harvard do not mean to establish an inferior college. It has been my privilege to stand very near to the late transactions between the Annex and Harvard, and I cannot doubt that her guardianship over her young ward will be just and generous. Is it not a little unreasonable to expect that the governing boards should at once explain to the public exactly what their course of action is going to be in dealing with an experiment, which is not yet begun and which involves so marked a change of policy in their administration? To those who have watched the working out of this agreement it seems far the best educational opportunity ever offered to women in this country. But should this new departure, so full of hope and promise, be met by a check now, — by a refusal or even a postponement of our right to give degrees under the authority of Harvard, it would take the heart out of our enterprise. We should be thrown back upon our old lines, upon the position of insecurity and doubt which we have held for so long, and which has been the chief hindrance to our progress.

We therefore hope that our petition for a college charter, supported as it is by the governing boards of Harvard and approved by her professors and teachers who have served us so long and so faithfully, will not be denied us by the Legislature.

The effect of Mrs. Agassiz's words and above all of her presence is described by President Eliot in the address at the Commemoration Service published below, and is therefore not dwelt upon here. There was no doubt in the minds of those present, as they watched the faces of the Committee, that her influence upon them was securing the desired legislation, yet Mrs. Agassiz herself with her usual modesty attributed the clinching of the arguments not to herself but to another. In the note on Professor Goodwin at the time of his resignation, which has been quoted above in part, she speaks of his influence at the hearing. "One of the grounds of the opposition of the remonstrants was our poverty. They asserted that the right of giving degrees should not be conferred upon an institution so poor, the future of which was therefore so insecure. To this plea Mr. Goodwin replied, 'The remonstrants are right as to the material

THE PASSING OF THE ANNEX

means of Radcliffe; she is not rich — perhaps she never will be. She only has the coöperation of a body of instruction such as cannot be obtained by any other college for women in the United States.' I remember that this closed the discussion very effectively." Mrs. Agassiz's own record in her diary for that day gives no indication of the slightest consciousness that she had delivered an epoch-making speech. "Hearing at State House — very satisfactory. Lunched with Sallie at the Mayflower. . . . To the Annex to see the students who were delighted at the success of the hearing."

A few days later Mrs. Agassiz received the following letter from the senior counsel for her opponents:

TO MRS. LOUIS AGASSIZ

Boston, March 13, 1894

MY DEAR MRS. AGASSIZ: The ladies whom I represented at the late hearing in regard to Radcliffe College have kindly sent me the enclosed, as they express it to me, "in token of their appreciation of the services you have rendered, not as a payment for strictly legal services."

I cannot use this acknowledgment so agreeably to myself or so nearly in accordance with their interest in the cause, as by asking that you would do me the honor to be the medium of adding it to the permanent fund of the College.

With cordial regards to yourself and grateful acknowledgments of your services for the Institution and the cause it represents, I am, with high respect and regard,

Sincerely yours,

GEORGE S. HALE

On March 23, 1894, the Governor signed the act for the incorporation of Radcliffe College.

The new relations with the University made a certain degree of reorganization necessary for the college. The Corporation and the Academic Board were both enlarged. The list of permanent officers was increased by the addition of a regent and a dean. Mrs. Agassiz continued to be president of the institution, Mr. Gilman became regent, and Mr. Warner remained treasurer. Miss Mary Coes, a graduate of the college and later its dean, was made secretary, an office which she continued to hold during the rest of Mrs. Agassiz's life; the college had no more devoted servant and friend, the students no more ready and interested adviser, and her faithfulness and quiet absorption in the affairs of Radcliffe ministered to Mrs. Agassiz in a thousand ways more constantly than probably any one, even Mrs Agassiz herself, could have told. The appointment of a dean, which constituted the most important change in the official personnel was felt to be a necessity attendant upon the development into a college. From the beginning of the Annex, Mrs. Arthur Gilman had acted as Chairman of the Students' Committee, and she and Mr. Gilman together had performed many of the duties that in a formally constituted college devolve upon the dean; but much of the voluntary service that had been rendered the Annex by its devoted friends had in the nature of things, when it became incorporated as a college, to be organized upon a more permanent and academic basis. It was the desire of Mrs. Agassiz that the college should have in the dean a social head, a person of such scholarship and experience in teaching that her presence would be of importance on all

THE PASSING OF THE ANNEX

the educational boards of Radcliffe, and an officer to whom all matters regarding the life of the students in Cambridge should be brought by them and their relatives for consultation and advice. "Nor will this," Mrs. Agassiz wrote in some notes found among her papers, "(at least, we surely hope that it will not) diminish in any way the friendly, we might almost say motherly interest which Mrs. Gilman has always taken in the students and which has been so valuable to them, while we also hope that it may in some measure relieve her of a responsibility which she has voluntarily and generously taken upon herself"; and in the same notes she continues: "It is difficult to define the duties of an officer who has been ready to accept so much and such various work as Mr. Gilman has cheerfully taken upon himself. Something of what has fallen upon him in the way of discipline and personal direction of the students will now naturally pass into the care of the lady in residence as general guide and adviser of the students." These tributes to the earliest friends of the college illustrate the spirit of loyalty and the appreciation of the efforts of others that were characteristic of Mrs. Agassiz.

So unusual was the combination and degree of the qualities demanded for the dean by Mrs. Agassiz and the Corporation that it seemed doubtful if the possessor of them could be found, until a member of the Council suggested Miss Agnes Irwin, who since 1869 had been principal of a widely known private school for girls in Philadelphia, through which she had become an important influence in the life of the city. The executive ability that had fitted her for this position was partly hereditary. Not only did she count Benjamin Franklin and Alexander James Dallas among her ancestors, but she had also had, especially on her mother's side of the family, a line of forbears who had won an enviable reputation in scientific, military, naval or diplomatic fields. She had herself the education that association and inheritance give in richer measure than any college, to which force and charm were lent by her intellectual and unusual social gifts, her ready wit, her strong religious faith, and her power of affection, and an air of natural distinction entirely independent of the accident of her position, made her presence additionally significant. It is no wonder that she was recognized as a suitable fellow-worker with Mrs. Agassiz and one whose coming to Radcliffe as dean would be a happy omen for the college. "I hope you will be glad to learn," she wrote to Mrs. Agassiz in her letter of acceptance of the office, "that I accept the place offered me with a deep sense of its possibilities and duties, and that I am proud and happy indeed to be associated with you in this work." On the envelope containing this letter Mrs. Agassiz noted: "Acceptance of Deanship, Radcliffe College. A blessed day for me. E. C. Agassiz." And in her diary she recorded for May 24 of that year: "Received Miss Irwin's answer accepting. An immense relief." "I know that we understand each other so well," she wrote to Miss Irwin a few years after her work at Radcliffe had begun, "that there is not and never could be a question of precedence of authority between us," and she has left many other expressions of her estimate of Miss Irwin's character and ability. "Under her guidance I believe the institution will always be dignified in its attitude and efficient in its work," she said later to a friend, and it was perhaps this reliance upon Miss Irwin's standards and

THE PASSING OF THE ANNEX

judgment that made her coming so great a relief to Mrs. Agassiz and so important an event in her connection with the college.

The ideals that Mrs. Agassiz had for the college, thus inaugurated, and the spirit in which she regarded its future are best set forth in selections from her Commencement address for 1894.

My Young Friends: I have not much to say to you this afternoon. Perhaps when a cherished wish is fulfilled, one does not feel inclined for many words. When we reach the summit of a height which we have been slowly climbing, not without difficulty and fatigue, our first feeling is, indeed, one of quiet satisfaction, rather than of excitement which seeks expression. Today we reach such a height, and a wider horizon opens around us, with larger opportunities. . . . I am not sure that we all understand the responsibility of success. In our elation at the fact, we forget, perhaps, its deeper significance as regards our own obligations.

We have all longed for the position we occupy today, — longed to be accepted by the old and beloved University, under whose shadow we ventured to begin our work, hoping for final recognition. Today that recognition is ours. Harvard has consented to receive our college as her ward, — has made herself responsible for our education and has given us her signature and her seal as guarantee thereunto. In this we may, of course, feel a just pride. We should not have had her approval had we not been in some degree worthy of it. She has opened to us new courses with a liberal hand; perhaps no University, either in this country, or elsewhere, opens a nobler course of instruction to women, than Harvard offers to her Radcliffe students of today; and while we are assembled here, on the last day of our present college year, knowing that the next term will open under new conditions, is it not well to take counsel together? to consider what the new aspect of our college instruction imposes upon us, as our most important academic duty?

It is no small gain to have a high standard held up before us. We all know what it is to follow a flag, if it represents to us a noble ideal. This is what Harvard has done for us, and it is a better gift even than the enlarged field of study, the higher grades of instruction which she offers us. In associating us so nearly with herself, — in sharing with us the wealth of her traditions gathered during more than two centuries and a half, she gives us a new stimulus to upright aims and conscientious achievement. In saying this, I do not think of scholarship alone, but of its uses, as helping toward a well-rounded character. Our scholarship will not be worth much if it does not lend itself in gracious service to whatever path in life it may be our lot to follow.

... It is my dearest wish for you all that Radcliffe College by her bearing (for institutions as well as individuals may have a dignified and noble bearing), by her simplicity and refinement of manners, by her fidelity to scholarship in its more comprehensive and liberal sense, should worthily serve the older institution by which she is adopted. This trust is yours, and I hope you will hand it down to successive classes, enriched by traditions of your own, such as may befit association with what is best and noblest in the records of Harvard University.

Mrs. Agassiz, it is to be observed, says nothing about her own part on the path up which the college had been "slowly climbing," and her silence brings to mind a story that Mrs. Curtis tells of her during her presidency. "Lizzie was never hampered with any consciousness that she herself held a position demanding any special consideration. I was present once at a little scene which amused me by showing this trait to some people who were entirely unaware of the character they were trying to exploit. It was at one of her afternoon teas at home and the visitors were either English or Americans who lived abroad. I was a silent looker-on, and very soon saw that she was being interviewed entirely unconsciously. They asked all sorts of questions. Had she done this? and accomplished that? And she would only tell of what had happened and nothing of what she herself had done."

But as we read the records given in the foregoing pages of "what had happened and what she herself had done," we see that the nature of Mrs. Agassiz's service to the college was twofold. She was influential in determining the policy of the movement almost from the day that she became associated with it, and she represented that policy in an exceptionally effective manner to the public. She was filled with a true reverence for Harvard University, due first, perhaps, to her associations with

President Felton and the group of men whom she first met under his roof, but more especially to the deep attachment of Agassiz to the college and his unflagging efforts for its development. Although Mrs. Agassiz's letters from Brazil indicate her interest in the condition of her own sex there, she was never one to spell "woman" with a capital W, and she gave her time and efforts not to the higher education of women in general, as a "cause," but specifically to Harvard education for women as a means of extending the benefits of the University to enrich the lives of women and so of children. Moreover, her interest in women's colleges was not independent of her interest in the Annex and was usually focused about the experiment in Cambridge.

It is true that any educational enterprise had a certain attraction for her because of Agassiz's character and reputation as one of the greatest teachers that Harvard has ever had; and it is largely in his enthusiasm for education, the ideals for the instruction of girls that he had expressed in the school, and his affection for Harvard that the springs of Mrs. Agassiz's activity in behalf of Radcliffe may be found. The school that she originated to assist him financially and which afforded her pleasure only in so far as they worked together in it, led her, according to her own testimony, to associate herself with the plan that resulted in Radcliffe College. Her relation to Radcliffe, therefore, which seems to form a separate chapter in her existence, does not in reality break the unity of her life, which found its completion by being merged in that of Agassiz; it was, on the contrary, the expression — to a greater extent, probably, than she was herself aware — of

THE PASSING OF THE ANNEX

her entire union with him, and it is scarcely an exaggeration to say that Radcliffe for no inconsiderable part of its foundations rests upon the devotion of a woman to her husband.

It was especially due to Mrs. Agassiz's loyalty to the University that she never ceased to emphasize the dependence of the Annex from its very inception upon Harvard alone, and that dependence as its sole reason for existence. Her confidence in the *Veritas* of Harvard had a large share in bringing about the final incorporation of Radcliffe College, and the personal affection and respect that she aroused attracted the already friendly administrative bodies of the University to the enterprise. It is practically certain that if Mrs. Agassiz had had no connection with the Annex, it would still have met with success; her contribution to the movement consisted in giving it, simply by being herself, an impetus, a dignity, and an unwavering standard that it could not have had without her.

In the same way her influence impressed itself upon the students. She herself said that her attitude toward them was characterized by an affectionate friendliness; theirs toward her was that of affectionate admiration and respect. None can be said to have had relations of intimacy with her, but, although her personal interest often came as a surprise to them, none failed to recognize that they had in her a friend to whom they might turn for counsel and sympathy. "I can never forget," a former president of the Alumnae Association of the Annex writes, "her gracious presence as she sat beside me at the Commencement dinners at which I had the painful duty to preside. A kind of *praesidium et dulce decus meum* she seemed to me, making my task lighter by her appreciative acceptance of my efforts."

The story has often been told of Mrs. Agassiz that one year when the Commencement exercises were held in her own drawing-room, and there was only one candidate for a diploma, as she handed her the parchment adorned as usual with a rose thrust through the ribbon that bound it, she put both arms around the astonished girl's neck and exclaimed, "We're proud of you, my dear!" And in the same spirit years later in Sanders Theatre when she conferred the first degree of doctor of philosophy given by Radcliffe College, she increased its value many fold to the recipient by her whispered, "So glad you have it, dear."

Her relation with the students, it should be said, was not one of daily intercourse, for she had no office hours and seldom met them except on public occasions and at social gatherings. After the Annex was installed in Fay House she saw them most frequently at the Wednesday afternoon teas which she established and which became a recognized college institution that she attended as long as it was possible for her to do so. These were held in the attractive, elliptical-shaped drawing-room, pleasantly shaded in spring and summer, and cheerful in winter with a blazing fire, fragrant with the delicate aroma of tea and lemon, and inviting with a special type of gay little Swedish cakes arrayed upon the tea-table. Here girls with scant experience of the world could meet pleasantly the friends of Mrs. Agassiz, attracted by her presence to the occasion; here an unfailing welcome was ready, given in tones that conveyed the very essence of kindliness even when the personality of the student was unknown; and here, best of all, was waiting the face, that as President Briggs has suggested, might well recall the lines of Waller:

> " Sweetness, truth and every grace
> Which time and use are wont to teach,
> The eye may in a moment reach
> And read distinctly in her face."

The picture of Mrs. Agassiz in her "widow's cap" and favorite white cashmere shawl gracefully drawn about her shoulders, seated by her tea-table in the drawing-room of Fay House, is probably that which first rises at the sound of her name in the minds of the students who knew her, although her appearance was perhaps more distinguished on the platform of Sanders Theatre at Commencement, when she emphasized the lady rather than the academic official by appearing always in a black velvet gown — the only woman, as one of the Cambridge clergy remarked, who could wear black velvet on the hottest day in June without loss of dignity. The Commencement exercises were to her the most dreaded of all occasions connected with the college, especially after they were transferred from Fay House to Sanders Theatre. Again and again her diaries record her troubled anticipations of the day when she must appear in public and deliver her address. "Great tremors before — immense relief after." "I feel like an emancipated woman, now that I need no longer look forward to that terrible ordeal in Sanders Theatre." It never ceased to be an agitating experience to her, and as will be seen from some of her letters published in a later chapter was the duty from which she most craved relief when the time for her resignation came.

In concluding the story of 1894, a year so memorable

for Mrs. Agassiz and for the college, a correspondence that took place in the autumn, as a sequel to the closer relation between Harvard and Radcliffe, remains to be mentioned. This correspondence has already been printed in the *First Annual Report* of the President of Radcliffe College and also in a published address by Charles Francis Adams, made at a meeting of the Massachusetts Historical Society held on February 14, 1895, in memory of Judge Ebenezer Hoar of Concord, Massachusetts. It is repeated here, since at the time it attracted a good deal of attention, and since Mrs. Agassiz's part in it is characteristically graceful.

TO MISTRESS LOUIS AGASSIZ

President of Radcliffe College, Cambridge, Massachusetts

Quincy, September 12, 1894

HONORED AND GRACIOUS LADY: This epistle is addressed to you from Quincy, because in the part of Braintree which now bears that name, in the burial place by the meeting house, all that was mortal of me was laid to rest more than two centuries ago, and the gravestone stands which bears my name, and marks the spot where my dust reposes.

It may cause you surprise to be thus addressed, and that the work which you are pursuing with such constancy and success is of interest to one who so long ago passed from the mortal sight of men. But you may recall that wise philosophers have believed and taught that those who have striven to do their Lord's will here below do not, when transferred to his house on high, thereby become wholly regardless of

THE PASSING OF THE ANNEX 269

what may befall those who come after them, — "*nec, haec coelestia spectantes, ista terrestria contemnunt.*" It is a comforting faith that those who have "gone forth weeping, bearing precious seed," shall be permitted to see and share the joys of the harvest with their successors who gather it.

I was a contemporary of the pious and bountiful Lady Radcliffe, for whom your college is named. My honored husband, Charles Hoar, Sheriff of Gloucester in England, by his death in 1638, left me a widow with six children. We were of the people called by their revilers Puritans, to whom civil liberty, sound learning, and religion were very dear. The times were troublous in England, and the hands of princes and prelates were heavy upon God's people. My thoughts were turned to the new England where precious Mr. John Harvard had just lighted that little candle which has since thrown its beams so far, where there seemed a providential refuge for those who desired a church without a Bishop, and a state without a King.

I did not, therefore, like the worshipful Lady Radcliffe, send a contribution in money; but I came hither myself, bringing the five youngest of my children with me, and arrived at Braintree in the year 1640.

From that day Harvard College has been much in my mind; and I humbly trust that my coming has not been without some furtherance to its well being. My lamented husband in his will directed that our youngest son, Leonard, should be "carefullie kept at Schoole, and when hee is fitt for itt to be carefullie placed at Oxford, and if ye Lord shall see fitt, to make him a Minister unto his people." As the nearest practicable conformity to this direction, I placed him carefully at Harvard College, to such purpose that he graduated therefrom in 1650, became a faithful minister to God's people, a capable physician to heal their bodily diseases, and became the third President of the College, and the first who was a graduate from it, in 1672.

My daughters became the wives of the Rev. Henry Flint, the minister of Braintree, and Col. Edmund Quincy of the same town: and it is recorded that from their descendants another President has since been raised up to the College, Josiah Quincy (*tam carum caput*), and a Professor of Rhetoric and Oratory, John Quincy Adams, who as well as his sons and grandsons have given much aid to the College, as members of one or the other of its governing boards, beside attaining other distinctions less to my present purpose.

The elder of my three sons who came with me to America, John Hoar, settled in the extreme western frontier town of English settlement in New England, called Concord: to which that exemplary Christian man, the Reverend Peter Bulkeley, had brought his flock in 1635. In Mr. Bulkeley's ponderous theological treatise, called "The Gospel Covenant," of which two editions were published in London (but whether it be so generally and constantly perused and studied at the present day, as it was in my time, I know not), — in the preface thereto, he says it was written "at the end of the earth." There my son and his posterity have dwelt and multiplied, and the love and service of the College which I should approve have not been wholly wanting among them. In so remote a place there must be urgent need of instruction, though the report seems to be well founded that settlements farther westward have since been made, and that some even of my own posterity have penetrated the continent to the shores of the Pacific Sea. Among the descendants of John Hoar have been that worthy Professor John Farrar, whose beautiful face in marble is among the precious possessions of the College; that dear and faithful woman who gave the whole of her humble fortune to establish a scholarship therein, Levina Hoar; and others who as Fellows or Overseers have done what they could for its prosperity and growth.

Pardon my prolixity, but the story I have told is but a prelude to my request of your kindness. There is no authentic mode in which departed souls can impart their wishes to those who succeed them in this world but these, the record or memory of their thoughts and deeds, while on earth; or the reappearance of their qualities of mind and character in their lineal descendants.

In this first year of Radcliffe College, — when so far as seems practicable and wise, the advantages which our dear Harvard College, "the defiance of the Puritan to the savage and the wilderness," has so long bestowed upon her sons, are through your means to be shared by the sisters and daughters of our people, — if it should so befall that funds for a scholarship to assist in the education of girls at Radcliffe College, who need assistance, with preference always to be given to natives, or daughters of citizens of Concord, Massachusetts, should be placed in the hands of your Treasurer, you might well suppose that memory of me had induced some of my descendants to spare so much from their necessities for such a modest memorial: and I would humbly ask that the scholarship may bear the name of

THE WIDOW JOANNA HOAR

And may God establish the good work you have in charge!

At the same time that Mrs. Agassiz received this letter the treasurer of Radcliffe College received an anonymous gift of two thousand dollars, afterward increased to five thousand dollars.

In reply, Mrs. Agassiz addressed the following letter to Judge Hoar as one of the descendants of Joanna Hoar.

Quincy Street, Cambridge, October 11, 1894

DEAR SIR: Very recently I received the most gracious communication from the far past, written with the mingled dignity and grace which we are wont to associate with our ladies of the olden time, yet not without a certain modernness which showed that she still keeps in touch with what is valuable in our day and generation. Through me she sends greeting to the young Radcliffe College, and a most generous gift to aid in the work for the education of women in which that institution is engaged.

A doubt as to the best way of acknowledging the gift and the sympathy it represents has kept me silent till now. But a friend suggests that you might put us in the way of searching that gentle Joanna Hoar who speaks across the lapse of time so cordially and sweetly. In that case will you express, if not to her, to some of her living descendants, the thanks of Radcliffe College for the scholarship which she has so generously endowed.

Perhaps I may be allowed to add my own respectful gratitude for her valued letter to me.

With great regard,

Most cordially yours,
ELIZABETH C. AGASSIZ

TO MRS. LOUIS AGASSIZ FROM A DESCENDANT OF THE WIDOW JOANNA HOAR

Concord, Massachusetts, October 15, 1894

DEAR MRS. AGASSIZ: I am honored by the receipt of your courteous letter. If, as I suppose, the Joanna Hoar to whom you refer is a lady from whom I am descended, I know no means of communicating with her. Even the messenger entrusted by the Post Office with a "special delivery" letter might decline to risk the chances of getting back, if he were to undertake the delivery in person. So I adopted the other alternative which you suggest, and stated the case to two of her most conspicuous descendants of our time, Senator George F. Hoar, of Worcester, and Mr. Charles F.

Adams, who has recently removed from Quincy to a house in Lincoln, just on the borders of Concord.

They look intelligent, but promise nothing; though both are members of the Historical Society, and perhaps know more than they choose to tell.

I am glad, however, that the old lady contrived a way to send Radcliffe a gift with her greeting.

Very faithfully yours,

In the address referred to above Mr. Adams "chose to tell" the story of the scholarship and revealed the open mystery that Joanna Hoar had made her gift through Judge Hoar himself. "He chose to give with an unseen hand," Mr. Adams said, "and to build his memorial to his first New England ancestor in his own peculiar way." He probably was well aware that in Mrs. Agassiz he had a correspondent who would meet his humor halfway and answer him in his own vein.

CHAPTER XI
EUROPE
1894-1895

DURING the fifteen years while the Annex was developing into Radcliffe College Mrs. Agassiz's manifold official duties did not by any means engross her entire time or form the most intimate claims on her attention. The conditions of her daily existence that we have seen prevailing between 1873 and 1879 essentially continued in this later period, accompanied by changes that time made in the lives of her grandchildren, who as they grew older did not grow any the less absorbing, and that illness and death brought into the family circle. Of these the most important to Mrs. Agassiz was the death of her mother in 1880. "Life is so different," she wrote to Frau Mettenius a few months later, "when we have no longer father or mother in the world. We are at first (however old we may be when the change comes) a little like lost children." Yet on the whole these years of which we are speaking, apart from Mrs. Agassiz's efforts for the college, contain little to record beyond the round of activities that were incident to a large social and family connection such as hers.

It was during this time that she became a member of the Ladies' Visiting Committee for the Kindergarten for the Blind, established under the direction of the Perkins Institution for the Blind, and began her service as treasurer for the Cambridge branch of the committee, which she continued for seventeen years, until after an illness in 1904 she was obliged to resign it. Her appeals for contributions from Cambridge, issued yearly in the form of leaflets, by their simplicity, directness, and freedom from sentimentality were effective at the time and are still interesting. Her own enthusiasm for the work among the children of the Kindergarten appears in the following letter.

TO MRS. CORNELIUS CONWAY FELTON

Cambridge [*May* 7, 1894]

... THE other day Alice Longfellow and I had a pleasant morning together; we drove over to the Kindergarten for the Blind and were wonderstruck, as one always is, however often he may have seen it, with the skilful work and the seeming enjoyment of these children. There are classes of little boys of seven or eight who are as versed in Longfellow's poetry as any children of real eyes could be. When Alice came in and they were told who it was, their faces grew radiant. They asked if they might recite something from her father's poems. The teacher seemed to think they would not remember on such a sudden call, but they were sure they could, and they recited eight or ten together, the "Blacksmith" (in chorus) without a mistake and with such sweet and intelligent expressions that you could not hear it without emotion. The teacher told me that last year (with Alice's permission) she took them to Craigie House. Alice was not at home, but they wanted to come in and look about. When they came to the old clock on the stairs, she said the children were touched as by some very sacred thing. They came down quite seriously, and after a moment with one accord as they stood quite silent at the foot of the stairs, they recited the poem about the clock. As you look at their work — their knitting and embroidery, their writing and sewing, and as you see their enjoyment of beautiful things, flowers, for instance, you cannot help thinking that they have, as Phillips Brooks said, some inner sense which stands them in stead of what they have lost.

No account of any series of years in Mrs. Agassiz's life is complete without some mention of Nahant. The summers there during the period of which we are speaking were scarcely less active for her than her Cambridge winters, as may be seen from some reminiscences of them written for the family by Mrs. Cornelius Conway Felton in an unpublished sketch called "Summer Days at Nahant," from which the following selections are made.

The house was placed on a slope of land so that one side of it was entered from the grassy lawn, without any driveway. The other side facing the sea was high enough to give a fine uninterrupted view of the whole bay and the Lynn shore. At first there was not a tree or a shrub on the place, but Aunt Lizzie's love for the beautiful soon prompted her to plant woodbine beside the porches and to begin a garden. She was a born home maker, and any abode of hers, even if for a day's visit assumed an air of cosiness as well as elegance. Everything was dainty, fresh, and in her housekeeping no friction was perceptible between mistress and maids. At any hour of the day or night a comfortable meal might be had. The newly arrived guest always had the warmest welcome, and while the traveller was refreshing himself Aunt Lizzie would sit and talk delightfully.

My husband tells me that when he and his brother were boys, they could have breakfast at any hour of the morning in order to go fishing or shooting. Boys were taken as much into consideration as any one else in the complicated household, which consisted of a dozen people regularly and often more when there were guests. A convenient feature of the Nahant cottage was that the rooms opened out of doors so that the occupants could enter and leave without disturbing other people. The Felton boys had their room at the end of the west wing, which proved a rendezvous for all their chums, where they met to talk endlessly. . . . It was a kind of Liberty Hall of which the memories are delightful. . . . Guests were always turning up unexpectedly to lunch, dine or pass the night, and one never had a sensation of making trouble even if the house were full — a bed could be made up in the laboratory for a grandson. One of Aunt Lizzie's delightful thoughts for entertaining children was that each might bring an intimate friend; so the variety of the rising generation that we saw was amusing and extensive. . . .

Aunt Lizzie delighted in her garden and until the last few years of her life daily spent several hours gathering and arranging her flowers. I like to recall her in her fresh white morning gown, basket and shears in hand, going leisurely with her rather stately

THE AGASSIZ HOUSE AT NAHANT

EUROPE

air from border to border, and then coming to the shady porch and arranging the flowers in different vases. Lemon verbena, rose geranium and heliotrope she always had in abundance, so that the rooms were fragrant with them and there were water lilies in August. At first her garden was of the simplest plan of flower beds arranged about the house, but ten years before her death she made a long grassy walk leading around the house between ornamental trees and shrubs. . . . Another pet plan of hers was a roof garden over the laboratory. . . . It consisted of a series of boxes put about the sides and across the roof, so that when the flowers were well started they joined each other, and you looked over a lovely mass of color to the blue sea and the Lynn shore. Aunt Lizzie studied the effect of her flower scheme quite intently till she arranged it to satisfy herself. Another pretty decoration for her porch was a glass tank in which she kept pond lilies, and she used nasturtium leaves, if she did not have lily pads.

Two interludes of travel interrupted these years spent for the greater part in Cambridge and Nahant. In the spring of 1892 Mrs. Agassiz went with relatives to the Pacific coast — a journey of three months that was a source of great enjoyment to her. The still greater pleasure that opened before her in the autumn of 1894, after the Annex had been safely transformed into Radcliffe College, is best announced by herself in the following note.

TO MISS GRACE NORTON

Nahant, September 25, 1894

... Do you know that I am going to Europe for the winter with my dear Shaws? I have known it myself for less than a week, and as I only returned from Newport last Tuesday, I have been rather busy and very bewildered — in a sort of waking dream. My plans were all laid for a winter in Cambridge and I was hardly prepared for this change of front. But the family chorus is in one strain, "You *must* go," and you can imagine that I could not go more delightfully.

Remember that my European experience consists of one week in England, one in Paris and four in Switzerland, that I know nothing of France, Germany or Italy — and to see the beautiful things that have been a dream to me all my life with Quin and Pauline! ...

Mrs. Agassiz sailed for Havre in October with Mr. and Mrs. Shaw, and two of their children. A month in Paris was followed by a winter in Italy; in the spring she went with her niece, Miss Mary Felton, and a friend, Miss Isa Gray, for a short visit to London, Cambridge, and Oxford, before joining Mrs. Richard Cary and Miss Cary, her sister-in-law and niece, in Venice for a few months of travel on the continent until October, when they sailed for home. Mrs. Agassiz's itinerary, it will be seen, led her along well-trodden paths and into the usual experience of the American traveller who makes the "grand tour" with ease of material conditions, meeting old and new friends on the road. It is her own spirit that gives individuality to the account of her travels that she has left in her letters and diaries. Although at this time she was preoccupied by many anxieties, her power of cheerful enjoyment, her incapability of grumbling, and her habitual self-forgetfulness provided her with the traveller's silver spoon no less at seventy-two years than in the days in Brazil and on the Hassler. In spite of her age she was undaunted by the exigencies of travel and unfoiled by lack of vigor from improving her opportunities for pleasure. When she was in the Dolomites and Tyrol, for instance, solitary mountain rambles in the early morning were her delight, nor did they afford her a reason for passing the rest of the day in *dolce far niente.* "A heavenly day," she recorded in her diary at Zell-am-See on August 18, 1895. "Breakfasted at 6.30 in my room. A beautiful walk. Packed. Afternoon, ascended the Schmittenhöhe, Helen [Mrs. Richard Cary] and I each in one of those queer chairs. The path excessively steep and none too safe. I walked down, but Helen who kept to her chair was upset, but not hurt." In her sight-seeing, in general, however, Mrs. Agassiz combined with the zest of one score the good sense of three score and ten years. In Paris and Italy she enjoyed the advantage of having an accomplished cicerone for the galleries in Mr. Shaw, whose long study and great love of art, as well as his experience and that of Mrs. Shaw in making choice additions to his valuable collection, had for many years supplemented her own admittedly slight acquaintance with painting and sculpture. "I have to thank Quin," she writes from Rome, "not only for bringing me to see pictures, but for teaching me all these years to enjoy them, for his pictures are really an education. I enjoy pictures now as I should not have done in my earlier days."

There were two visits that Mrs. Agassiz definitely planned to make for her own gratification in the course of her travels, one to Montagny where the Swiss relatives of Agassiz were still living, and the other to the colleges for women in Cambridge and Oxford. It is significant of her interests that her only two personal desires for her year abroad were connected, one with the great affection of her life, the other with her faithfully accepted public responsibility. For the rest of her travels she expressed no individual plans or preferences, in spite of the fact that she had previously seen almost nothing of Europe. "I do not incline to make plans," she wrote, "rather to confine my outlook to shorter intervals — as Sydney Smith has said, 'not farther than from dinner to tea.'"

A few extracts from letters written during this year abroad are given here, which reflect in one way or another traits and interests which were an inherent part of Mrs. Agassiz's true self — her delight in music, her pleasure in friends connected with her past, as, for example, in meeting Francesca Alexander and her mother in Florence, and in London Lady Harcourt, who as Miss Lily Motley had been a pupil at the Agassiz school, her love for Nahant that called as loudly in Venice as in Cambridge, and her devotion to Agassiz that made every scene connected with his early years sacred.

TO MISS SARAH G. CARY

Hôtel Meurice, Paris, October 29, 1894

OUR days are arranged somewhat after this fashion. Breakfast independent, or we each order it, as we come out of our rooms — of course the French breakfast first, and a heavier one at 12.30. After early breakfast Paunie [Miss Pauline Shaw] and I generally do something together. Often we take one room at the Louvre and devote ourselves to that, after getting the first outline sketch from Quin. These quiet mornings there with ease and leisure for what we like best are delightful. This morning ... coming out from [St. Germain l'Auxerrois] we crossed one of the bridges, standing long to watch the craft on the river — the passenger boats going to and fro. And then on the other side we followed the Quais, where they sell the old books and engravings, music, etc., and past the Institut (I thought how often Agassiz had gone out and in there), and along the old street of quaint, queer shops, and then returned across another bridge and by the garden of the Tuileries home to our hotel.

There is something very attractive in wandering about on foot in this independent fashion, mousing out things for ourselves — much better than going about in carriages, I think, and I am glad to find that I can do a good deal on foot.

TO MISS MARY FELTON

Hôtel Meurice, Paris, November 20, 1894

WE have done and seen much since I wrote you, of which the two things that I remember with the deepest interest are an afternoon at Chantilly, the place of the Duc d'Aumale, and next a morning at Notre Dame (high mass). It is a wonderful thing to hear the great organ at its deepest and fullest roll through those wonderful arches, where as you look down their full length all things grow dim and distant at the farther end. Since I have been here, I have come to be deeply interested in the history of Paris. It is a wonderful story taken from the beginning to this present *fin de siècle*, and there are so many monuments of the past, still preserved, still beautiful, still picturesque; they are like stepping stones to cross this gulf of time, and they make the whole connected and in a way comprehensible. If ever the history of a nation can be made clear, one ought to understand something of the history of France in Paris.

Rome, Hôtel Royal, December 6, 1894

You did not know that I was entering Rome yesterday on my seventy-second birthday. Italy and Rome — was not that the most beautiful birthday gift that Pauline and Quin have ever given me? Yes, at last I am in your Italy, dear Mollie, and I thought of you so often yesterday as we pursued our way from Turin, leaving the snow mountains still in sight for the cultivated plain, and then through Genoa and Pisa and along the coast to Civitavecchia, reaching Rome at 11.30. I felt with you that it is an enchanted land. The descent into the plain of Italy, and the vast extent of beautifully cultivated land with its soft green furrows and rich brown soil between, every field a picture, and then, as you have always said, the human interest gives it such a charm — the little towns clustered so close upon the rising grounds, the churches on seemingly almost inaccessible heights — and then when we came to the seashores! But it is of no use to write about it. I am sure a mere word calls it all up to you.

Rome is still closed to us. We arrived in pitch darkness and are greeted by rain today, and no glimpse of ruins or of the Rome of my imagination in sight. But yesterday was enough for one day. I can well afford to wait, and meanwhile we are settling in to what will be our home, I suppose, for two months.

TO MISS SARAH G. CARY

Hôtel Royal, Rome, December 8, 1894

THE morning after our arrival a dripping rain greeted us. Yesterday was again a rainy day, but in the afternoon we went to St. Peter's thinking that the great church would have its own light and atmosphere independent of weather — and so it was. As Quin lifted the heavy curtain for us to pass in, I thought of what Mother wrote me after first seeing that wonderful interior, "No one's church — the World's church." I always thought it a very expressive phrase and Quin said he thought it would be difficult to describe it better.

How impossible it is to represent the great things of the world by any artificial means! When I saw the Yosemite every photograph ceased to have any relation to it, and so it was with St. Peter's, and so the next day with the Coliseum.

TO THE STUDENTS OF RADCLIFFE COLLEGE

Rome, December 11, 1894

MY DEAR YOUNG FRIENDS: Far away as I am from Radcliffe College you are often in my thoughts. I see you at your work, in your Clubs, in your social gatherings and especially at the Wednesday teas, where I long to join you and to share in the talk that goes on around the tables. Could I be transported there, I should have much to tell you of the old story of which these ancient cities speak to us still, bringing the past so near that it sometimes seems more vivid than the present. Of course we all know the facts, or a great part of them, but to be on the spot makes our dry knowledge a living reality. I felt this in Paris, where the new is lost in the old (at least, it was so to me), and still more here, where the dead ruins make the life of the city.

But I did not mean to talk to you of myself and of what I am seeing and enjoying, but rather of the pleasure I have in hearing that all goes well with Radcliffe and its students. This year seems to me of greater importance in the history of our college than any preceding one except the first. That was the initiative step in what was really a far-reaching undertaking, though at the moment it seemed hardly more than a doubtful experiment; this year marks the conclusion of that period and the opening of one which rests on a sure foundation.

I am confident that you all appreciate this new aspect of our undertaking and will help the officers of

Radcliffe in their resolution to keep our college up to a standard worthy of its relation to our old University. To this end we must work together with single-hearted sincerity of purpose. Sending you an affectionate greeting across the sea for the New Year, I am always

                Your old friend,
                    ELIZABETH C. AGASSIZ

TO MISS SARAH G. CARY

Hôtel Grande Bretagne, Florence, April 5, 1895

YESTERDAY we all went to such a pretty festa (for Easter) given by Mrs. Alexander, and Pauline sharing, for the poor school in which Pauline has been interested. The children had a dinner first (about seventy there were), and then all were collected in the schoolroom to receive their gifts. Each had three presents apiece and an orange. And then there was a surprise which Pauline had prepared — a plant in flower for each child. That carried the day — nothing they had received seemed to give them the pleasure that these growing plants did. So they went off, a floral procession, each child bearing his or her pot all in bloom. Indeed I hardly know how they managed to bear away all their treasures. They had full hands and full hearts, I think. The rounds of applause were loud and long.

Hôtel Meurice, Paris, May 13, 1895

YESTERDAY I had a very pretty excursion to Fontenay-aux-Roses, where there is an establishment for training normal teachers. It is all gratuitous and was quite interesting to me, though the ideas about women's education were so limited as compared with ours that I was a little puzzled. But the whole visit was pleasant, and there was so much warm expression from one or two of the professors about Agassiz. It carried me back to old times. The little town of Fontenay is very picturesque, and the park and garden attached to the school were charming.

In her diary, after noting the visit to Fontenay-aux-Roses, Mrs. Agassiz adds: "It touches me to see how strong the feeling about Agassiz is wherever education is going on."

Harvey's Hotel, Curzon Street, London, May 27

OF all the time-devouring places London is the most exasperating. I have not been able to write a home letter since I came, and now I can barely do more than copy the entries in my little diary, only just to say where I have been.

On arriving here I found a cordial note of welcome from Lily Harcourt, asking me to lunch the next day. You have no idea how affectionate she was — full of the old memories, the days of her mother and father and our relations in the past. She is a very lovely, loyal friend. The lunch was the usual family lunch, so that it gave me a very pleasant opportunity to see her husband and her son.

"The Bull," Cambridge, June 1

THUS far had I written, but the fates intervened and I was interrupted, and never could catch on again. So

EUROPE

I pick up the thread here. I was telling you about my first visit to Lily Motley. Her husband was very cordial and extremely amusing. He came in when lunch was half through from his office, bringing with him a very pleasant man who works with him. They were making up that mysterious package called "The Budget," so Lily said, and were fearfully busy. Sir William, though a Liberal, seemed by no means in sympathy with modern reforms; bicycles and higher education for women were equally under his ban, and he said the nineteenth century had become intolerable and the twentieth would be worse, and he was glad to think how soon he should bid good-bye to both. He and his party are very unpopular. "I am old and likely to go out of office soon." It is curious how one gets interested in the local political talk when one is on the spot.

... My next will be from Oxford, and I shall not be sorry. Pleasant as it all is, I shall be very glad to drop social and educational responsibilities and be off with Mollie to Italy and Venice.

Mrs. Agassiz's visits to Cambridge and Oxford had a direct influence upon her policy in regard to the establishment of halls of residence at Radcliffe. In 1897 she gave an account of some of her experiences at the English colleges for women to the Emmanuel Club at Radcliffe, from which the following extracts are made.

When you first arrive in Cambridge, if you stay, as we did, in the old tavern, The Bull, your first outlook upon the street will give you the sense of antiquity, of something belonging to the past, grown gray with time and softened by age which we expect to find in the old university towns of England. To me Cambridge had a wonderful picturesqueness, and a kind of rural quality suggestive of quiet and scholarly seclusion. Oxford is more before the world. You will be asked whether you have seen Oxford before you are asked whether you have been to Cambridge. Yet, to me, the latter had a charm of its own that brings it very near to one's affections.

The following morning we went early to Girton. . . . We were most cordially received by Miss Welsh, the Principal or so-called Mistress. . . . The instruction in the colleges for women at Cambridge and Oxford is by no means given altogether by the professors and teachers of the Universities. Much instruction is given by ladies, many of whom have themselves been educated at the colleges where they teach. I must add that the presence of these ladies and their relations with the students seemed to be extremely pleasant. They shared in their sports and recreations and had a very friendly and genial companionship with their pupils. . . .

You will want me to say something of the girls' personal arrangements. They have generally at Girton a sitting-room with bedroom adjoining, occupied, as the case might be, by one student or two. The rooms looked very pleasant: a certain portion of the outfit, as beds, table and desk, all of the simplest description, is provided by the college, but the rooms are made cheerful by what the girls themselves have added, in the way of pretty tables and chairs, with draperies and screens, their favorite photographs, etc. I think you all know the look of a college girl's room, and I did not see that they differed much from ours. The grounds are large and prettily planted; there are lawn-tennis grounds and spaces laid out for croquet. Whether golf reigns there I did not learn, but the general aspect is certainly very attractive. The distance of Girton from the University, about two miles I should think, struck me as objectionable. There are no tramways or any regular line of coaches, and the college is obliged to provide carriages for driving the students into the town for all lectures. I heard nothing of bicycles there, though I should think it would be not only a quicker but a more economical way of making the short journey. . . .

Returning from Girton we went the same afternoon to Newnham upon invitation. Mrs. Sidgwick, who is Principal at Newnham, is a shy, reserved woman, the very impersonation in appearance and manners of the English gentlewoman, so gentle and seemingly timid that one wonders to find her in so responsible and prominent a post. But I fancy her decision and force of character are well balanced with her gentleness of manner. She and her husband, Professor Sidgwick, make their home at Newnham, having an apartment in the main building. Her position is simply one of choice, arising from her interest in the University education of women. She is of the Balfour family, — is the sister of Arthur Balfour now a member of the English Cabinet. Her fortune is large, and she gives most generously to the institution in the management of which she takes so prominent a part. Professor Sidgwick is wholly at one with her in this and teaches in the College. He is as witty as he is learned, a very agreeable, genial man, and of course his residence at Newnham is a very important factor in the success and growth of the institution.

At this first visit we had not time to see the whole building. It was toward the close of the afternoon, and after a cup of tea in her drawing-room Mrs. Sidgwick took us at once into the grounds, where a competitive game of lawn-tennis was going on. Our hostess evidently took as much interest in it as the girls themselves, though her sympathy was impartial, having good wishes for both sides. The game over, we walked about the grounds and came upon one or two pretty teas spread out in the shade under the trees. At one, I remember, tea being over, the girls were blowing soap-bubbles into the air and over the grass.

This short visit gave me of course but an outside glance, and the next day I spent the whole day there with my friends and travelling companions, Miss Felton and Miss Gray. We lunched with Mrs. Sidgwick and several of the resident ladies of the College. Here again, as at Girton, I felt that the presence of these ladies, their easy, sympathetic companionship with the students, must form no small part of the education which the girls receive at Newnham. Among these resident teachers is Miss Gladstone, daughter of the statesman, an exceptionally pleasant woman of much personal charm. Then there is Miss Clough, daughter of the poet, and Miss Fawcett who carried off the honors of the Mathematical Tripos one year from all competitors, and was, I believe, Senior Wrangler for that year, and there were several others whom I saw and knew less, but who were very pleasing. Miss Clough and Miss Fawcett were students at Newnham before they became resident teachers.

After lunch Mrs. Sidgwick took us over the building and showed us not only the lecture and class rooms, but also the girls' quarters. Here they have no sitting or study rooms, but the chambers are ample and comfortable, and are occupied singly or as double rooms. In order to give them by day the air rather of a parlor than of a chamber the beds are broad couches, which when covered by afghans and well cushioned serve as sofas during the daytime. Still I think the Girton arrangement is the pleasanter, and I am not sure that the sofa in the long run takes the place of a bed.

The day of our visit was a fortunate one for us, because the graduating class was just coming back from final examinations, and the successful ones were of course the centre of interest. I remember seeing Miss Fawcett as she caught sight of a student who had received special honors with her Tripos spring on a window-seat, throw open the sash, and greet her with the greatest warmth. A little later in the day we dined in the girls' Hall, where instead of a single table extending from end to end there were a number of small tables arranged for groups of eight or ten at each. Of course the examinations were the topic of the hour, and I believe they were to have a dance in the evening to let off the exuberance of their joy. One pleasant habit I observed in all the Colleges. There was a sort of sitting-room, or as they called it conversation-room, very cosy and comfortable, which seemed open to all where they gathered after dinner for a cup of coffee. Here we ended our pleasant day, and it was my last visit to Newnham.

But I cannot leave Cambridge without a word on other things beside the Colleges for Women; of its ancient Colleges and Chapels, its pretty bridges over the river Cam, where the students row and have their fun, of the shady and peaceful old courts around which the Colleges are built. In June when we were there the flower season is in its glory and the students' balconies and windows are full of color among the dark ivy which clothes the walls.

We had a glimpse also of a college student's room, for a young friend invited us to take tea with him after Vespers. It was a cheerful, comfortable half-study and half-sitting-room, but by no means [so] luxurious as many of our students' rooms. Perhaps this was an individual case, but I was told it was not considered "good form" to have very elegantly furnished rooms.

I had but three or four days in Oxford and but for the feeling that you may wish to have such a glimpse as I can give you I should hardly venture to speak of my personal experience there.

The aspect of things at the Oxford Colleges for Women was of course in a general way the same as at Newnham and Girton — their internal arrangements, recitation rooms, library, etc., and their pretty chambers looking out on pleasant grounds, though not so extensive as those at Newnham and Girton. I dined at Somerville with Miss Maitland in company with all the students, and passed a pleasant evening with her and them. I was hospitably entertained also at Lady Margaret Hall and at St. Hugh's, but to give you an account of my days there would be to go over the same ground as at the Cambridge Colleges for Women. . . .

Of course we spent some hours in the Bodleian Library. To give you the least idea of its picturesque interior or of the impression it makes upon you would be impossible. I will pause a moment to tell you an incident which struck me as curious. We were going through the Library under Mr. Pelham's guidance, and he stopped to point out a portrait of Mary, Queen of Scots, said to be the most authentic in existence. In connection with it he told me this singular story. On some public occasion when the crowd was likely to be great in the Library, they had a squad of police to prevent any injury to their many treasures. One of the professors passing through the Hall where this portrait hangs saw the Chief of the Police looking intently at this picture. The professor, struck by the man's interest, stopped beside him a moment and said, "It is an interesting portrait, is n't it?" The policeman answered, "I don't know who it is — I was only looking at it professionally." "How do you mean, 'professionally'?" asked the professor. "Well, you see," said the man, "in my work I often come into contact with criminals who stand high socially. They do not belong to what is called the criminal class. She looks of that kind. I know the expression well." The professor then told him who she was. I do not know whether the man knew enough of her history to be aware that she had been accused of crime and that a shadow of doubt still hangs over her. Perhaps he did not see the coincidence between his own comment and her sad life.

TO MISS SARAH G. CARY

Hotel Brunswick, London, June 10, 1895

It gives me such a strange feeling to be on the other side of my Cambridge and Oxford visits. I looked forward to it all with pleasure but not without a certain sense of anxiety and responsibility. It has all been simply delightful. Everything has been made very easy for me, and I have seen and learned more than I could have hoped to do. It has stimulated my interest in our home work, and I shall be surprised if it does not prove of serious value to me on my return. After all, I think it helps one very much to see what others are doing on the same lines on which you are yourself working. Our last day was one of the best in Oxford. In the morning I had a pleasant visit at the Max Müllers', — did not see him, because he was not well, but she is a charming person. I had once or twice spoken to her of a paper of her husband's, which always interested me very much — I think you have heard me speak of it; it came out in Littell, and after a while I lost it and have ever since been trying to find it among his collections of short papers, but never succeeded. The morning I went to bid them good-bye she looked for it and showed me one or two that she thought might be the article I liked so much; but I remembered my favorite phrases word for word, and they did not correspond. But just as we were leaving in the late afternoon a package was brought to me — a volume containing the paper I had been seeking this many a year from Mr. Müller himself, and my name on the fly-leaf, "with the regards of the author." I don't know when anything has given me so much pleasure.

Good-night and good-bye. I shall write next from Venice. I am with you at Nahant "every day and hour," as the old song says.

Casa Biondetti, Venice, June 22, 1895

I THINK that our life differs from that of many visitors to Venice. Being all women and all of one mind, we are absolutely irresponsible as to hours and rules. Every one breakfasts when she sees fit, and as we have the most amiable of cooks and housekeepers in our *padrona*, she never minds any amount of unpunctuality. A life so free from conventionalities and at the same time so sympathetic was never shared I think by a household of half a dozen people.

But with all the charm of Venice, I think the greatest happiness of my life here is the thought of Nahant. To picture you all on my piazza or yours, to think of Carrie driving up to your door or mine, all this completes and fills out my experience this summer. Nor does the beauty of Nahant fade in the wonderful picture. I remember our sunsets and ask myself even here if anything can be more beautiful, and I think with delight of being there again. To be sure one must allow something for the love of a lifetime, the place where you were almost born and have spent all your summers — that counts for something.

TO MRS. ARTHUR GILMAN

Venice, June 23, 1895

DEAR MRS. GILMAN: Before this the quiet of vacation has fallen upon Radcliffe, the last words are spoken for the year, and I hope that you and Mr. Gilman are preparing for summer rest. Perhaps you have already gone.

I am afraid that you and he will have felt that in being absent from Commencement I have neglected my Radcliffe engagements. But the truth is that when I left, although my plans were uncertain, I had it in mind, should circumstances be favorable, to visit the English colleges — Girton and Newnham and the rest. I did not do quite all that I had hoped, but I passed a week in Cambridge and one in Oxford. I am very glad to have done this, and I feel that I learned a good deal which may be helpful, — not so much concerning the methods of instruction (they differ so widely from ours as regards general arrangement that they could hardly serve as models for us), — but regarding the domestic life. In that respect I made careful inquiries for I feel that one of the most pressing questions for us is that of a home or homes for such students as must find lodgings in Cambridge. In regard to the size and distribution of room in such house or houses as we may build, my views were a good deal modified by what I learned from Mrs. Sidgwick, Miss Gladstone and the other ladies resident in the different halls.

You know I have always been in favor of small houses with few students — not more than ten or twelve. Mrs. Sidgwick is strongly in favor of a greater number — not less than twenty to twenty-five — not more perhaps than fifty. She has no experience in the other method, but her objection to it in theory seemed to be chiefly that the smaller number limited the choice of acquaintanceship, and also that individual peculiarities which might be trying in so small a community would be merged in a larger one. In this matter also the cases are hardly parallel; we could never have as they have a number of resident ladies like Mrs. Sidgwick, Miss Gladstone, Miss Clough (daughter of the poet), Miss Fawcett, and others whose names I do not recall at this moment. Of course their presence gives the tone to the whole community, for they live in very delightful, it seemed to me intimate relations with the students, while allowing them much freedom. At Girton the arrangements seemed much the same. I feel that this is a pressing question and will need much consideration. It would be a misfortune should we make any mistakes in our buildings.

I hear that there is much doubt and discussion as to the future arrangements for our athletic grounds and some idea of choosing a place where all our buildings — college, gymnasium, dwellings, laboratories, etc., as well as land enough for sports and athletics — could be combined. I confess that I should be very sorry to leave the Fay House, — but the question is a wide one, and I know too little of what has been going on this winter to venture upon any discussion of the pros and cons.

For all these things we are going to need a great deal of money. But I suppose that when we have finally made up our minds as to the best method, we shall be able to find the means to carry it out.

I hope that all is well with you and yours. Best wishes for your summer from

Yours most cordially,
ELIZABETH C. AGASSIZ

TO MRS. LOUIS AGASSIZ

Cambridge, June 30, 1895

MY DEAR MRS. AGASSIZ: The year's work is over, and my first thought is to write to you and to tell you how much I have missed your presence here, and how anxiously I have striven to do all that would satisfy you without appealing constantly to you for advice and suggestion. I think, on the whole, everything has gone well, and just now the future of Radcliffe looks very bright indeed. There is so much interest and sympathy expressed and we hope we have *gained* friends during the past year, as well as *kept* those we had. Whatever *feeling* remained after the organization last spring is, I think, in many cases, dying away, and it is generally recognized that the alliance with Harvard is close enough for all practical purposes. The students who have come up for the entrance examinations these past three days, are more in number than ever before, and most of the schools send up larger classes; the girls look very nice and I don't believe that we shall have a larger freshman class than we can manage. That is our present solicitude; for this year we had no room at all to spare, and next year we shall have not quite enough. . . . I think we must make up our minds now as to our future policy with regard to staying where we are (this we should certainly do for years to come), or looking to some other site for the College of fifty years hence. In this is involved (to my thinking) the question of some other form of lodging the students who come from a distance. The present scheme answers for some, but not for all; if we are to have any number of students from the Middle and Western States, or from that part of New England which feels the influence of New York, we must have some mode of living that is at once less expensive and better suited to their wishes and habits. As it is, there is a danger of our becoming simply a "local college," and that would be a great waste of our opportunities; for there is no denying the fact that we do offer preeminent advantages in the way of instruction. But why do I trouble you with all this now, when I am hoping so soon to see you back? We hear that you mean to come home the end of August; perhaps you will lengthen your stay a little later, but we shall have you next winter. I say *we*, but I really mean *I*. How we did miss you at Commencement! We tried in every way to do what you would like and as you would like it; and I shall always regret that you did not see Sanders Theatre *filled* with friends on that first occasion, when we had hoped for not more than a few. It was all so cordial and sympathetic — every one will tell you that. . . .

Ever your attached
AGNES IRWIN

The first Radcliffe Commencement in Sanders Theatre, held there by invitation of the President and Fellows of Harvard College, to which Miss Irwin refers in the above letter, was an event of great importance in Mrs. Agassiz's eyes. To the uninitiated it may seem strange that she should have felt such deep emotion at this step as the following letter indicates, but it was intended as a public demonstration of the more intimate relations now established between the two institutions and as such was significant.

TO MISS SARAH G. CARY

Casa Biondetti, Venice, July 8, 1895

... TODAY comes a letter from Lily Cleveland, bringing me such a pleasant surprise, with full accounts, both her own and newspaper reports also, of the Graduating Exercises for Radcliffe in Sanders Theatre. I think my usual correspondents must have meant to heighten my pleasure in this most unlooked-for piece of news, for no one has ever suggested the transfer of the Radcliffe Commencement to Memorial Hall, and yet I am sure there must have been much discussion and deliberation between our Academic Board and the Corporation before the two decided upon the matter. There could not be a more positive recognition of Radcliffe by Harvard than this. It sets the seal upon our final adoption. It really has made me feel very happy. When I think of our first little Commencement with four graduates in Ellen Gurney's library and of this consummation I can hardly believe it. She and Gurney have gone beyond college ceremonies and have entered upon new Commencements, — but I wish they knew it. I really longed for their sympathy.

I feel more and more satisfied that it was well for me to be away this year. It has given Miss Irwin an independent ground. Of course I should never have hampered her in any way, but she would naturally have deferred to me as the older officer. But I am so glad about the ceremonies at Sanders Theatre. They seem to me to have been concluded very simply with quiet dignity. The fact that our Commencement is transferred in this way to the place where all the Memorial days of the University are kept will settle many doubtful questions about the occasion which were always coming up on its annual recurrence. I fancy we owe this very much to Mr. Eliot's influence.

So you see my mind is much at peace about Radcliffe matters, and I feel more and more inclined for the restful influences here which creep into my life more and more — a little like the Lotos-eaters, perhaps, in the land where it was "always afternoon"; but I give myself up to it for the time being very contentedly.

Perarolo, July 26, 1895

... THERE were three or four interesting masses sung in St. Mark's on successive days just before we left Venice, and I went to all but one. The first was at sunset, an hour which is so beautiful at St. Mark's because there are high windows which throw the light shortly before sunset into the upper part of the church and light up those wonderful mosaics and make them as fresh as yesterday with their gilded backgrounds. The music was very fine and the scene is always so engrossing — the figures moving about or kneeling, the priests coming and going, the mingling of rich and poor. But in Venice where are there not pictures? In the boats, on the church steps, in the by-ways — those little narrow *calle*, where the land traffic goes on, — the markets, etc., — one grows monotonous in calling attention every minute to these things, which from their frequency might seem commonplace, but every group is different. I could never see a grass boat coming in from the islands with its green load built up in perfect symmetry, fifteen feet high perhaps and as many long, with the boatmen leaning against it below or standing on the top to steer with their long poles, without a new sense of pleasure.

Our leave-taking was quite impressive — all the three gondoliers brought bouquets to each one of us, and as our *padrona* said, we had quite the air of a floral procession.

The change from the sirocco of Venice to these mountain solitudes where the air is pure and fresh and full of vitality is wonderful. We are now at Perarolo, the sweetest little town with mountains on either side and a rushing river, where the women are washing their linen and the men are collecting the timbers brought down on the stream and putting them on rafts to transport them.

Cortina, Val d'Ampezzo, August 2

... My chief pleasure here (and it is a very great one), is in my morning tramps. I sometimes wonder whether [if] you were here, you would join me in my early cup of tea and be off by seven o'clock. As my companions are not given to this style of enjoyment, I go alone, and there is something rather fascinating in the solitude. Occasionally I meet — not exactly with adventures for they do not deserve so grand a name, — but with incidents which are sometimes interesting, and at least amusing. Yesterday morning at the end of my ascent (which was accompanied by magnificent views with endless changes of light and shade all the way) I stopped before the door of a chalet and asked leave of the mistress who was standing outside to rest a little there. She led me along the shaky floor of one of those low-roofed balconies so characteristic of mountain chalets, offered me a rough seat (which at the moment was as delicious as a stuffed arm-chair), and brought me a cup of milk. I drank a little and then put it down simply because I did not think it wise, heated as I was, to drink the whole at once. Evidently she thought I found the cup too coarse, for she took it up (I was dreadfully afraid she was going to take it away) and brought the milk back in a little glass tumbler, to my great relief — not that I minded the cup, but I was very loath to relinquish the milk. While I sipped it she sat down on the door sill and sewed. Her work consisted in embroidering the most hideous coarse bags, one of which I bought to show my gratitude for her hospitality, and my sympathy with her poverty. She took me into her little home, where she lived, so far as I could make out, with an only child, a boy of seven or eight. To make my story what it should be, that home ought to have been as neat as it was ill-supplied with the necessities of life. Truth compels me to state that its dirt equalled its poverty. But the misery was unmistakable and so, ugly as it was, I was glad to buy my bag as an excuse for giving her a little lift out of her difficulties by paying more than her work was worth.

On the afternoon of the same day we drove to a superb view, called the Belvedere, to see the sunset from the top of a great cliff. One could drive up, but as they told us there was a short cut through the wood, Mollie and I thought we would take that path instead of making the steep descent by the carriage road. The path proved to be a kind of rough staircase in the face of the cliff. However we clambered down its picturesque windings safely enough, — only Mollie said, "What would Sallie say to me, if she knew I had led you into a scramble like that?"

Englischer Hof, Munich, September 8, 1895

... On Monday we came to Munich. Were you ever in Munich? To me it has the most homelike feeling because here Agassiz and Alexander Braun and all their brilliant young companions had their University life, of which Agassiz told me so much and so often, and which is told so vividly in his home letters. I have been to the Sendlinger Thor, near which he lodged in the house of the old naturalist, Döllinger, but I cannot find out which house, though there are some very old ones there. But there have been great changes; the old gate remains, but most of the landmarks belonging to that time have disappeared.

The long-anticipated visit to Montagny followed the stay in Munich. "Arriving yesterday," Mrs. Agassiz wrote in her diary on September 18, "Olympe brought me to the little chamber which Agassiz and I occupied in 1859. It was overwhelming at first, but still I felt very happy to be here."

TO MISS SALLIE CARY

Hôtel Normandie, Paris, September 29, 1895

I CANNOT tell you how delightful my stay with the Swiss family has been. It was rather agitating to go, for a whole world of young people has grown up (and indeed they have come into the world) since I was at Montagny in 1859 — and most of those I knew there are gone. I felt therefore a little strange and as if they would feel me to be more or less out of the circle. It was never so for a moment. I felt completely at home and as if I were a member of the household at once.

The old Montagny house is quaint and picturesque as ever. It is a family centre, and while I was there no day passed without members of the family dropping in to spend the day. And then we all dined together, and the afternoon was spent in the shady garden full of flowers, where the tables stand always ready for tea or coffee, and where the young people were gay and full of fun, and the older people quietly talked over memories of the past, aroused in part no doubt by my coming which brought the family together perhaps in greater numbers than usual. At all events I felt myself quite at home with young and old. I shall tell you much more about it when we can talk instead of writing. But I am so very glad that I was able to go.

And now here we are in Paris; the personal things I so wished to do, and which seemed to me to have a certain responsibility, as my visits to the English colleges, the arrangements for seeing the Swiss family, these all lie behind me, and we are here to await the steamer and attend to various practical matters.

On October 18 Mrs. Agassiz sailed for New York from Cherbourg. The record in her diary for October 26th tells of a contented home-coming to Quincy Street. "Left New York at 12 o'clock. Sallie and Carrie to meet me at the station. Drove home and had time to dress and arrange flowers before Alex, Rodolphe, and Max came. A delightful evening with Alex alone — the boys at a college dinner. Coming up to my room at the end of the evening, found the E. C. Agassiz scholarship. It was the crowning joy of my return." This scholarship came in the form of a gift of $6150 to Mrs. Agassiz from friends who desired to show their sense of what she had done for Radcliffe and for women; the money was given without restriction except that the scholarship should bear the name of Elizabeth Cary Agassiz.

CHAPTER XII
RADCLIFFE COLLEGE
1895–1904

THE conditions that Mrs. Agassiz found prevailing at Radcliffe on her return from Europe are set forth in the letter from Miss Irwin quoted above, and they were summed up more succinctly by her in her report as Dean to the President of Harvard University for the year 1894–1895. Here she stated that the two great material needs of Radcliffe College were "better academic accommodations and opportunities for physical culture." The same necessities were also emphasized by President Eliot at the Radcliffe Commencement exercises in the following year, when he pointed out that Radcliffe would not require a large theatre, an extensive library, a great observatory, or vast collections in natural history, since Harvard had acquired all this equipment for her; "nevertheless," he added, "Radcliffe needs laboratories of the best sort for teaching purposes; it needs departmental libraries; it needs a gymnasium and lecture halls of its own; it needs houses, not too large, and plenty of them, in which its students may live in a tranquil, wholesome way. Now all these things cost money; therefore Radcliffe needs great endowments, and needs them at once." These words of Miss Irwin and President Eliot mark the beginning of a phase in the growth of Radcliffe that directly affected Mrs. Agassiz in two ways. Hitherto she had been the protagonist of the college; it was she who had placed its needs before the public from time to time, and she who had been its representative before the world. In Miss Irwin she now had an able second, who discerned and vigorously expressed the necessities of Radcliffe, which by its closer connection with Harvard received added support from the influence of President Eliot. Furthermore it is evident that the college, having now attained to a recognized academic status, had reached a period in which material acquisition must be its immediate object, and that the ability which its president had shown in developing its organization must now be directed toward its mechanical equipment. It will be noticed that in this, the second part of Mrs. Agassiz's administration, although she was less active publicly than she had been in behalf of Radcliffe, her influence, discretion, and judicious foresight made themselves felt at every step that the college advanced, her ideals added sentiment to the brick and mortar of every building, and the affection that she awoke among her friends continued to react for the benefit of the college that she loved.

How the needs set forth by Miss Irwin and President Eliot were in a measure met within the next few years can be told for the greater part in the words of Mrs. Agassiz. It should be said in preface that since the purchase of Fay House the college had by degrees acquired in addition to the 20,000 square feet bought then nearly four times as much land, most of which lay in one piece of property and all of which was in the immediate vicinity of Fay House.

The story begins with a letter from Mrs. Augustus Hemenway to Mrs. Agassiz and requires for explanation so far as the college is concerned merely the statement that the Radcliffe gymnasium at this time occupied a small wooden building in the rear of Fay House on Mason Street. Mrs. Hemenway was well known in Boston for her philanthropic interests, practically all of which had one definite and specific aim — the cultivation among girls of the pursuits and powers that tend to the making of better homes; her beneficence was therefore directed to the encouragement of industrial and physical training as a part of education. The fact that her husband had given the Hemenway Gymnasium to Harvard University doubtless suggested to her the plan that she proposed in the following letter.

TO MRS. LOUIS AGASSIZ

Boston, December 20, 1896

DEAR MRS. AGASSIZ: In making a visit to Radcliffe lately I was struck with the inadequacy of the gymnasium, and in looking across the street and seeing what friends had done to make Harvard what it is, I felt that we were not showing the same appreciation of our women that had been so freely bestowed on the boys.

I do not know what plans you have for a gymnasium or for the future of Radcliffe, but I am sure you have an immediate want for a larger building, and I should like to give, if my means permit, a permanent gymnasium to Radcliffe and have the pleasure of seeing it used and enjoyed soon — that is, if your plans are sufficiently matured as to the College's future to allow of its being rightly placed. Will you please mention this to no one, but if things open toward the building of it, I shall be ready to begin at any time. As

I see it, the need is now, and I should like to meet that need and enjoy the results.

>Sincerely yours,
>
>HARRIETT L. HEMENWAY

TO MRS. AUGUSTUS HEMENWAY

Cambridge, January 3, 1897

DEAR MRS. HEMENWAY: . . . It is now absolutely settled that we remain on our present location. It is probable that another large lot on the square of which the Fay estate makes a part will fall into our hands shortly — probably next spring. . . . You see, therefore, dear Mrs. Hemenway, that the site may now be chosen at any moment for a suitable gymnasium building. Our present idea is in general to have our academic buildings including a gymnasium built around the circumference of the square and enclosing a quadrangle on which we already have some few trees. As we have not the means to build the whole at once we shall put the buildings up in sections as needed, but with such reference to the final aspect that when completed they will be harmonious and symmetrical. We want our buildings to have a certain distinction and dignity, but also to be practical and thoroughly adapted to the work to which they are dedicated, — a consideration which is sometimes neglected by skilled architects, who are naturally not so familiar with the inside working as those who are intimate with the daily occupations and needs. . . .

I need hardly say that the mere hint of a suitable

gymnasium gave the greatest pleasure to the members of our Council.

With grateful regard — for the hope you have held out makes me very happy, I am

Cordially yours,

ELIZABETH C. AGASSIZ

The story is continued in Mrs. Agassiz's Commencement address in June, 1897.

Last year at this time we were in no slight perplexity as to certain decisions regarding Radcliffe College. We were deeply attached to the Fay House which had served our needs so long; but we were well aware that we had reached its utmost limits as regarded the accommodation of our classes and the general demands of the institution.

The ground surrounding us was and is occupied by various holdings standing very near each other. There were two private schools beside a number of dwelling houses. . . . Curiously enough in about three weeks from that time three of these lots fell into our hands most unexpectedly. . . . I may add here that, since the above-mentioned acquisitions, we have secured two other lots, and that there can now be little doubt that the somewhat irregular square lying between Garden Street and Brattle Street and bounded on its side lines by Appian Way and Mason Street will eventually be our college ground. We can therefore safely decide upon retaining our present home on a spot endeared to us by many associations and extremely convenient also for our educational work, for which we rely wholly upon Harvard and her corps of instructors.

Thus freed from anxiety about our future location, our ultimate college plan becomes our next consideration. This now exists only upon paper and I fear it will be long before it takes a more tangible shape. Yet I think, when completed, it will make a harmonious whole and will have a charm of its own. . . .

We hope, in short, that our college will have a certain dignity and picturesqueness which will atone for its want of more striking features and more extensive grounds. Our most imperative need is that of laboratories, which may I hope be met within a reasonable time. Next may come a Library building where we can place our ever-increasing working Library, numbering some 10,000 volumes, in security from fire.

Our buildings must of necessity be erected gradually and separately according to our means and our most pressing wants. But in whatever succession they may appear, they will from the beginning hold definite relations to each other and to the general architectural scheme of which they form a part, thus, securing, as we hope, unity and fair proportion in the end.

On Commencement Day of the next year Mrs. Agassiz was able to announce Mrs. Hemenway's gift of the Gymnasium, the first building in the series constituting the architectural scheme of the college, and also another important gift.

Today the news is brought me of another gift, the announcement of which will be welcome to our students, and I think to our general audience as well. Certain of our alumnae and of our special students (a society known as the "Annex '95 Club") generously undertook with the coöperation of our graduates to raise money for the building of a Hall of Residence for Radcliffe. They proposed their plan to us (that is, to the officers and Council of Radcliffe) about a year ago, and appointed a committee and took other measures toward its accomplishment. They were proceeding hopefully when the breaking out of the war [with Spain] brought this project with many others to a standstill. They felt that it was impossible at such a moment to raise the sum of $50,000, and for less than that they were assured that their scheme could not be successfully carried out. It looked as if the plan so full of promise for Radcliffe must be indefinitely postponed, if not given up. Today, however, I am allowed to say that the Club has received from Mrs. David P. Kimball a gift of $50,000, the whole sum needed for the execution of this pleasant purpose.

I knew that it would give you all great pleasure, and for myself it is a great gratification to record these facts concerning our graduates and students. The life of every college must be in a great degree dependent upon the affection and loyal service of her students, and we have the happiness of seeing that long after their college course is ended, our graduates are still in active sympathy with us, sharing in our work and aiding the progress of Radcliffe by every means in their power.

On March 24, 1898, Mrs. Agassiz's diary records: "To Radcliffe for Council meeting. Had casting vote on the matter of position of new gymnasium with reference to Fay House. The casting vote seems to me a great responsibility but I gave it in favor of retaining the larger space at the James Street end of the gymnasium lot." By the following December the building had been erected and its formal opening, at which Mrs. Agassiz made a brief address, took place on December 17. This is the last incident to be chronicled for 1898. The following letters speak for themselves of the most important event that befell Radcliffe in 1899.

TO MISS IRWIN

Castle Hill, Newport, July 31, 1899

MY DEAR AGNES: My children agree with me that the time has come when for their peace of mind as well as my own, I must withdraw from my official connection with Radcliffe College.

Looking back upon the last twenty years I feel as if my share in the work had been as nothing compared with that of the Council, the Academic Board and in a more general though not less important sense the Faculty of Harvard. They have made our college what it is and have turned an educational experiment into an institution of learning. My feeling is one of deep gratitude to them and I wish I could give it any adequate expression.

Let me add that your coöperation and sympathy

have enabled me to keep my position some years longer than I could otherwise have done. I can never thank you in words for the relief and support that you have given me.

      Your affectionate friend,
          ELIZABETH C. AGASSIZ

My resignation takes effect January 1, 1900.

TO MRS. LOUIS AGASSIZ FROM MISS IRVIN

Gray Pine, North East Harbor, Maine, August 15, 1899

DEAR MRS. AGASSIZ: I was not absolutely unprepared for your letter, as I had just heard from Mr. Higginson that you were writing to me and that your "decision must be accepted." I have, nevertheless, been profoundly disturbed by your determination to resign, and I have thought over the matter and tried to be as *fair* as possible. I know you have earned your repose; still, I do feel that we might and could and would take off every one of your burdens if you would remain with us even in name! The Commencement speech is the one black spot, is it not? You need never make one, I think. But I don't wish to urge you. I wish to do only what you think best. . . .

No one can fill *your* place. What you have been to us as President, no one else can be. I mean in kind as well as in degree. I think we are all of one mind about that. What *you* can give us is given by *you*. Could and would any one else as President give us that? I feel sure that no one would. . . .

TO MISS IRWIN

August, 1899

My dear Agnes: Your letter has just come and is extremely clear and helpful. . . . I do not think that I ought to entertain the idea of continuing to hold my present place. I have always felt that deeply as I was interested for Radcliffe, my family claims and responsibilities must come first — and I think I ought to yield to the wish of my children and also to that of my sisters in this matter. I admit that I could be relieved of any important demands upon my strength (indeed I have become so relieved since you came), and that even the Commencement nightmare might be laid to rest and something substituted in its place, more like the usual college commencement. But while others might exonerate me from all responsibility, I should not exonerate myself. I should remain in an undecided attitude questioning how much to do, how much to leave undone. Such a doubt is a fatigue. I have another feeling, namely, that it would be an immense satisfaction to me to see the institution going on as I know it would go on. I should have a sense of security about it that I should never have, if I left the change till I was fairly broken down, giving it up simply because I must.

TO MRS. LOUIS AGASSIZ FROM MAJOR HENRY L. HIGGINSON

Manchester, August 29, 1899

Dear Lady President: Is it wise to prepare for illness and death? Is it wise to leave the struggle and dust of the day and sitting back in one's chair to watch the new century go on, and see if one's bundle of mistakes lets one caution, advise, cheer the wage-earners, greedy to accomplish and thereby to lift the cause of humanity a bit higher in their turn? 'T is all that they can do, and no time while at work is to be lost in self-contemplation or in striving for prizes and honours. And in my philosophy the old and tired onlookers can greatly help. I do think these above things are wise, and I feel no real doubt as to your course. Miss Irwin's wish to keep you still is affectionate, natural, excellent, but even she does not think it best. Go in peace! You have been a great boon to the College, have indeed given it birth, and you can now bless it in your own fashion. It has led a peaceful and beneficent existence, thanks to you — with your temperament, your aims, your thoughts and your training. . . .

TO MISS IRWIN

Nahant, September 19, 1899

DEAR AGNES: . . . If there were no strings pulling the other way I know that my sympathy and love for you and my affection for Radcliffe, would win me over to believe that I could, if I only would, stay on. But in such important matters (especially when one's own feeling is engaged) we must listen to the judgment of those outside; and my own people, together with some sense of failure in myself, combine in urging me to give up my nominal office. I think and believe that the change in my actual relation to the college, and as I hope, dear Agnes, to you, will not be so great as you think. If it suits you, I want to keep my teas just as before (adapting the period of their duration to your judgment). This will I trust keep up my friendly relation with the students and lead perhaps to other intercourse with them.

Cambridge, October 19, 1899

DEAR AGNES: Thank you with all my heart for your note, — that we have grown to be such friends is indeed a happiness to me, and I only hope we may still work together as dear friends may without other tie. It grieves me more than I can say to think of causing pain to the colleagues with whom I have worked so long in the most harmonious companionship, — and yet I am sure that I am right in taking this step before it is forced upon me. It does not seem so great a change to me as to my co-workers perhaps, because I have so strong a hope that I may still keep my personal relation to Radcliffe, still be in touch with all its interests and with the students — and more than all with you, dear Partner.

Your affectionate old friend,

ELIZABETH C. AGASSIZ

I have written a letter to President Eliot — It seemed fitting to apprise him myself of the change.

TO MRS. LOUIS AGASSIZ

Shady Hill, Cambridge, November 10, 1899

My dear Mrs. Agassiz: I am sorry that the enclosed paper has not reached you sooner. . . . I mean to have a better copy for you, but I will not wait to have it made before sending to you this report of the action taken by the Associates of Radcliffe on your resignation.

I hope that you will approve their proposal and grant their wish. I fully sympathize with you in the feeling which must accompany so grave a step as the laying down of a duty which has filled so large a part of life, and thus sympathizing I also feel very strongly that this proposal of the Associates may be a mode of softening the change for you, and the continuance in sentiment for them of a most happy relation.

I venture to say for myself that my strongest tie to Radcliffe is that which you make. . . . I leave a thousand things unsaid.

Affectionately yours,

C. E. Norton

The enclosed paper to which Mr. Norton refers was a copy of the following minute unanimously adopted at a meeting of the Associates of Radcliffe College held on November 1, 1899:

The Associates of Radcliffe College have received with the deepest regret the letter of Mrs. Agassiz by which she resigns the office of President of the College.

Recognizing that her wishes in the matter are to be absolutely respected, they accept her resignation, without attempting to alter her decision. They are, however, unwilling to consent that her formal official relation with the College should hereby be broken, and they request her to accept the position of Honorary President of the College, in which, freed from responsibility for the discharge of specific duties, she may still afford to the active officers of the College the benefit of her counsel, and still give to the College the honor of having her name at its head.

The Associates cannot deny themselves the privilege and satisfaction of expressing to her their sense of the perfect manner in which she has discharged every function of her office, and of the entirely happy relations which she has maintained with the officers, the teachers, and the students of the College, and with the public at large interested in its welfare.

To this official expression they desire to add the warmest expression of their individual gratitude and affection.

> CHARLES ELIOT NORTON
> ANNIE LELAND BARBER
> W. E. BYERLY
> MARY H. COOKE
> JOHN C. GRAY
> JAS. B. GREENOUGH
> SARAH W. WHITMAN
>
> *Committee on behalf of the Associates*

The proposal of the Associates that she become Honorary President was accepted by Mrs. Agassiz, and her resignation from her active duties, which devolved in large measure upon Miss Irwin, made no difference in the regular order of affairs at the college. At the Commencement exercises of 1900 Professor W. W. Goodwin delivered the address. "It closed," Mrs. Agassiz writes in her diary, "with a few words of affectionate remembrance of my personal relation to the college which were very touching to me as coming from such an old friend." These were the "few words":

During our academic life of twenty-one years we have had the high privilege of being under the leadership of the gracious lady who now lays down the active work of the presidency. From the beginning Mrs. Agassiz has been at once our chief guide and the life and soul of our undertaking. Full of the enthusiasm of her earlier years, enthusiasm which was inspired from no ordinary source, she has brought to us the treasured traditions of the past, and wisely taught us how to use them for the inspiration of the present and the future. Herself trained as a scholar and a teacher, she could always give us the best advice as to what we should do for the higher education of women and what we should not do. It is to her influence as much as to anything that our success and our present position in the academic world are due. In our private deliberations and also in the critical times when we needed a wise and dignified representative in public, we have always felt her steady hand at the helm. I feel that no words can express our estimate of the value of her services, or the respect and the affectionate regard which we feel for her; and now that she feels entitled to resign her more active work to others, we congratulate ourselves that she is willing and able to remain as our honorary president, and I am sure it is the unanimous prayer of all our friends that in this new relation she may long be with us as our best friend and our best adviser.

An adviser to the College Mrs. Agassiz continued to be in the next important advance made after her resignation. This step was the purchase in May, 1900, of some 300,000 square feet of land lying between Shepard, Linnaean and Walker Streets and the college property on Garden Street; here, on Shepard Street, within five minutes' walk of Fay House the site was selected for the hall given by Mrs. Kimball, which was called Bertram Hall, in memory of her son, who had borne her own family name, Bertram. This investment was a source of great satisfaction to Mrs. Agassiz, for the college thus acquired a Homestead where there was ample room for future dormitories as well as space for open-air sports.

Bertram Hall was begun in March, 1901, and was ready for occupancy when the college opened in the autumn. With Mrs. Henry Whitman as chairman of the committee who had it in charge, and Mr. A. W. Longfellow, Jr., as architect with freedom to carry out his designs, its artistic excellence in every detail was ensured, and it was, in fact, almost the first public building that had been erected in Cambridge for many long years that is architecturally agreeable. Extracts from Mrs. Agassiz's diaries show what gratification she derived from it, and how it speedily began to have the atmosphere that she desired for it under the influence of its first and for seventeen years its only mistress, Miss Eliza M. Hoppin. "It is too delightful — absolutely satisfactory and so cheerful," she wrote on December 21, 1901. In the next year, on February 10, she records: "In the evening to Bertram Hall. Dined with the students. It was really delightful. I never saw a happier set of girls — dancing and singing after dinner till eight o'clock when they all went to their studies." Another description of an evening there is given on January 13, 1903: "Went to dine at Bertram Hall. It was really charming — a pleasanter, more cheerful, better bred set of young girls I could not wish to see. The dinner was nice and very prettily served; the talk round the table was pleasant and intelligent. After dinner they showed me the game of ping-pong, after which I went around to see them in their rooms — pretty chambers and studies connected. It was all very satisfactory."

The formal opening ("a great affair for us, though very small in itself," Mrs. Agassiz writes in her diary) took place on January 22, 1902, at which Mrs. Agassiz made an address, giving first a sketch of the events leading to Mrs. Kimball's gift, the purchase of the Homestead, and the plans for enclosing it by eight dormitories, of which Bertram Hall was the first. The remainder of the address expresses Mrs. Agassiz's ideals for the Halls of Residence of Radcliffe.

While we are here to celebrate more especially the opening of a home for our students, we must not forget that we are also inaugurating a new chapter in the history of Radcliffe College. The domestic and social life which, with the help of the students themselves, we may build up in the homes we hope to provide for them, seems to me hardly less valuable than the academic education offered them by Harvard University. It should be at least the fitting accompaniment of their scholarly attainments.

Great as our pleasure is in being able to offer for the first time a home of their own to our students, we are nevertheless aware that many of them have formed delightful associations, and have come under the happiest influences in the homes opened to them by the kindness of Cambridge families. For this we and they are deeply grateful. But in Bertram Hall and in the other halls of residence which we hope to establish in connection with it, the attitude is and will be somewhat changed. Here in Bertram Hall, for instance, our students instead of being guests are hostesses. It is their *own* home, where under permission of the Mistress they can exercise a certain hospitality. We all know that the character, what we may call the bearing, of a home is something which it derives from the quality of its inmates. The maintenance of such a character in its highest sense will depend upon the students themselves, — upon their own refinement, simplicity, and dignity. Toward this we will gladly help them, and we shall feel more closely drawn toward them, and they will feel, we hope, more nearly allied to us for the very reason that we work together toward this end. But we would have them all remember at the same time that it is *their* home during the years of their college life; that a home implies responsibility; that their highest ambition with reference to it should be to maintain a standard of good breeding, of kindly intercourse and consideration for each other, which give after all under any social conditions the keynote to gentle manners.

In a community brought together under one roof by a common interest and kindred occupations, and not by kith and kinship, the bond is of course not as close nor can the relations be as spontaneous as between the members of one family. But a respect for such reserves as may leave each student in quiet possession of her room at her own will and pleasure, for her own studies or occupations, need not hinder the formation of intimacies or the growth of friendships which may last a lifetime. In the encouragement of such genial and pleasant companionships, with due consideration for each others' individual tastes and preferences, it seems to me that a very happy and a mutually helpful life must grow up here.

The very conditions under which our new Hall and home exists are suggestive of the best influences. It is, as I have told you, the gift of a dear friend of Radcliffe College; known as Bertram Hall, it is consecrated by a beloved name; it is pledged to worthy occcupations and interests; and it may well stimulate those who live under its shelter to sincere, cheerful, and sustained effort. Accepted in this spirit it can hardly fail to be a happy home where the higher qualities both of character and culture may be held in religious reverence and developed side by side.

December, 1902, brought Mrs. Agassiz to her eightieth birthday. The celebration of the occasion was intimately connected with Radcliffe. In the autumn of that year her children and grandchildren, knowing that her dearest wish was for a Students' House at Radcliffe, offered unknown to her to give the college $50,000 for that purpose, provided that an equal sum were raised before the fifth of December, Mrs. Agassiz's birthday, in order that the building might be presented to her as a birthday gift. Another novel and beautiful tribute was prepared by Major and Mrs. Higginson who arranged for a concert to be given in her honor by the Boston Symphony Orchestra and the Choral Art Society in Sanders Theatre on the evening of the birthday. "It is a lovely plan, but I have sworn that I would never have one of these semi-public birthdays," Mrs. Agassiz wrote in her diary when she learned of it, "but this time I must yield, not without dread." The day when it came proved memorable in her experience, and her acceptance of it highly characteristic, as extracts from her diaries and letters show.

December 1, 1902. — The week opens and I try to turn my thoughts away from the eightieth birthday. I dread the celebration. . . . But one often shrinks from what seems quite pleasant in the actual experience. I am, however, nervous and agitated in the prospect and so afraid that I may have a cold or be out of condition and disturb every one's plans.

December 2. — This week, although it comes in festive guise is an anxious one.

December 4. — Tomorrow is the great day, but I feel calmer as it grows nearer. I am trying to keep quiet and tranquil.

In the meantime a committee of forty-one friends had undertaken to collect the money required for the Students' House, and as a result of their efforts $116,000 was given or pledged within the time designated. In the words of the committee it was intended as a testimonial of "the respect of the community for a woman who has given a shining example of distinguished public service perfectly performed." "The house was given," as President Briggs said later, "not so much to Radcliffe College as to her for Radcliffe College; and into the building of it went such affection as man or woman has rarely won." The matter was kept a profound secret from Mrs. Agassiz until the morning of the fifth of December, when she received the following note from Mrs. Henry Whitman.

TO MRS. LOUIS AGASSIZ

Boston, December 5, 1902

MOST BELOVED LADY: What joyful news do you think there is for you this happy day? Simply that I have to tell you that a little company of family and friends — *all* your lovers — have ready a hundred and eight thousand dollars to build a Students' Hall at once and call it by your name, as a birthday gift, and in token of their everlasting love and gratitude.

Yours ever more and more,

S. W.

"The day is here," Mrs. Agassiz recorded in her diary, "and the greetings by telegram and note and the lovely gifts make it a day in Paradise. But a fairy gift — a pure surprise, — dropped into my hands, crowned this beautiful day in my life — $116,000 for Radcliffe College for a Students' Hall. I cannot believe it; it is too good to be true." It was typical of Mrs. Agassiz's interests that on this day when above all others her thoughts might have been centred on herself, though deeply stirred by the expressions of affection that she received, her emotions overpowered her and her composure gave way only when she learned of the gift that was not personal but for Radcliffe. "Mother is none the worse for all this," Mr. Alexander Agassiz wrote to his daughter-in-law, describing the concert, "in fact would like a second festival, provided it could be as lucrative as the first"; and Mrs. Agassiz's diary testifies to the disappearance of all her apprehensions in the happiness of the evening, when she characteristically believed that the applause that followed her as she left the theatre on the arm of her son, was as much a demonstration in his honor as in hers. A few selections from her diary and from letters written at the time complete the record of an occasion, the spirit of which was happily expressed by Mrs. Henry Whitman in a note that she wrote to Mrs. Agassiz a few days later, "Oh, all the beauty of this birthday! It will always hang like a star in my heaven."

December 6, 1902. — The day I have so feared was one of the most beautiful I have known, not only for its personal happiness, but because it brought such a munificent gift to Radcliffe — more than the building for which we have so longed as giving us new facilities for our work, more than that, because the Students' Hall gives us assurance of stability, of permanence; it consolidates our relations to Harvard, and will lead to our completion as one of its recognized departments.

December 7. — The birthday concert on Friday was perfect. Every one says as a musical occasion very rare and very perfect. After the concert grandchildren and children, and a few friends and neighbors came in. It was very easy and pleasant. And now I have only to say that my birthday was without a flaw, and that I fully enjoyed it. One of the dearest things that happened was that Alex took me in and led me out. That made it so much less personal for me. I felt so proud and as if the honors were for him rather than for me.

TO MRS. LOUIS AGASSIZ

Cambridge, December 4, 1902.

MY DEAR MRS. AGASSIZ: At Mr. Higginson's suggestion I tried — and gladly tried — to write some verses which might be sung with Mr. Gericke's music, at the concert tomorrow. Not hearing the music sung or played, I could only follow the metre of the older words; and I did not succeed in fitting my words to the music. I send them to you, however, with every good birthday greeting.

Sincerely yours,

L. B. R. BRIGGS

E. C. A., DECEMBER 5, 1902

Worthy wearer of his name —
Loved, though long departed —
His whose learning, rank and fame
Left him simple-hearted,

Thine the age that sweetens youth,
Softens each affliction;
Heaven's everlasting truth
Lights thy benediction.

Never song by poet sung
Stirred the gladdened hearer
Like the soul, that ever young,
Brings the Godhead nearer.

When our years fly on apace,
When our hearts are colder,
May we, thinking on thy face,
Graciously grow older.

Grow like thee in tranquil heart
Touched by Time's caressing.
When we choose the better part,
Eighty brings its blessing.

L. B. R. BRIGGS

TO PROFESSOR L. B. R. BRIGGS

Quincy Street, December 13, 1902

DEAR MR. BRIGGS: In turning over the many letters of my birthday I have found your verses and your kind note, and though the verses did not adapt themselves to the music or the music did not fit itself to them, I shall never cease to feel that they made a part of the beautiful and affectionate commemoration of my eightieth anniversary.

I have so much to thank you for, but I should find a difficulty in putting it into words. But what I cannot say I hope you will understand and will see that I have deeply felt the sympathy expressed in your verses both for my earlier and my later life.

With grateful remembrance,
    Sincerely yours,
      ELIZABETH C. AGASSIZ

TO MRS. LOUIS AGASSIZ

DEAREST MRS. AGASSIZ: I am honored by your letter of thanks (which I did little to deserve) signed in your own dear, clear hand. You can hardly imagine unless you put yourself in our place, the impetus of enthusiasm with which we followed up the plan of giving you a birthday pleasure, whoever first put it in motion. The programme of your concert moved me a good deal; it seemed to speak of by-gone years, and your music with your sisters, and of the beneficent reign of Dresel. . . .

There is but one regret for me, which is in the thought that future generations of Radcliffe girls cannot have that example of "the gracious and sympathetic side of life," the dignity and refinement which its first students have been so fortunate as to enjoy. But I trust that when years (many happy ones, I hope) have robbed the college of that perfect type, the tradition may abide as a perpetual stimulus. Do me the favor, dear lady, not to notice this missive, as I know that you are buried in similar ones. It is but a weak expression of the affection and admiration which you have had for a half century from me and mine.

Yours faithfully,
SARAH B. WISTER

TO MRS. LOUIS AGASSIZ

95 Irving Street, December 5, 1902.

DEAR MRS. AGASSIZ: With our whole heart we wish you a happy birthday, and a long series more of them to follow. For forty years *I* have known you, dear Mrs. Agassiz, always the same, spreading benedictions around you by your sympathy, intelligence, cheerfulness, and activity; and I hate to think that such a presence should ever leave the scene. I am sixty; — let me breathe a prayer that we may both live twenty years longer, in plenary possession of our faculties and expire on the same day!

With tenderest affection, your old friend,
WM. JAMES

95 Irving Street, December 15, 1902

DEAR MRS. AGASSIZ: I never dreamed of your replying to that note of mine [of Dec. 5]. If you are replying to all the notes you received on that eventful day, it seems to me a rather heavy penalty for becoming an octogenarian. But glad I am that you replied to mine, and so beautifully. Indeed I do remember the meeting of those two canoes; and the dance, over the river from Manaos; and many another incident and hour of that wonderful voyage. I remember your freshness of interest, and readiness to take hold of everything, and what a blessing to me it was to have one civilized lady in sight, to keep the memory of cultivated conversation from growing extinct. I remember my own folly in wishing to return home after I came out of the hospital at Rio; and my general greenness and incapacity as a naturalist afterwards, with my eyes gone to pieces. It was all because my destiny was to be a "philosopher" — a fact which then I didn't know, but which only means, I think, that if a man is good for nothing else, he can at least teach philosophy. But I'm going to write one book worthy of you, dear Mrs. Agassiz, and of the Thayer expedition, if I am spared a couple of years longer.

I hope you were not displeased at the *applause* the other night, as you went out. *I* started it; if I hadn't some one else would a moment later, for the tension had grown intolerable.

How delightful about the Radcliffe building. Well, once more, dear Mrs. Agassiz, we both thank you for this beautiful and truly affectionate letter.

Your affectionate
WM. JAMES

On December 10 the entry in Mrs. Agassiz's diary reads: "Today met the Radcliffe students, just for a little hour of interchange about the new hall. I hardly know whether they or I are more happy in this new prospect for the college."

The informal address that Mrs. Agassiz made to the students on that afternoon follows:

I have called you together this afternoon because you and I and Radcliffe have received a beautiful gift in common, and I think we should talk of it, and ask each other what we should make of it. What influence shall it have upon the future of our college; for it is not only the gift of a building, it is not only one step forward, it gives solidity and permanence to our whole scheme of existence as a college, our future is secured by it and a seal is set, as it were, upon our work.

Such a building as our Students' Hall is the promise of growth and development; it makes one feel that the essential needs will yet be fulfilled, such as the Library for instance, for we have no Library building, though we have thousands of books to put upon its shelves, and other provisions for Laboratories and Recitation rooms.

You all know how much a Students' Hall has been in your thoughts and mine; you all know that friends within and without Radcliffe College have worked for it, but their efforts have been unavailing, and I confess that I was deeply discouraged.

Suddenly, on one beautiful day of my life, the means were put into my hand, the whole means in a most generous measure, and without conditions — a fairy gift, if ever there was one, for it came as a pure surprise.

I call it mine, because it was given to me for you, to fulfil a wish that I had long cherished for the students of Radcliffe, the accomplishment of which I feared that I might never see.

For a moment I could not believe what my eyes and my ears declared. One must have experienced it, in order to understand what it is to have a desire of your heart suddenly granted, the road opened without obstruction; so did this come, as if one had said, "Here is all you need for your Students' Hall, you may turn the first sod tomorrow if you like."

And now the very name of your new hall indicates not only your share in it, but your responsibility towards it. Education is never complete without its domestic and social side. This building is to represent to you the refinement and charm of a home, while it will give you many advantages in your studies. Yet I hope that in this building, side by side with your college instruction and in keeping with a happy and cheerful life, there will grow up the domestic and social qualities without which no education is perfect. It rests with you, for whose pleasure and well being it is intended, to make the best use of this building, and it is to be not only a Students' Hall but a students' home.

You are all aware that the one distinction of Radcliffe lies in the fact that our teaching force is exclusively drawn from the faculty of Harvard. We have the whole body of instruction of our old University, and this we owe to the generosity of Harvard, to the sympathy and interest of its professors and teachers; therefore, to Harvard, we owe the allegiance and loyalty of a younger to a much older institution, and we must contribute our share to her laurels.

Let us strive, therefore, to maintain a high standard of excellence, not only in study, but in gentle manners and in all that contributes to a home in the best sense.

A little later Mrs. Agassiz sent to the contributors to the Students' Hall the following letter of thanks:

To the friends who by their exertions and contributions collected the fund for a Students' Hall at Radcliffe College.

36 *Quincy Street, Cambridge, December* 25, 1902

MY FRIENDS: A long cherished wish of mine for Radcliffe College was fulfilled in the most touching way on my 80th birthday.

Knowing the needs and desires of our students, I have long hoped that we might provide fitting conditions within the precincts of the college for the maintenance of a social, domestic, and, as it were a family life among them, side by side with their daily studies. Friends within and without the College, and even the students themselves had worked toward this end but had failed thus far of success. Suddenly by no effort of my own, on one fair and beautiful day of my life, the means for this purpose were put into my hand. The impossible became the possible. The road opened before me clear of all obstructions. Indeed, it seemed that the ground might be broken tomorrow for the building which should represent to our students the refinement and the charm of a home. By virtue of this gift we hope that the more gracious and sympathetic side of life without which no education is perfect, may accompany our academic instruction.

I should vainly attempt to express here my own gratitude or the thanks of our students for this rare gift tendered to them through me. The future history of Radcliffe must speak for us all. May their loyal work, their well-bred manners and the dignity of their life in this new Hall, show that this act of generosity has been understood and deeply appreciated by the students of Radcliffe as well as by its officers and its Honorary President.

ELIZABETH CARY AGASSIZ

With the gift of the Elizabeth Cary Agassiz House (a name which Mrs. Agassiz confided to her diary was "quite a mouthful") the college found itself in possession of three of the four buildings that had been pronounced essential to its welfare — the Gymnasium, a Hall of Residence, and a Students' House. It may be added here that the fourth, a Library, was later provided chiefly through Miss Irwin's influence with Mr. Andrew Carnegie, who offered to give $75,000 for a building provided an equal sum should be given as an endowment — an amount that was contributed by the alumnae and other friends of the college. This building Mrs. Agassiz did not live to see.

The site for Agassiz House was chosen in the Radcliffe Yard, next to the Gymnasium, and to Mrs. Agassiz's great satisfaction the architect selected for the building was Mr. A. W. Longfellow. On April 6 of the next year she noted in her diary: "A most interesting meeting concerning Elizabeth Cary Agassiz House. I think the plan is admirable and very ingenious considering the various uses to which it is to be put." Before work upon the house was begun, however, other events occurred, which should be recounted in their turn.

In the spring of 1903, Mrs. Agassiz decided that Radcliffe had grown beyond her strength and that it was best to resign her position as Honorary President. Her resignation was presented to the Council on May 26 and in deference to her wish was accepted to take effect at the end of the academic year. At the same meeting, in order to strengthen and emphasize the connection between Harvard University and Radcliffe the Dean of the Faculty of Arts and Sciences in the University, LeBaron Russell Briggs, was nominated as President of Radcliffe. At a meeting of the Associates on June 10, Mrs. Agassiz presented her formal resignation and Dean Briggs was unanimously elected President. "What Mrs. Agassiz has been and still is to Radcliffe College, no one needs to say," Miss Irwin wrote in her report for the year to the President of Harvard University. "What Mr. Briggs has been to Harvard College in the past, what he surely will be to Radcliffe College in the future, no one can know so well as the President of Harvard University." Letters and other material that have to do with these changes and show the spirit in which Mrs. Agassiz shared in them follow.

TO MRS. LOUIS AGASSIZ FROM MAJOR HENRY L. HIGGINSON

Manchester-by-the-Sea, May 13, 1903

THE committee, as you know, wishes to have Dean Briggs as President — but it needs to know what positions and duties and rights you wish, if any. You are honorary president and are expected to perform certain duties. My notion has been that you would prefer the pleasures — after all these years of service and of essentialness (to coin a word) I think that you should reap the joys only — hold your teas, if you like, know what is going on, but feel no weight and be held to no meetings or consultations.

But you are grown up and will decide. Will you send me a line at an early time and settle the matter — and tell me if you prefer to resign everything but your joys?

TO MAJOR HENRY L. HIGGINSON

I SHOULD like to give up *all*. My age and my deafness make even the small share I have retained in the work very difficult of fulfilment. I can never cease to love Radcliffe College and to take the deepest interest in its concerns, but I am really no longer strong enough to take any share in its direction. I cannot trust myself nor can I be depended upon to take part in any of the meetings (as Council, Associate meeting, boards, etc.) and especially not in the public functions, as Commencement and the like. In fact I should like to give up *all* my responsibilities of that kind and only to be admitted as a loving spectator and listener when I am able to be present. To tell the truth I am trembling now at the thought of Commencement and of coming forward on the platform to give all those degrees. I am delighted to hear (I so understand your note) that the Committee are agreed in wishing to have Dean Briggs as President. I hope it will be clearly understood that as President he will preside at all meetings — Council, Associates' meetings, etc., etc., etc. We need a presiding officer to give clearness, promptness, and decision to our work.

I do not think I need make any exception about teas or other social functions, because I know that I shall always be welcome at them when I can join in them.

On June 10, at the meeting of the Associates mentioned above, Mrs. Agassiz submitted to them the following letter of resignation:

To the Associates and to the other official boards connected with the government of Radcliffe College:

THE time has come when I feel that it is not only best for myself but essential also for the interests of Radcliffe that I should withdraw from her counsels. In doing so I would send a word of farewell and of gratitude to my colleagues. Among them are some with whom I have shared the fortunes of Radcliffe from her initiation twenty-four years ago till now.

They remember with me those early days when her life seemed a precarious one, when her only wealth consisted in the quality of her instruction (drawn wholly from the Faculty of Harvard) and in the enthusiasm of her students. Indeed, the real inspiration of her life in those early years and of her subsequent growth has been the hope of becoming more and more closely allied with the University; sharing its intellectual outfit, its traditions, its associations. That hope has been our guiding star, which we have never lost from sight at any time.

First through the sympathy and generosity of the professors and teachers, then through the recognition of the President and Fellows of Harvard (its governing boards), we have been brought to the very gates of the University, until we have now our full share of that organized body of college instruction which is the pride of our State, which our young men are taught to love and honor. In that affection and reverence our students of Radcliffe have become their worthy rivals.

In leaving Radcliffe (so far as that is possible, since her future must always be dear to me), I am happy to feel that our next step is one of the greatest importance and value for her, according, moreover, with the policy which we have pursued from the beginning.

In electing a member of the Faculty (and the second officer of the University) as our President, we put ourselves in immediate touch with the whole educational force of Harvard, and we gain a position of absolute security and permanence under her protection. Therefore, the choice of Dean Briggs to be the

President of Radcliffe gives me much pleasure and entire satisfaction.

I am grateful for the length of years which has allowed me to see the fulfilment of our cherished hope for Radcliffe in this closer relation of her academic life and government with that of Harvard. With cheerful confidence in her future which now seems assured to me, with full and affectionate recognition of all that her Council, her Academic Board and her Associates have done to bring her where she now stands, I bid farewell to my colleagues.

At the same time, I thank them for their unfailing support and encouragement in the work which we have shared together in behalf of Radcliffe College.

ELIZABETH C. AGASSIZ

June 10, 1903

EXTRACTS FROM THE DIARY OF MRS. AGASSIZ

June 11, 1903. — I hear that the meeting went well at Radcliffe and Briggs is elected. I hope I am right in believing that this is a great step upward and onward for Radcliffe. I am sorry to hear from Henry Higginson that he believes our building at this time would involve a loss of $20,000 on account of the high price of material and labor. This is a great disappointment.

June 12. — The papers have full and pleasant articles with regard to the election of Dean Briggs as President of Radcliffe — my successor. This means that Radcliffe is affiliated more closely than ever with the educational force of the University of Harvard. Already this has been from the start our one distinction. This makes it more marked and ensures permanence and a marked character for our little institution.

TO MRS. LOUIS AGASSIZ

Cambridge, June 12, 1903

MY DEAR MRS. AGASSIZ: Mr. Briggs was elected unanimously, of course, on Wednesday evening, and he has this morning notified Miss Coes of his acceptance. But it is no longer a secret, as it was "announced" yesterday evening at Mrs. Moore's musical party, and you will probably read it in the "Transcript" before you read this....

Your resignation had its solemnizing effect, I assure you. A committee of three has been appointed, Mr. Gilman, Mrs. Cooke and Miss Longfellow, to express to you the feelings of the Association. Your letter was like *you*.

I hope you are comfortably toasting your feet over a fire and looking at the sea.

Yours sincerely,
AGNES IRWIN

TO A COMMITTEE OF THE ASSOCIATES CONSISTING OF MR. ARTHUR GILMAN, MRS. JOSIAH P. COOKE AND MISS ALICE M. LONGFELLOW.

Nahant, July 1, 1903

MY DEAR MR. GILMAN: Will you and the other members of your committee accept for yourselves and for the Associates of Radcliffe College my thanks for the expressions of friendship which I have received from them all through you?

Whatever I have done for the College has been done by means of the coöperation and sympathy of all my colleagues and Associates. Indeed I must say that we have worked together with such good-will and readiness, in such affection for Radcliffe and such confidence in each other that it is difficult to say how or by whom the result has been obtained.

However this may be, I shall ever feel grateful to the friends who have worked with me for Radcliffe during the last quarter of a century. Not a shadow rests upon the memory of our allied company held together as it has been by one common aim and interest.

With warm regard to you who have conveyed to me the affectionate farewell greeting of my colleagues and Associates.

Faithfully yours,
Elizabeth C. Agassiz

Cambridge, June 18, 1903

Dear Mrs. Agassiz: I have now informed myself about the Radcliffe situation as regards the President and the Honorary President. You are still Honorary President, and I do not see why you should resign that position at all, but much reason why you should continue to hold it indefinitely....

Let me repeat that I hope very much that you will not feel it necessary to give up the Honorary Presidency. The office seems to me to be analogous to that of Professor Emeritus. Now the name of a Professor Emeritus adorns our annual catalogue until his death. No duties attach to it, but if he chooses he may give instruction. No duties would attach necessarily to the office of Honorary President; but if you chose to take part in social functions you would do so in that capacity. The retention of your name seems to me very desirable, and I am sure that both the graduates and the undergraduates of Radcliffe would greatly prefer this arrangement.

Sincerely yours,

CHARLES W. ELIOT

The suggestion contained in the above letter of President Eliot, though never formally adopted, was put into effect, and Mrs. Agassiz will always remain in the hearts of those who knew her the President Emerita of Radcliffe.

A draft of the following undated letter lies in the pages of Mrs. Agassiz's diary for 1902. The note from President Eliot, which is given below immediately after it, was evidently written in reply.

TO PRESIDENT CHARLES W. ELIOT

MY DEAR MR. ELIOT: Just a word (which you must not answer in these days of countless letters for you) to tell you that I have never failed to be grateful for all you have done for me and for Radcliffe. Personally your presence at our Commencements has given me a sense of support and protection in my official position without which I should have felt quite unnerved. I was always very proud and quite self-possessed when I went up to the platform on your arm. But apart from that I am anxious to tell you that I have appreciated and understood your policy towards Radcliffe from the beginning. During the first ten or fifteen years when the Governing Boards had not recognized us and when the more aggressive reformers were urging us to force the gates of Harvard and demand recognition, I knew that this delay was prompted by a loyalty to the old University which was the first duty of Harvard and her officers, — that they could not recognize us until they were satisfied that such recognition would involve no change of policy in the old University, nor any difficulty in her government.

When you did recognize us it was in a large and a generous spirit, and I confess that our present attitude fulfils my brightest hopes. How could our little craft be moored more safely than she now is against the great body of instruction which represents the learning and the teaching of which the state and country at large are so proud? Forgive me for taking even a few moments of your time just now and believe me,

Truly and gratefully yours,
ELIZABETH C. AGASSIZ

TO MRS. LOUIS AGASSIZ

Cambridge, July 2, 1903

DEAR MRS. AGASSIZ: I thank you for your very friendly note of June 30. My impression is that Radcliffe College has got on fast, and is now in an excellent position. In fact, I do not see how it can be improved, so far as its organization and instruction go. You ought to take solid satisfaction in your work for it.

> Sincerely yours,
> CHARLES ELIOT

TO MISS EMMA F. CARY AND MISS LOUISA FELTON

Nahant [June 26, 1903]

I HAVE longed to write to you both, but time has been at high pressure for the last week, and notes and letters have been at a discount. One thing I will say, — that this my last Commencement [June 23] (which has kept me awake and frightened me out of my wits for the last three weeks) proved to be one of the happiest experiences of my long connection with the dear Radcliffe, which I now leave where I have so longed to see her, in closest touch with the intellectual outfit of Harvard, sharing her government, her instruction, her traditions and associations.

President Eliot was admirable — full of sympathy, eminently satisfied and pleased with our choice of a new president from the Faculty, which of course sets the seal upon our relation to Harvard. Mr. Ropes [Professor James H. Ropes], who was our officiating clergyman and who read the annual address, touched upon a point to which no one has ever before alluded, though it has often been in my own mind. He spoke of the College (Radcliffe) as a natural growth out of our old school. So it has always seemed to me. But for the school, the college (so far as I am concerned) would never have existed. The training of the school prepared me for the later work and has always been associated with it in my thought. Mr. Ropes brought this out (associating with it the influence of Agassiz as a teacher) in the most delightful way. The giving of degrees followed in the usual way, but I did not make my address.

When all the official ceremony was over, Miss Irwin, Mrs. Whitman and I drove in together to the Vendome where the Alumnæ dinner took place — 170 women, I think, Dean Briggs, the only man! After dinner I opened the speaking with a short address; others followed, but I must tell you that our ceremonies were interrupted by a very pretty incident. We received a message from the Harvard class of '83; they were having their annual dinner in an adjoining hall and would like to send us greeting. Of course this was accepted with great pleasure. Presently half a dozen of these gentlemen (some of whom I knew) came in, bringing three or four of the most superb baskets of roses (Jacqueminots) that I have ever seen. The first was presented to me, the others at other parts of the company. They then introduced themselves as the class of '83, wished us everything for the future fortunes of Radcliffe and a pleasant evening on this our graduating day, and bade us good-bye. Nothing could be more friendly or more dignified and respectful; it struck me as a new note never sounded before, — a sort of fraternizing, as it were, — which meant a good deal. With that our evening ended.

TO MRS. WILLIAM B. RICHARDSON, PRESIDENT OF THE RADCLIFFE COLLEGE ALUMNAE ASSOCIATION

Nahant, June 30, 1903

MY DEAR MRS. RICHARDSON: You must let me tell you how much I enjoyed the evening with our Alumnae, and how charmingly I thought the whole occasion was presided over by you. It was a lovely close to my social relations with that pleasant company of students which have made year by year so great a part of the interest and charm of my life. I do not speak of the "close" as if it meant the end of that companionship, for I trust that I shall meet our students often and often in close and cordial association. I only mean that the bright and pleasant meeting of the Alumnae ended the day for me delightfully.

With affectionate remembrance,

ELIZABETH C. AGASSIZ

On June 24 Mrs. Agassiz had written in her diary: "The day I had so much dreaded is over and was one of the happiest I have known in my connection with Radcliffe. And now my presidency is over, and Dean Briggs is installed, and I feel that the position of Radcliffe is assured." "Now that I am losing courage in these later days," she wrote at this time to a friend, "it is a joy to feel that there are younger people to take up the cares and responsibilities and bear them along with fresh hope and faith," and the following letters still further illustrate her attitude toward her successors. The fact that Mrs. Briggs was a graduate of Radcliffe was especially pleasant to Mrs. Agassiz.

TO MRS. L. B. R. BRIGGS

December 9, [1903]

MY DEAR MRS. BRIGGS: My stupid influenza which clings to me like a brother still keeps me at home.

I had hoped to meet you this afternoon, but my cold and the weather are equally unfavorable. Perhaps you will not be at Radcliffe yourself, but I care to tell you how sorry I shall be to miss you, should you look in, — and to tell you also how great a help and pleasure it is to me to see you there. You seem to me one of us, — the natural associate of our early days. How happy we should have been then to know that Radcliffe would so soon have the position she holds now!

I have wished to say all this to you so much that I write instead of waiting to see you when my cold leaves me free. As to the teas much as I like to see you there you must always remember that one of their good points is that no one is bound by them, — the tea-table stands there ready for use by the students and their friends, even if their elders are otherwise occupied or engaged.

With affectionate remembrance,

Your old friend,
ELIZABETH C. AGASSIZ

May 8, [1904]

DEAR MRS. BRIGGS: It was a great pleasure to have your note after the Radcliffe dance the other evening. I was very sorry not to go and very glad that you were there. It is such a good thing that you are in sympathy with their pleasure as well as with their studies. The fact of your having been a "college girl" yourself is so valuable for them and for us. I remember that an English instructress from one of the Oxford Halls for women said to me, "Try always to have a college-bred woman among the officers — you will find it an immense help." I think she was right.

With affectionate regard,
    Yours truly,
      ELIZABETH C. AGASSIZ

During the time that the reorganization of the college was being effected, owing to the exceptionally high cost of building, the work on Agassiz House was being delayed, and it was not until March that, according to the record in Mrs. Agassiz's diary, the clearing of the site, which had been begun in the summer of 1903, was resumed. The building was not completed until 1905, when on June 16 it was opened for inspection by invited guests, and on June 19 the Auditorium was dedicated by the first performance of *Marlowe*, a play by Josephine Preston Peabody, a former student of the college. Like Bertram Hall the building owed its perfect appropriateness for its purposes and its beauty of proportion and detail to the architect and to the unerring taste of Mrs. Henry Whitman, who, although she did not live to see the work completed, has in it, as

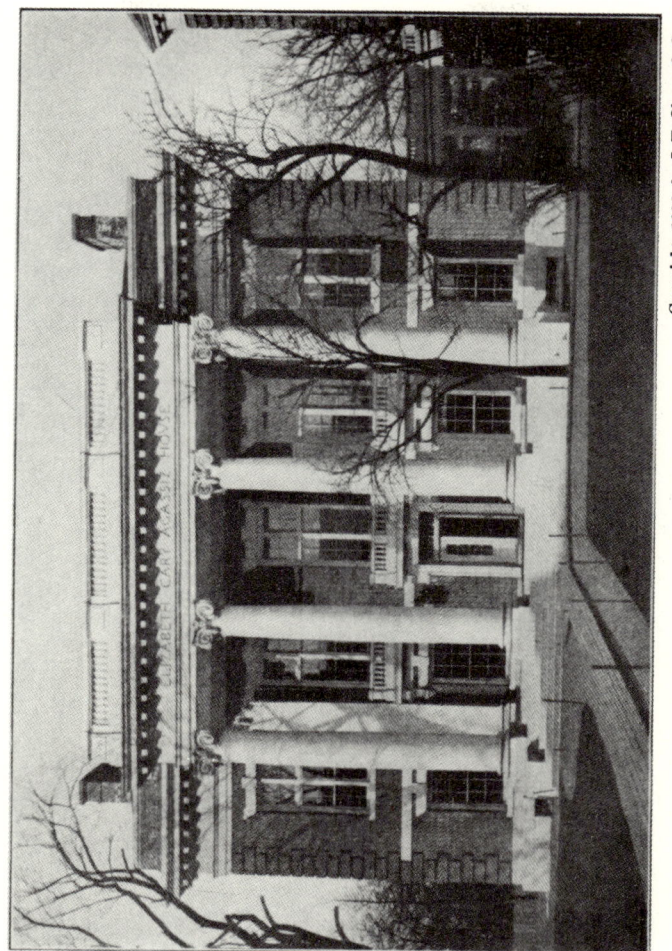

ELIZABETH CARY AGASSIZ HOUSE, RADCLIFFE COLLEGE

Copyright, 1906, by J. F. Olsson & Co.

in Bertram Hall, left a worthy memorial of her unusual gifts.

With the death of Mrs. Whitman the summer of 1904 opened sadly for Mrs. Agassiz. Few, if any, associations into which her connection with Radcliffe had led her, had become dearer to her than that with Mrs. Whitman. This association began in the days of the Society for the Collegiate Instruction of Women, when in 1886 Mrs. Whitman was elected to the Corporation; in 1892 she was made a member of the Executive Committee of the Society, and in 1894 a member of the Council of Radcliffe College. During all these years she gave unstintingly of her time, her influence, and her best gifts to the college. As an artist, she will be known to future Radcliffe students by two fine specimens of her glass that they may often have before their eyes — a large window in Memorial Hall and a small window in the Whitman Room in the Radcliffe College Library. The glowing richness of the former and the delicacy and simplicity of the latter are no less an epitome of her character than the figures of Love, Courage and Patience that from the Radcliffe window give her lasting message to the brief college generations that pass in swift succession beneath it. Her earnest religious faith was as essential a part of her nature as her artistic gifts, and her vitality, which expressed itself in a remarkable power of work and unfailing courage, was however under too perfect control to betray her into a loss of tranquillity. Her vivid interest in human lives, added to an attractive presence, made her an agreeably dominating personality. These exceptional traits, and her calming yet stimulating presence bound Mrs. Agassiz peculiarly to her, and their constant intercourse was a continual source of enjoyment to her in her life as President of Radcliffe College. A few of the entries in her diary at the time of Mrs. Whitman's death follow.

Nahant, June 19, 1904. — A note from the hospital makes every one anxious about Sally Whitman.

June 22. — Bad news from Sally Whitman, dear, dear Sally, — is she going where all the mysteries are solved — the great secret?

June 26. — Sally Whitman died yesterday at the hospital. How impossible it seems! And now no more our "again," but dead silence.

June 28. — Yesterday the last farewells were said to such a friend as is rarely found.

Within a few days after the last entry Mrs. Agassiz suffered a cerebral hemorrhage, which threatened serious consequences. She remained at Nahant in the hands of physicians and nurses until the end of September when she came back to Quincy Street, after which she began slowly to improve, but was obliged to lead the life of an invalid for the greater part of a year and never regained the vitality lost during the summer. When Agassiz House was completed she was too feeble to attend the opening. The following spring on May 13, she wrote in her diary: "I hope Pauline will take me to the new Radcliffe Hall tomorrow," and on May 14, "Yes Pauline came and took me over the Hall named after me. We had a lovely morning together. It is a beautiful building, without and within. Architecturally dignified and of fine lines and proportions; within, fittings convenient and serviceable — suited for the purpose and meaning."

Among Mrs. Agassiz's papers there has been found a half-sheet which in its feebleness would seem too sacred for publication were it not that it contains the last recorded words which she desired to speak to the students of Radcliffe, and which are therefore her parting message to the college. On the outside of the sheet is written, — "Something that should I have to join in the opening ceremonies for the new students' building at Radcliffe I should like to say —"

I do not mean that our relation to Harvard should give us the faintest feeling of superiority but only a deeper feeling of responsibility. We cannot hold the position without accepting the responsibility.

It will be difficult for me to speak here within the walls and under the roof of a building given first as a gift to me and second [as] a gift through me to the students of Radcliffe. When I came before them the next day to tell them that I had received so beautiful a gift, I felt that we took as it were a pledge to each other, binding us to the best uses of this new home — not only while we enjoyed it, but that we would also establish traditions by force of which it would be consecrated also in time to come as worthy of its donors.

Today I feel like renewing that pledge. Indeed I believe that we —

CHAPTER XIII
THE RADCLIFFE TRADITION

We love to personify our colleges. Harvard is to me as truly human as the men and women that I meet from day to day; a human being of heroic mould,

> "A daughter of the gods, divinely tall,
> And most divinely fair."

Radcliffe College is human too; and when we think of her we see — what better could we see! — that gracious lady who has lived and loved and worked for Radcliffe College from the beginning, of whom the old poet might have thought in prophecy when he wrote,

> "No spring nor summer's beauty hath such grace
> As I have seen in one autumnal face,"

who is herself an Alma Mater, — an Alma Mater in whose "through-shine" face, as the same old poet might have said, rests all that is sweet and true.
LeBaron Russell Briggs (*June*, 1904)

WE have seen what Radcliffe College owes to Mrs. Agassiz in its organization and externals; in its traditions the debt is still greater. Its traditional ideals are those that she expressed first of all in herself. She rarely put them into words except in her public addresses. Selections from some of these have appeared in the preceding chapters, but others are added here which set forth more fully her convictions in regard to the education of women.

COMMENCEMENT ADDRESS, JUNE 23, 1896

... I THINK sometimes that in the discussions concerning women's higher education which stir the air in these latter days, we hear and talk too much of the claims of women, too little of the responsibilities involved therein. We are making a claim; do we always remember that we are also giving a pledge? Granted that the whole field of literature and science shall be opened to women educationally, as it is to men, and that it shall form a part of their training for life, the question then comes up, What added service shall they bring in acknowledgment of this larger and more complete outfit? If in receiving a man's education we were simply expected to duplicate a man's work, the problem might at least theoretically be easier of solution. But taken in the larger sense, with the greater variety and freedom of occupation now opening to women, our first task (at least so it seems to me) is to adapt the new means put into our hands to the conditions and methods of a woman's life, which must be in a great degree her own, and in accordance with her natural endowments and limitations. We have to show that the wider scope of knowledge and the severer training of the intellect may strengthen and enrich a woman's life, and help her in her appointed or her chosen work, whatever that may prove to be, as much as it helps a man in his career. Wherever her future path may turn, whether she be the head of a house or hold some official position in a school, a college, or a hospital (I only name things with which she is so often associated), wherever, in short, she may rule or serve, her rule and her service should be the wiser, the more steady, gentle and healthful, because she has been trained to clear and logical methods of thinking, because her powers of concentration and observation have been cultivated. . . .

I repeat that we must think of instruction as something that may transcend itself, something that has higher issues than the mere acquisition of knowledge. If it does not build up character, if it does not give us a more urgent sense of duty, a larger and braver sympathy for what is noblest in life, — in short, if it does not make lives better and homes happier — then it has done its least and not its greatest work, then we have missed its highest inspiration.

COMMENCEMENT ADDRESS, JUNE 27, 1899

... So many farewells to the nineteenth century, so many greetings to the twentieth, will be heard on all public occasions in the next few months, that one hesitates to enter upon a subject which is, as it were, already bespoken, and may perhaps be in danger of becoming commonplace by repetition. And yet, though it may be said in a certain sense that every day ends one century and begins another, the milestones that men set up to mark their artificial divisions of time are deeply impressive, especially when they connect themselves with permanent institutions, which, in their future growth and expansion, are likely to touch the finer issues of civilization and of social life; and therefore it seems to me worth while to remember here and now what the last hundred years have done for women, and to remind each other that today our Commencement falls for the last time within the closing gates of the nineteenth century.

Among the numerous and startling changes that

have marked this century, the progress in the education of women has been singularly striking and novel. For one whose life has kept pace with that of the century, beginning with its earlier years and sharing now in its decline, the retrospect as regards women is simply amazing. I do not forget in saying this that at all times and in almost all countries some one woman has made her mark intellectually here and there, has been known and acknowledged as an exceptional power in her day and generation. I speak now not of such rare instances, but of women in general and their opportunities. . . . Even now, after twenty years of experience and observation at Radcliffe, I still find myself surprised at the possibilities opened to women by their admission into the range of academic instruction. I was vividly reminded of this the other day. Having gone to the Harvard Observatory on a chance errand, I happened upon a class of our own students who have been working there this year under Mr. Edmands. He was absent on that day, and Mrs. Fleming, whose work in the photographic department of the Observatory has made her name known to astronomers everywhere, had taken his class for him. I joined them, and for one pleasant hour was a student with them. Mrs. Fleming was just showing them what I had especially wished to see, the image of a star which, until recently revealed by the photographic telescope, had never been seen by human eye, although, since its discovery, its position and magnitude have been computed by astronomers. Something of the method, by which the photographic instrument is made thus to serve the work of man I had heard from Mrs. Fleming before. It is impossible to reproduce the charm of the narrative as told by her; the fitting of the blank photographic plate into the glass at evening, the setting of the telescope to the prescribed area over which it is to travel before daylight returns, the winding of the clock which is to control its motion, the examination of the plate in the morning, and the finding possibly a new star included in the record of the night's work, — it is all of transcendent interest.

We may ask of what use the knowledge of such a discovery and of its results may be to the student unless he or she is to be an astronomer. As much use as any knowledge which exalts and enlarges one's conception of the infinite, and carries us, if but a little way, into the measureless regions of the unknown. That the ingenuity of man should reveal to him the existence of a world which lies beyond his utmost field of vision, however aided artificially; that the intellect of man should compute the position of this world and determine its relation in space, — seems like bringing the seen and the unseen into touch with one another. It is an object lesson which appeals alike to reason and to faith. I have no right to dwell, however lightly, on these mysteries. I only use the incident of that hour at the Observatory, which seemed to lift the veil for a moment from the hidden things of life, as an illustration of what characterizes the whole subject of enlarged education for girls and women, namely,

... the multiplying of their chances in life, whether for purely moral and intellectual ends or for practical uses. In short, I came away more than ever wondering at the stimulating influences poured in upon women through the doors and windows so recently thrown wide open to them. ...

Such are some of the gifts of the nineteenth century to women. The further development of these gifts and their noblest use as they open out in the twentieth century into new occupations and interests must largely be determined by women themselves. The field is wide and the opinions are various; and I share too much perhaps in the predilections and traditions of the century which is ending to be a good judge of the questions under discussion, as, for instance, regarding professional or political work for women. I am confident of one thing, however, which is that the largest liberty of instruction cannot in itself impair true womanhood. If understood and used aright, it can only be a help and not a hindrance in the life-work natural to women. It can never impair, but rather will enlarge and ennoble, the life of the home. I remember the saying of a very sweet, a very wise, and a truly learned woman who was by force of circumstances obliged to undertake the work of the house with her own hands. When compassionated for this by a friend, she answered, in the spirit of old Herbert's poem, "No one can prevent me from talking with the angels while I sweep the room."

Be sure that the love of books, love of nature, love of everything beautiful or interesting in art or literature or science, may go hand in hand with even the homeliest domestic duties, as they may also give a dignity and charm to a home of comparative ease and leisure. Look upon your years of college study as the outer court which may give entrance to the inner temple of life. So considered, your university education will prove a strong friend and trusty ally in the years to come. Such is my hope and best wish for you all.

The ideals inaugurated by Mrs. Agassiz were kept steadily in view by her successors when the reins dropped from her hands. We may see how sympathetically they were accepted and transmitted by Miss Irwin if we turn to her address at Commencement in 1895, the year of Mrs. Agassiz's absence in Europe.

. . . Much, very much, has been done for us, and the College can never be grateful enough to the friends and teachers who have made it what it is — but the *students* of the Annex deserve much; faithful, diligent, docile, loving to learn and learning because they loved it; needing no spur or goad, craving no prize or reward; running a race, not the race in which all run and only one obtains the prize, but the race in which the runners pass from hand to hand the lamp of life that it may never cease to burn. Moved by the genuine love of learning and by no baser motive, such were the students of the Annex, such are the students of the ideal College for man or woman. And of such students as these we hope to hand down the "self-perpetuating tradition."

THE RADCLIFFE TRADITION

The women who have gone far on the road to learning and who wish to go farther are not many, it is true; in the very nature of things pioneers and leaders must always be few. But the hope of our civilization lies in the few: in the men and women who have the strength and courage to press on and up into the clearer sky, the purer air. Thinking of these things, have we not reason to be proud of the past and hopeful of the future? We have lived and grown strong by the kindness of friends in Harvard College and out of it; they have never failed us, surely they never will; we may rely — may we not? — on the sympathy and interest and generosity of the community in which we live. If much is given to us, much will be required of us; but in the past we have been faithful stewards, and in the future I think we shall not be found wanting. New paths may be opened to us; I feel that we shall have strength to tread them. New questions will be put to us; I trust that we may have wisdom to answer them. New burdens will be laid upon us; I pray that we may have courage to bear them. We have never forgotten that our "practical" business is to make our students good members of society, to fit them for the world; not the world of yesterday, but of today and tomorrow, the world which has need of the best in every one of us. We have tried to teach them that wisdom is better than knowledge and that "wisdom is a loving spirit"; we ask for them that they shall have what they deserve, no more, but no less, and we are glad to remember that it was the wisest of men who said of a good woman: "Give her of the fruit of her hands, and let her own works praise her in the gates."

An even higher ideal, an even finer tradition for Radcliffe College to preserve has been best expressed by President Briggs in words referring to Mrs. Agassiz: "To a member of a graduating class there can be no better advice than this: Make your life like hers. In detail it cannot be; in incidental privilege it cannot be; but in principle it can. Fix your mind on the principle; make it a part of yourself, the controlling part; learn to apply it in its purity to every task of life, and take the tasks one at a time. Then the factitious and the unessential drop off as a garment; the knots are suddenly untied; the complex becomes simple; the impossible is done."

CHAPTER XIV
THE LAST YEARS
1895–1907

IN order not to interrupt the account of Mrs. Agassiz's last decade at Radcliffe College, nothing has been said about her personal life during this period. Yet in these later as in her earlier years, her closest interests lay apart from the college that she so faithfully served, and formed a separate chapter in her experience. They centred in her family, and the joys and sorrows that came to her children and grandchildren were the events that touched her most keenly. Her social instincts, her sympathy with children that was as keen after as before she was eighty years old, her calm acceptance of sorrow, her freedom from morbidness, her pleasure in books and above all in music, her unqualified affection for Nahant still remained with her, as she gradually withdrew from some of the more active occupations in which she had previously been engaged. One year melted into another with little to differentiate it from its fellows, and although the extracts from diaries and letters that follow are in general widely separated from each other in date, they serve, in the lack of other records, to represent the continuity of her thoughts and occupations, and read consecutively they convey an impression of the way in which, blessed with her own goodness, she was passing her old age.

June 5, 1896.—Reached Nahant before tea. Heavenly peace.

June 8, 1896. — It is delightfully serene here. I enjoy every minute.

January 30, 1897. — College Tea. Dramatic Club. Both were remarkably pleasant. The College Tea is really an excellent means of bringing together the college society. The settlement has grown so large, there are so many young teachers with still younger wives that it is almost impossible for the older ladies to meet and greet them. This solves the difficulty and we are all gradually learning to be quite at home with each other [Mrs. Agassiz was *persona gratissima* at the teas held weekly during term time in Brooks House for all members of Harvard University and their families, where she usually formed the centre of a circle of young men, with some of whom she made lasting friendships].

February 8, 1897. — In the afternoon after a cup of tea Sallie and I drove in to the Adams House where we had comfortable rooms and dined and went to the opera where we heard *Meistersinger* very well given. Returned to our "inn," and after a mild supper went quietly to bed.

February 9. — Breakfasted late, having altogether the feeling of "ladies of leisure." To lunch with Nannie. Then a few errands and back to the Adams House; read up our *Fidelio* librettos before dinner and then to the theatre. I had never heard so beautiful a presentation of *Fidelio*, and how wonderfully beautiful it is! A bit of supper while we talked it over, and then to bed.

June 10. Nahant. — Violent storm. Georgie Cary

[a niece of Mrs. Agassiz] came down to dine and we had a nice afternoon together. When she went I made a little music. I wish it were like old wine, the better for keeping, but it gets fearfully broken and rusty in places.

TO MISS ELIZABETH H. CLARK

Nahant, May 29, 1897

DEAR MISS CLARK:... Everything is prospering in the sunshine after the soft rain. My laburnum tree is in blossom and my purple irises most beautiful. I am getting ready for you, as you see. If I can only coax the roses out by June 15th!

July 29, 1897. — A violent southerly storm with tremendous rain. I have been in the Arctics with Nansen all day. What a fascinating book!

January 5, 1898. — Yesterday to Nannie's funeral. I came straight home and spent the rest of the day in all sorts of business to be cleared away. It was the best occupation and helped to bring one back into the everyday current of life. I spent the day by myself and put my house in order.

In February, 1898, a heavy sorrow came to Mrs. Agassiz in the death of her sister, Miss Sallie Cary; "the world seems so strange and different without her," she writes in her diary, "the best, the truest, dearest sister, strength and support to us all."

March 12, 1898. — To Council meeting. One must begin some time to take up the thread of life again, but it is hard. One feels the attitude as something unnatural, and after control comes the break-down.

April 22. — The war with Spain, if not declared by word of mouth, is nevertheless known by the hoarse notes of the guns in preparation — an unholy war, for it is not justified by the circumstances. What will be the end no man can say.

Nahant, May 21. — Emma called for me and we went together to the train for Lynn. It was a strange experience, we two together — all that were left of the old Nahant household.

June 1. — The papers say that our ships are bombarding Santiago de Cuba. "War is Hell" is well said.

July 5. — News of victory for us in Cuba — Cervera's fleet destroyed. Santiago must be in our power, but, oh, the tragedy of it, the suffering!

TO MISS GRACE NORTON

Nahant, August 3, [1898]

... One thing has surprised me in the things written or spoken about Sallie, and that is that people who, one would say, had hardly seen and known her familiarly enough to receive a distinct impression of her rare qualities have said the most discriminating things about her. . . . Her singing was the expression of what was so pure, so noble, so true to herself and to others in her own nature. Life goes on and I have a great deal to make me happy, but there is something beside — homesickness is the best name for it, perhaps — but we must not dwell on that side.

Nahant, August 24, 1898

YES, it is a very intangible, inexplicable ripening of life that makes itself felt as we near the end, and which is very consoling and reassuring. It is difficult to say (even to one's self) exactly what it means, but one rests in it with a certain quiet acceptance that brings strength.

December 14, 1898. — "Queens" [a small club of old friends] at Clem Crafts'. It was very pleasant; our relation to each other is so simple and affectionate and the talk is very refreshing. The women are so bright and interested in all sorts of good things.

February 9, 1899. — Went to the concert in the evening. Aus der Ohe played and then we had the enchanting Brahms waltzes. The best waltz is like life, — a touch of pathos surging to the surface, mingled constantly with the gaiety and the movement.

February 26, Sunday. — Tomorrow will be just a year since Sallie passed out of sight. The real anniversary was the twenty-seventh, but Sunday seemed more like it, because she died on Sunday. I had just risen this morning and let in the daylight, when just outside my chamber door rose the sweetest, softest music — voices singing the trio, "Lift up thine eyes unto the mountains." Sallie and Mary and I used to sing it so much together, especially at the Channing Hospital. At first the surprise was so absolute, the music so low and far away it seemed to me to come from heaven — as if I were half there. It was overwhelming — but it is well to have the flood gates opened sometimes to a grief which most of the time you must suppress. It helps, and then it seems so much more natural than to go on your way seemingly unchanged. It was very beautiful, and it was Mrs. Gallison's loving thought. She came to me with two of her pupils and waked me with the heavenly music, but she did not know what associations it had for me and Mary and Sallie.

September 29, Nahant. — Every spare minute for the last fortnight I have been reading the Browning letters, entering "where angels fear to tread." It is an extraordinary experience, a laying bare of souls. You cannot help but read, though it seems such an intrusion.

October 11. — The little girls lunched with me after passing most of the morning playing with their new stoves. Then we went to walk together and passing a rather poor looking house by the roadside, where in the yard there were crowds of hens, chickens, ducks; we went in and the good woman of the house allowed the little children to feed them; they were enchanted. A little farther on we made a visit to some pussies on the steps of the piazza, and then returning we met Mama on horseback, and she gave them a ride. So the afternoon was quite eventful.

June 25, 1900. — Went to see Mr. Eliot and he told me of Alex's letter concerning the gift from himself, Quin, Ida and Pauline, $100,000 for completing the façade of the Museum of Comparative Zoölogy. What a joy it would have been to their father!

In the latter part of the summer of this year an indefin-

THE LAST YEARS 373

able change in Mrs. Agassiz's physical condition took place; she had no illness, but various minor indispositions left her visibly older and she remained more or less of an invalid through the autumn. Yet although the years then first began to exact their toll, she was able to resume many of her activities before the winter had passed, and the account of her visit at Hamilton given below as well as the record of some of her days shows that she by no means lost all her earlier vigor in 1900. Time treated her gently, but beginning with the late summer of that year," the leaves look pale, dreading the winter's near."

October 13, 1900. — Had a quiet morning. Dined or lunched early after reading score of Beethoven mass. Went to rehearsal. Did not feel fatigued.

October 23. — A book when I am alone. I am finding refuge in the Carlyle literature. I have read it all before years ago, but it not only bears but gains by a second reading — the four volumes of Froude, the Letters and Memorials, the Reminiscences — wonderful presentation of a life.

October 25. — Oh, how wonderful is this experience of old age! No one knows till they reach it how passing strange — on the brink of the Unknown! I remember dear Sallie's pregnant saying, "How much do you know of tomorrow? it is as much closed to you as the greater future."

December 24. — Governor Wolcott's funeral — the whole town in mourning for a man beloved and respected by every one, "stainless and fearless." Christmas at Shady Hill — an interesting occasion always — cheerful and informal, in the spirit truly Christmas. [Christmas Eve at Shady Hill, the residence of Professor Charles Eliot Norton, became a Harvard institution after 1886, when Professor Norton inaugurated the custom of receiving informally all students from a distance, who were passing the holidays in Cambridge.]

January 1, 1901. — The new century began last night at midnight. I am so sorry that I did not hear and see the celebration at the State House. It seems to have been so beautiful in spirit and so impressive. The trumpets from the State House, the singing joined in by the multitude, the Lord's Prayer in which the crowd joined. It was all serious and the crowds of people quiet and serious. Today I have been at home, and indeed yesterday, for much as I wished to see and hear what went on at the State House I did not dare.

January 30. — Reading all day — Barrett Wendell; a very readable book, especially for one who has lived as I have through the greater part of the century. His short sketches of the authors whom he associates with the growth of the history of America amount to brief memoirs. His generalizations go too far, perhaps, in the parallelism of the literary, social and political development of the country, but it is a very thoughtful, suggestive book.

February 20. — A rather full day. Dentist. Lunch with the "Queens." French lecture, M. Deschamps — delightful. Sallie Whitman to dine. Evening, meeting of the Associates of Radcliffe.

March 22. — To my dear Lizzie [Cabot] Lee. So

strange that we should be two old women talking of the days when we were young.

TO FRAU CECILE METTENIUS

November 6, 1901

... THE old pantheistic idea of "God in Nature" ... holds a very beautiful truth, no doubt; — a divine being ever present in the world he has made. But when you try to specialize (I would almost say *materialize*) this thought, it escapes you and is lost in the vast distance where these great mysteries lie; they are intangible — in trying to hold them we lose them. This "new thought" may perhaps be leading through scientific research to some unlooked-for revelation, but I do not hear any confirmation of these theories of Christian Science and the like from the men who are the closest investigators. They come rather from the outsiders than from the laboratories where the researches are carried on. The only man I know who has given his name to this new aspect of speculation is our dear friend William James, the psychologist. I think he does believe in the healing power of some of these "Christian Scientists" and does believe that their methods may lead to good in the end. But I will not talk farther of these vague and as it seems to me crude views.

December 5. — My birthday — seventy-nine. Flowers and love from every side. I should be and am very grateful.

December 6. — All went well yesterday. I think it

was felt to be pleasant. Such days are exciting, but they leave lovely memories. Dinner, ten in all, counting myself. Kate made a beautiful cake — no candles; seventy-nine were due, but that would have made a deep hole in the candle-box, beside being a very serious comment upon my old age.

January 5, 1902. — Having finished Martineau's biography I am now reading his *Study of Religion*. Far be it from me to say I understand it.

January 11. — Still reading Martineau's *Study of Religion*. It is very interesting, but I confess that all the efforts to prove that the presence of evil in the world is part of the beneficence of God seem to me futile; that without a sinner, for instance, you cannot have a saint, — without sensitiveness to pain we cannot have sensitiveness to pleasure. When we think of the nameless crimes committed on the earth together with the open record of horror and suffering one would think that no being at once beneficent and all-powerful would make a world which includes such possibilities. Perhaps the other life when we come to it may explain this one. But all these arguments drawn from the idea that good is impossible without evil (which is just what we believe Heaven to be) seem to me a begging of the question. Is Heaven then impossible without Hell? — One would answer "impossible *with* Hell," since the knowledge that others are in mortal suffering while you are free from all pain or sorrow would in itself impair all conscious enjoyment of your own happiness. And yet there is "a soul of good in all things evil." For good may we read God?

January 12. — Martineau says striking things, as this — "For *character* to lose its hold on the affairs of men and serve the anarchies of impulse is no more possible than for the sheep to drive the shepherds." However his justification of the Providence of God in the permission of crime and cruelty in the world fails like all such arguments to satisfy one. Of slavery, for instance: — if slavery is intended to work out a good result in the end, it is none the less impossible to think of it as an instrument in the dealing of an all-wise, all-beneficent creator with his creatures. Better to leave the mystery unsolved than to admit such an explanation.

January 26. — We passed the morning at Mrs. [John L.] Gardner's. There is but one thing to be said, — what the newspapers call her "palace" is simply a beautiful creation. It must always be a delight for every lover of art and architecture, and its very presence in the city is a benefaction to the community, for it sets a standard of ideal beauty, largeness of conception, combined with such exquisite charm and grace of expression as can never be overlooked. No building erected for artistic purposes can be hereafter built in Boston without reference to this work of Mrs. Gardner's as a standard, a measure of comparison.

TO MRS. JAMES T. FIELDS

Hamilton, March 25, 1902

MY DEAR FRIEND: I cannot resist the temptation to answer your card by a note. Your tempting invitation finds me at Hamilton which at this season means deep in country life, for only the village people remain here through the winter.

My grandson Rodolphe and his wife have gone to England. . . . They will be gone for two or three months, and I am here to look after their two dear little girls during their absence.

I have a sense of rest here which is very refreshing, and not lonely, since I have the companionship of the dear children who are most obedient and affectionate. They are just at the age when story books are their delight, and that is such a delightful occupation both for reader and listener. When not reading to them I am reading to myself, and to have undisturbed time for books is a great luxury. Our lives for the most part are too busy. Then it is a great pleasure to look out on the pine woods so close about us, on the blue bits of water bordered by trees, on the low hills and the open meadows — there is no fine scenery but a rolling country with pasture land and well wooded; it is very restful and pleasant.

Farewell, dear friend, and my love to you and Sarah [Jewett].

Yours always and always,
ELIZABETH C. AGASSIZ

The visit at Hamilton proved an occasion of great happiness to Mrs. Agassiz. There are few more attractive pages in her diary than those in which she records from day to day the doings of the little girls, and they admirably illustrate with what felicity she put herself on a level with children and truly felt with them in all their interests.

March 18, 1902. — Marie and Rodolphe got off this morning, and the children and I and Jackie also were at the dining-room window with waving of hands and handkerchiefs, and barks thrown in. I said to Jackie, "You'll miss your master badly, Jackie," to which Marie added as a supreme consolation, "Yes, but you'll have Grandma." After the travellers had gone the children unpacked with me, and as they found many small surprises for themselves in my baggage they were quite pleased. This afternoon the weather cleared and they had their walk and then we read together and now they are fast asleep.

March 22. — There is little to say. — A sort of pause has come in my life, and it has a great charm for me thus far. In the early mornings I am reading the book that Pauline likes so much — *Religion and Democracy*. It is certainly a striking book — suggestive to me, at least. But there is a certain sense of effort about the style — a striving after originality of form and phrase, — sometimes one would say a touch of Emerson, but without his simplicity and unconsciousness. The thoughts are certainly strong and large. One has a sense of completeness in the universe as a whole. And yet, — and yet, — the mysteries remain.

March 24. — A beautiful day, and I lengthened my walk a little. But walking when you are old is a very different thing from walking when you are young. The springiness, the elasticity is all gone, — an immense pleasure has become a duty, and yet it is better to keep it up if one can.

March 25. — The children as well as myself have had a lovely day with "Aunt Pauline." She was sweet with them. We cut out animals and played menagerie with our paper wild beasts and circus with our harlequins and riders in pasteboard and fine costumes (the paper animals prove to be a great success). After Pauline had gone we read *Rosy's Travels;* very tranquillizing.

March 31. — Received *Ulysses* from Ida by this day's mail and read it breathlessly through the whole morning. The old legend is undying, since it awakens poetry and imagination and beauty in these days which are called prosaic.

In a letter written to another friend during her stay in Hamilton, Mrs. Agassiz says:

My occupations consist chiefly in reading fairy stories for the children and making clothes for their dollies. I wish you could see them — they are very dear little persons.

They have just come into possession of a little lamb. They have named it Flossie on account of its soft white wool, and I am commissioned by them to buy a bell and a blue riband for its neck when I go to town tomorrow.

I do not know that there is anything much nicer than the companionship of little children, and I find it quite difficult to tear myself away from my quiet life here, as I shall do tomorrow for a day or two.

The occasion referred to in the following selections was the opening of the Geological Section of the Harvard University Museum, after the southwest corner of the façade, which had been given by the children of Agassiz in the preceding year, had been finished. The event was important, for it marked the completion, except for a part of the south wing, of the building that had been the aim of Agassiz, whose plan for the Museum had had a far wider scope than its original name, the Museum of Comparative Zoölogy, implied.

June 12. — Meeting; Museum, speeches, etc. All went off successfully. — As I looked at the building of such magnitude as to be really impressive — and picturesque too with its drapery of vines, — and as I saw the crowds flocking towards us, I thought of [Agassiz's] shanty built of rough boards — not large enough to hold half a dozen people, its only furniture a kitchen table and a few pine shelves against the wall — and compared it with the huge building containing one of the finest collections of Natural History in the world; it seemed to me impossible that the one should have been the beginning and, as it were, the foundation of the other.

July 16, Nahant. — Reading French at sight. It seems a little absurd to be pursuing modern languages when you are face to face with your eightieth birthday. I wonder why I do it.

August 16. — I have heard such good music at Emma's this morning. They sang things which carried me back to the old days irresistibly. What a strange thing it is to live things over, to find them as real and true as ever in your memory, and yet not be sure that you shall have them again.

January 24, 1903. — There was a man who said, "If it were not for my pleasures, I could get on very well." Sometimes the same reflection in which wit and wisdom are combined comes to me. Take Tuesday next for example; — Lunch at Clem Crafts'. Return home for tea, 4–6. Go back to town to Ida's; with her to see *Julius Caesar* in the evening. All are tempting, — one is rather much at eighty years of age — unless one has a temperament like my dear Julia Ward Howe.

January 27. — Lunch at Clem Crafts' very pleasant. Returned for afternoon tea at home. Then to Ida's, went with her to see Mansfield as Brutus in *Julius Caesar*. I did not care for him; stilted and posing, with no distinction, nothing noble in bearing. The actors of Shakespeare of my youth had much elegance both in their reading and action. Their diction and delivery were noticeably fine; witness Macready, Booth, Wallack, Fechter — you could not forget their phrasing of certain passages.

February 6. — Brooks House tea this afternoon. I really think these teas are going to help in bringing the older and younger society of Cambridge together — that is, the society of the College. After all what is the life of Cambridge but the life of the students and the cultivated men who make the background of their academic education? That forms the whole community, and it surely ought to form a homogeneous one. This will go far to make it so.

November 10. — Opening Germanic Museum, afternoon. German play, evening. Ida and Henry to dine.

I am glad that this celebration of the Germanic Museum was so dignified and worthy of an occasion which really was one of great significance for Harvard with a somewhat wider importance also. Ida told me that among the speakers William James outdid himself. The closing address was his, and after the somewhat long speeches of the earlier afternoon he dismissed the audience in the best of humors by his wit and lighter touch. His wit has always a literary refinement and a certain elegance in the turn of phrase, while it is also perfectly spontaneous and natural.

January 3, 1904. — A cold and stormy day which I devoted to William Story's Life. It is an extremely interesting book, not only for the given subject, but for the entourage, the stage setting. The scheme of the book is ingenious and original — the whole is presented as part of a vanished past, out of which the "Dramatis Personae" loom up, evoked as it were from the mists and haze of time, — so many "ghosts" as the author calls them; and so they seem indeed, outlined against the vivid foreground of Italian life and color and movement. Henry James's intricacies of style render it somewhat difficult of interpretation, but happily the people of whom he treats are simpler than he is, and much of the material consists of the very frank familiar correspondence.

January 4. — Was reading today Miss Crawford's account of John Eliot and his Indians. It is picturesque and effective, and she feels that had his plan been carried out the Indians would have been made an integral and serviceable part of the American nation.

Here I think she is entirely mistaken. The whole history is a story of failure, — a failure which makes the volume in the Harvard Library containing John Eliot's translation of the Bible into the Indian tongue one of the saddest sights in the world. One of the noblest and at the same time one of the most futile efforts to Christianize and civilize a savage people, it ends in a volume that no man can read, which remains a curiosity. Now and then some one asks to look at it, but only from that point of view. I do not think it has ever been used in the religious instruction of the Indians except by John Eliot himself.

January 21. — The children came today; much enchanted. When after lunch they said, " What shall we do this afternoon?" I answered, "You like to help Amelia about her work; she may have something to unpack." They were enchanted — especially when they dived into the boxes and found dollies and beds and chairs and washstands, etc. They quickly arranged a bed chamber for the new children, and had a lovely afternoon with them. I begin to find the convenience of a telephone. I sent a list to Schwartz for what I wanted, and had the whole set before the children arrived, to my great joy as well as theirs.

February 1. — I think the children are very advanced in their music — they write it very nicely, drawing their lines and making their notes neatly and their intervals correctly. It is a very good beginning.

February 3. — The children left me this morning. It has been a lovely fortnight with them, and I hope they will come later. They have been making and I have been renewing acquaintance with Miss Edgeworth, — Simple Susan, Lazy Lawrence, Barring Out, and all the rest of it. It is really pleasant to return to these old friends. For my own reading, I have been deeply interested in Morse's Life of Holmes. Toward the end of his days one sees that he, too, came face to face with the great mystery. Dying do we leave this life a "futile failure" and return to unconsciousness, or do we meet another life full of infinite possibilities?

February 11. — A black woman, or rather mulatto, came to see me yesterday about a negro school in Alabama. When we had finished about the school, she said, "You have been kind to me; I wonder if I could give you pleasure by singing for you the songs of my people." Of course I was glad. She went to the piano and touching a few chords began to sing. I have rarely been more moved. It was not dramatic, still less melodramatic. It was to the last degree genuine and unconscious. The first word or line, "Were you there when He was crucified?" was overwhelming. Not from its pathos — not from any attempt to make it touching, — but it was a person in the very time asking the question of another who might have been there. I can never forget it. It was as if I might have been present myself.

April 24. — This has been the most heavenly Sunday. We were all at Luly Dresel's to hear a trio written by her father when he was about twenty and looked upon by Mendelssohn and Liszt and Schubert as a most promising young musician. This trio was then played in Berlin, — brought forward by these older musicians and thought by them a remarkable production for so young a man. This was rehearsed — ah, such a delightful afternoon. We seemed behind the scenes, as it were, while the musicians discussed and criticized and analyzed their work. And then came songs of Dresel's; it seemed to us that he must be there.

In the summer of 1904 the record in the diary is interrupted by Mrs. Agassiz's illness, and after this she was never again able to resume the ordinary course of her life. Although she was not constantly confined to her room or even to the house, her days were substantially those of an invalid. "The record for every day is much the same," she writes in her diary on January 21, 1905. "The variety comes from flowers sent in by friends — the visits of dear people who come to see me and brighten up my imprisonment — many pleasant little incidents." Not the least of these "pleasant incidents" were the visits of children, in whom her joy remained unabated, and who flickered like little flashes of sunshine across the gray hours of her invalidism. It was about this time that she stationed a large woolly lamb of many charms in her window to delight the eyes of a neighbor's baby, it being understood that when he was able to call upon her, walking alone, he was to become its proud possessor. "The dearest children from Hamilton," the note in her diary for January 18, 1905, reads. "I had some paint-boxes for them made up in the form of little handbags and containing everything that juvenile artists could need. They were so pleased, and they ask for so little — just to sit in my room and read aloud to me — enough to make them quite happy." And on St. Valentine's Day of the same year she records a call from a young lover, — "It was a Valentine visit; dear little fellow, he was so pleased to bring me a bunch of lilies of the valley, and he took home as his own Valentine a box of very fine paper soldiers." Flowers, too, never ceased to be a delight to her. "Orchids — such heavenly things," "flowers of the most enchanting kind," "orchids — lilac, purest amethyst and pale yellow — a beautiful combination" — these are some of the terms in which she records the gifts that gratified her. Her diaries also contain numerous entries, showing the extent of her reading during much of this time, and how greatly she was able to enjoy it.

January 17, 1905. — I have a great deal of pleasant reading: Morley's *Gladstone*, unfinished. *John Andrew*, brilliant story of an interesting and very momentous life. *Roma*, Maude Elliott — to the last degree interesting. *Norton and Ruskin* — a rare friendship, recorded in letters. *Montaigne*, Grace Norton — from various aspects and points of view, a very scholarly work — a help to any one who would fain be better acquainted with Montaigne and his friends, not only as men of letters and as men of the world, but as companions and co-workers.

March 8, 1905. — Mimi [Mrs. Theodore Lyman] brought me glorious carnations. She sent me the Stevenson letters a day or two [ago] and I have been reading them ever since; very entertaining. She brought me also to read aloud a letter from Alex — There was a passage which spoke of our relation to each other (his and mine) which I could hardly read myself without emotion.

April 8, 1906. — I am reading for the second time Newman's *Apologia pro Vita Sua.* I confess I have found it difficult to understand how a man of so powerful, so logical a nature could enter into the Catholic Church. Does he himself give us a clew? He says (p. 44 of the *Apologia*), "From the age of fifteen dogma has been the foundation principle of my religion. I cannot enter into the idea of any other sort of religion." How then should he find himself landed elsewhere than in the headquarters of dogma, creeds, sacraments, sacramental rites?

May 22, 1906. — I am re-reading Emerson's biography by Eliot Cabot. How far away and how delightful those days seem!

May 25. — Finished Emerson today. He and his comrades made a most interesting set of men, and Eliot Cabot has put them together in a very effective and human sort of way.

After 1904 Mrs. Agassiz did not return to Nahant, but on the advice of her physicians spent the remaining summers of her life with her niece, Miss Louisa Felton, who owned an attractive cottage at Arlington Heights. Although Mrs. Agassiz at times thought wistfully of her beloved Nahant, she greatly enjoyed the beautiful view from Miss Felton's verandah over woodland and distant hills, and at the end of her first season there, she wrote to a friend, "It has been a summer of health and happiness for me and I am grateful for it." Eighty-three is not an age at which new surroundings, however desirable, are usually welcomed, and it was doubtless the fruit of Mrs. Agassiz's lifelong habits of adaptation that she accepted the charms of Arlington Heights with the appreciation that she expresses in the following letters.

TO MRS. JAMES T. FIELDS

Quincy Street, Cambridge, April 1, [1905]

MY WELL-BELOVED FRIEND: The glimpse of Sarah [Jewett] and yourself in that dear South Berwick note from you took me down to the riverside and gave me all the country sights and sounds in which you are rejoicing. I too have had a lovely visit with my Emma and I understand from the few lines for her in your note how well you know our lives together, between music and books and the mingled past and present which we share. You will have heard perhaps that I am again leaving my beloved Nahant this summer and going to my niece Lisa Felton, who has a dear little nest on Arlington Heights commanding one of the finest views I know. Night is really a revelation of Heaven trembling with countless worlds above you — but I will not try to describe it though I wish you could see (it) with me.

I went there last year at the command of the physicians — "high and dry," — such was the air they ordered and it certainly proved most salubrious, — beside its beauty in point of situation.

I am just now expecting my son from across the water. He has had an enchanting winter on the Nile; after seven winter voyages of most laborious work among the Coral islands of the Southern Pacific he has at last taken a vacation which he has greatly enjoyed. Now he is coming home for his Newport summer.

I hear only dimly from the world outside; but I have tidings now and then of Radcliffe and its affairs from Miss Irwin and from our President — Mr. Briggs, one of the faculty. He is a charming man and a great favorite with the students. When I remember our small beginnings — without buildings or books or apparatus which makes the outfit of an educational institution, I can hardly believe that we are as it were anchored against the whole teaching force of Harvard. But I must not run on.

Hoping that I may have the happiness of seeing you both as the warm weather sets us free,

Your loving old friend,

E. C. AGASSIZ

"The carriage is just about to arrive," she wrote to another friend a few weeks later, "in order to take this old lady to her summer residence on Arlington Heights. I am almost reconciled to leaving Nahant for that beautiful summit, where stretches of woodland alternate with distant towns and villages, lost at last in our big Boston and its far away harbor; and then comes night, crowned with the constellations and sometimes with the morning or the evening stars."

One of the advantages of Arlington Heights was its accessibility to Boston, so that Mrs. Agassiz was not deprived of the visits from step-children and friends, which were a great source of pleasure. No account of these years would be complete without a mention of the devoted companionship given her by her only remaining sisters, Mrs. Curtis and Miss Cary. Mrs. Curtis's visits were her continual delight both in anticipation and in retrospect, while Miss Cary's music never lost its charm for her. "I long to see my Emma," she writes from Arlington Heights in September, 1906, "to hear her play Chopin, so full of passion and sweetness as his music is, with a touch all her own. Some one said one day on hearing her for the first time, 'I have heard all the virtuosos who come to Boston, but here is something I do not recognize — a personal note which I hear for the first time.' I know it well and long for it."

To the end of her life Mrs. Agassiz's affections remained strong, and in the few following letters, found in draft among her papers and among the latest that she wrote, the note of friendship sounds as clear and sweet as an evening bell.

TO OWEN WISTER

Arlington Heights, [*June*, 1906]

DEAR OWEN: You will think I have neither read nor enjoyed your book [*Lady Baltimore*], and yet I have done both; but an invalid (especially one whose failure makes part of her eighty-three years) has to postpone many things. To tell the truth when the book was brought to me it recalled the time when you were just on the threshold of life, when you used to look in upon me sometimes in the evening, having the kindness to give me a lesson in Wagner — I was, and still am, a very poor scholar on that ground. The older music is to me the dearest. I remember the programme in an afternoon in the Conservatoire in Paris: — *Ave Verum Corpus*, Mozart; *Gloria*, Palestrina; *Fifth Avenue*.

But I want to talk to you of your book and tell you how much I loved it. I, too, when I was before the river used to float down to the beach, the soft bells following me with their soft thrill. At that time Mr. Agassiz was living at the island, having the privilege of a cottage there to be used as a laboratory, and the girls and I used to go down to pass Sunday with him. And so, you see, this book had a special and personal charm for me and I thank you doubly for sending it to me. It is the delightful renewal of many old and pleasant associations.

Good-bye, and may a blessing ever follow you and yours.

  Think of me always as
    Your faithful old friend,
      E. C. AGASSIZ

TO PROFESSOR CHARLES ELIOT NORTON

(Written after Mrs. Agassiz had received *Henry Wadsworth Longfellow*, containing Longfellow's chief autobiographical poems and a sketch of his life by Norton.)

[1907]

MY DEAR MR. NORTON: How shall I thank you? You have called up the fairest memories; you have knitted a chain which I had thought dissevered, from the "Prelude" to the closing lines,

> "And as the evening twilight fades away
> The sky is filled with stars invisible by day."

Its earlier chapters are interwoven with Shady Hill and all its attractions. Need I say how much of the happiness of my personal life is owed to that delightful circle, where the men were so intelligent and so kindly, and the women so cultivated and sweet?

Such were some of the brighter rays that lighted Mrs. Agassiz's last years; but " the ship was nigh unto the harbor, and the pilgrim was reaching the city, and life was close unto its end." Slowly the day was fading, yet the clouds that gathered at evening never shrouded, even though they dimmed, the rare and delightful qualities that had been hers since the morning of life. Through the late winter and the spring of 1907 her strength gradually failed, but in June she was able to go to Arlington Heights. Three weeks later, on June 27, the release came, and her spirit returned unto God who gave it.

CHAPTER XV

COMMEMORATION ADDRESSES, AGASSIZ HOUSE
DECEMBER 8, 1907

ON the afternoon of Sunday, December 8, 1907, a meeting in memory of Mrs. Agassiz was held in Agassiz House. President Briggs presided and the speakers were Miss Georgina Schuyler of New York, representing the Agassiz School, Professor William Watson Goodwin, Professor Charles Eliot Norton, and President Charles W. Eliot. Perhaps nothing that was said that afternoon better conveyed the influence of Mrs. Agassiz's personality than the closing sentences of the few words spoken by President Briggs:
"If it is true that

'Prayer is the soul's sincere desire,
Uttered or unexpressed,'

whoever came into her presence prayed; and his prayer was, 'Create in *me* a clean heart, O God.'"

The addresses follow.

MISS GEORGINA SCHUYLER

ALLOW me to express to the Faculty and the students of Radcliffe College the gratification of a pupil of Agassiz School that the School is to be represented here today, and her appreciation of their indulgence in listening for a few minutes to the recollections of fifty years ago. It is the beloved and revered memory of Mrs. Agassiz, that unites School and College, that

THE AGASSIZ GATE, RADCLIFFE COLLEGE

brings us all here, and encourages me to address you, however inadequately.

For, to go back from Radcliffe College to Agassiz School is something like going back to the nursery. Yet the nursery holds an important place, and surely the good seed sown in Agassiz School has blossomed in Radcliffe College!

To the seventy school-girls or more, between the ages of fifteen and eighteen, who every morning came running up the staircase to the third story of Mrs. Agassiz's home in Quincy Street, to their cheerful, well-lighted, well-warmed, and well-ventilated classrooms, the phrase "Higher Education of Women" was unknown. Yet, like M. Jourdain, who had spoken prose all his life without knowing it, we *had* the Higher Education offered to us. Indeed we had the Highest Education: the daily contact with superior minds imbued with a desire to impart their knowledge to us, to give us high standards, to awaken wide interests. And thus we school-girls had a glimpse and foretaste of the good things that were coming to women all the world over, and we can especially rejoice in Radcliffe's adult strength, in its organized growth and power.

In her *Life of Louis Agassiz*, Mrs. Agassiz gives a few pages to the School. It owed its existence, she states, as many another school has done, to the desire of the wife, the son, the daughter, to lift a burden from the head of the family. The plans, she relates, were discussed in secret between the three, but, when the conspirators with many misgivings unfolded their plot, to their surprise Agassiz seized upon the idea with delight — said his name must appear on the circular — he himself would give instruction. This hearty coöperation of his made the School. At that time, 1855, he was widely known in the United States, not only as an eminent scientific man but as a most interesting lecturer. Although it was a day school, pupils came from far and near. I recall a group of intelligent girls from St. Louis who took the highest courses we had. There were also pupils from Buffalo, a few of us from New York City, but the large proportion came from New England, from Boston and vicinity.

The School opened in 1855, closed in 1863, and was a success in every way, educationally and financially.

Associated with Professor Agassiz in teaching was Professor Felton, afterwards President of Harvard College. Professor Felton's mind was a storehouse of information from which, like the householder in the Bible, "he brought forth out of his treasure things new and old." He taught History, English literature, Rhetoric, Greek, Latin, Greek history, American history. But, apart from his regular courses of instruction, the incidental facts he told us have remained with us for a lifetime, recurring to illuminate our own experiences, whether of reading or of travel, and I cannot but recall, also, the courtesy and kindness shown by this distinguished and scholarly man to us ignorant girls.

Mr. Alexander Agassiz had the classes in mathematics, geometry, trigonometry and chemistry, lectures on astronomy, and on chemistry with experiments. Miss Helen Clapp, afterwards head of the well-known school in Boston, taught Latin, botany with Gray's text-books, and arithmetic. Miss Clapp's winning personality endeared her to every pupil in the School. She was associated with it from beginning to end, and was greatly valued by Mrs. Agassiz. Miss Katherine Howard and Miss Emily Howard, Miss Augusta Curtis and Miss Katherine Ireland were also teachers in the School. Miss Le Clère, an admirable teacher, had the French classes and lectures in French literature. Professor Schmidt, of Harvard, had the German classes; Professor Luigi Monti, of Harvard, the Italian. Mr. Gurney, later Dean of Harvard University, taught Greek. Professor James Russell Lowell and Professor Child of Harvard lectured to the School, and there were lectures on art by William J. Stillman.

To Mr. Alexander Agassiz, in addition to his classes, was entrusted the business management of the school. Miss Ida Agassiz, now Mrs. Henry Higginson, gave able and devoted assistance when the School opened, and later, by teaching French and German. One of the younger pupils of our School was Pauline Agassiz, now Mrs. Quincy Shaw, who has done more for education than any of us, through the introduction of the Kindergarten system into the Public Schools of Boston, and by other educational work.

Naturally, the central figure of the School was Professor Agassiz himself. He had a genius for imparting what he knew. This, joined with his personal charm, the beauty of his animated face, his enthusiasm for his subject which he inspired in others, made the great attraction. For eight years, with few interruptions, he gave daily lectures to us girls, always illustrating by specimens, maps, and by drawing on the blackboard in his incomparable manner.

His courses of lectures comprised zoölogy and botany, geology and embryology. These lectures included the classification of plants and their geographical distribution. He also gave us his famous lectures on glaciers — he having originated the glacial theory — and an elementary course of anthropology and ethnology.

It was a wonderful gift of his to keep a classroom of girls alert and interested while describing the structure of a jelly-fish, the distinction between Discophora and Ctenophora. Mrs. Agassiz is kind enough to say of us: "He never had an audience more responsive and more eager to learn than the sixty or seventy girls who gathered at the close of the morning to hear his daily lecture, nor did he ever give to any audience lectures more carefully prepared, more comprehensive in their range of subjects, more lofty in their tone of thought."

He spoke several times of the difficulty of translating to us, in simple terms, the technical language of Science, so that we could understand him. He gave us a deep respect for the laborious collecting of scientific facts and a mistrust and dislike of what is superficial. At the same time his ideality appealed strongly to us, and some of us listened with tears in our eyes as he unfolded his theories and emphasized his belief in the ability of the mind of man to trace in Nature the creative thought of God. "What I wish for you," I can hear him say in his clear tones, "is a culture that is alive, active, susceptible of further development. Do not think that I care to teach you this or the other special science. My instruction is only intended to show you the thoughts in Nature which Science reveals, and the facts I give you are useful only, or chiefly for this object."

And now to speak of Mrs. Agassiz, the hostess of our School, for so she seemed to us. To her fell the administration, the discipline of the School. The fact that there were no marks for good or bad conduct, a new departure in those days, made this all the more difficult. Though keeping herself in the background (she taught no classes — she never addressed us), it was her ceaseless vigilance, her constant watchfulness, that smoothed the path for the teachers, that kept going the daily routine of the School in its orderly succession. But more than this, she had it so at heart, that we girls should get the benefit of our teaching, that we should see and appreciate what was given us, that, unconsciously, perhaps, she made us feel it. Above all, we were *trusted*, — both as to our conduct and the amount of work we did, — and, as a whole, we responded to her confidence in us.

Her kindness to the girls who came from a distance, and had no relatives here, but boarded in Cambridge, was marked. But there was one merry little party that came out from Boston every morning in an omnious reserved for them, which trundled down the hill of old Beacon Street, stopping at many doors, on through Charles Street to the house of Dr. Oliver Wendell Holmes, and so on out over the bridge to Cambridge, — a merry little party which was very much afraid of Mrs. Agassiz. They felt her eyes constantly upon them and there was no reprieve. "My dear Mary," laying her hand on the culprit's shoulder, "you must study your French verses," this the mild penalty for repeated whisperings in English, in a school where French was supposed always to be spoken.

When we first entered school she received each one of us. She told us she would always be there, — always to be found by us if, for any reason, we needed her. When the term closed, I recall a few words of commendation and encouragement which she doubtless gave to each pupil, sometimes a message to our parents. Every day she looked in upon the classes — locked in and passed on — and when the Agassiz lecture came she sat, as one of the listeners, more diligent with her note-book than any of us.

For, with her, Agassiz School was a formative period. The seed sown there was to develop into Radcliffe College and come to its full and beautiful fruition on that eightieth birthday, five years ago, of which the permanent material memorials is this Elizabeth Cary Agassiz House where we are now assembled.

On that birthday, nearly fifty years had elapsed since the opening of Agassiz School, more than twenty years since her love and solicitude had been awakened in behalf of the Harvard Annex, which ultimately was to become the Woman's College of Harvard University. That day witnessed the fulfilment of an important career, the rounding out and perfecting of a noble exceptional character. It is a privilege, it is an education to let the mind dwell upon that character, but other friends of hers, here today, will speak of this. What she was to Radcliffe, you know. What she was as the head of Radcliffe, you have witnessed. That noble presence — that poise — that dignity — that graciousness of manner which veiled the force of her character — her reticence — her kindness — all this Radcliffe knows — but Agassiz School had it too! As she told us, *she was always there* — as in a sense she is here today. God grant her influence, and the blessing of it, may be *here* — for years and years to come.

PROFESSOR GOODWIN

THE earliest distinct recollection I have of Mrs. Agassiz is a very pleasant one. When we were beginning, more than thirty years ago, to read Greek tragedies and comedies to the Harvard students, I was about to read either the *Antigone* or the *Frogs* one evening, when Mrs. Agassiz and Mrs. Robert Storer came into the room with their Greek books and followed the reading most attentively. I could not have had a more delightful addition to my audience. These ladies represented a company of cultivated women, who read the classics intelligently and with pleasure, long before there were any women's colleges to teach them. Mrs. Storer, who survived Mrs.

Agassiz only a few weeks, with her sister, Miss Elizabeth Hoar, and other Concord ladies, more than seventy years ago, read all the Greek and Latin authors which their brothers were studying here in college, and through long lives they never lost their love of classic literature. One of these brothers was our beloved and revered Ebenezer Rockwood Hoar. It was hardly a year ago that Mrs. Storer (who was then nearly 90 years old) asked me to lend her the *Hippolytus* of Euripides "in good large Greek type."

This period of classical study in Concord began before Mr. Emerson made that town his home. Indeed it may well be thought that the attraction of this cultivated society helped to draw him thither. I remember with pleasure another one of my Greek readings, before which I found Mrs. Samuel Hooper, with her niece, Mrs. Gurney, toiling up the long staircase of Harvard Hall with their Greek books to hear a comedy of Aristophanes. Mrs. Gurney herself was a brilliant example, in the second generation, of the scholarly company of ladies into which she was born. Her coming to Cambridge made an era in our intellectual life. She brought into it a fresh vitality which I shall never forget. I never undertook any important work in connection with my professorship without consulting her as well as her husband, and I never failed to receive the best advice. She became at once most devoted to our new women's college, and Mrs. Agassiz always depended upon her in every forward step which was taken. She was one of a class of ladies who one year entered their names as students of the "Annex," paid their fees, and read Greek poetry with me in my study. I feel that this occasion would be incomplete without even this inadequate tribute of appreciation to her services in our cause. It is pleasant to think, as we recall these older times, that through her first President Radcliffe has inherited some of the atmosphere of this simple, dignified society.

When we were getting ready to give the *Oedipus Tyrannus* in Sanders Theatre, in 1881, Mrs. Agassiz took the greatest interest in all the preparations. She frequently attended the rehearsals, and her advice about the musical performance and the choral songs was always of the highest value. Her knowledge of music made her an authority upon many of the hardest problems with which we had to deal. Once she gave me a solemn warning which alarmed me a little, when she thought that "the music was running away with the play." "I know you will not suspect me of being prejudiced against music," she said, "but I am really sometimes afraid that at the end you will find that you have only a beautiful opera with a Greek play attached to it." But after she had heard the first rehearsal of the play as a whole, she at once took back her warning, saying, "It's all going to be splendid." (I suspect, however, that her warning had already been of some effect.) At the public performances it was seldom that we did not have the satisfaction of seeing her in her special chair in the centre of the front row.

It was a most important step which the ladies and

gentlemen who were informally discussing plans for the collegiate education of women in Cambridge took in February, 1879, when they invited Mrs. Agassiz to be one of their committee. She accepted this invitation at once; and thus began her close connection with this important movement, to which she devoted her best energies for the rest of her life. As soon as there was any formal organization of the managing committee, she was made its President; and after its incorporation as the Society for the Collegiate Instruction of Women and again as Radcliffe College, she remained its President and gave her life and soul to its welfare. No words of mine can even attempt to express her great and lasting services during this period of more than 28 years to the cause of sound learning and especially to the higher education of women in this country. Her long experience as a teacher of girls, her almost unerring practical wisdom, and the unfailing common sense which she always brought to the difficult problems which constantly faced us in our almost unexplored way, have done more, in my opinion, to make Radcliffe College what it now is, than all other causes combined. But beyond and above all this was that gracious personality which always made itself felt in everything that she said or did, and gave an indescribable charm to all her intercourse with both teachers and students. We are soon to listen to the striking story of her powerful aid, in 1894, in rescuing us from the greatest danger to which we were ever exposed, when our wise conservatism in gratefully accepting the generous conditions offered us by Harvard College brought us into bitter conflict with those who wished us to insist on a more complete union with the College than most of us thought to be either necessary or expedient. It was that same strong personality of Mrs. Agassiz which then saved us from defeat and gained us a victory even greater than we hoped for. And the result has amply proved the wisdom of the action then taken. I think it would be hard to find any one connected with the teaching of Radcliffe who now thinks that we should have gained anything if our elementary instruction had been merged with that of the undergraduates of Harvard in the College classes. On the other hand, we felt that the admission of our graduate students and other advanced scholars to many of the most important graduate courses in the University was the greatest privilege which could be given us; and Mrs. Agassiz appreciated at once that this open door would ultimately admit us to all that we could reasonably ask. The first year's trial (in 1894–1895) fully confirmed her judgment, when Radcliffe was able to offer 63 graduate courses of high rank, of which $53\frac{1}{2}$ were given in Harvard University, where our students were admitted to the same classes with the men. This early announcement of graduate instruction in the University classes gave Radcliffe College a distinction of which no other college for women in this country could boast, and it gave most encouraging promise of future facilities for even the most advanced university study.

The words with which Mrs. Agassiz closed her

first report as President of Radcliffe well show her appreciation of what had already been done, and of the wider and brighter prospect which our incorporation as a college offered for the future:

"I wish it were possible for me to make, in broad and simple language, a statement of the force and efficiency of the instruction given here from the beginning. The standard has always been high and inspiring, and it has told upon the whole character of the institution. It has enabled us to accomplish the purpose with which we started, — that of making a large and liberal provision for the education of women according to their tastes and pursuits, and according also to their necessities, should it be needful for them to use their education as a means of support. With this hope we started; and the position of Radcliffe College today may well assure us of its final fulfilment, even in a larger sense than the present. The University has taken us under her charge, has made herself responsible for the validity of our degrees by the strongest official guarantees, while the liberal interpretation she puts upon her own pledges shows that they include more than they promise. Even in this first year she opens to us a greatly enlarged field of study, including a far larger number of advanced courses than we had hoped for. We may well say that, since the opening of the institution fifteen years ago, no year of its history has been so important as the present, for it gives us what we most needed, security and a certain and safe future under the guardianship of Harvard University."

PROFESSOR NORTON

IN looking back over the long, happy and beneficent life of Mrs. Agassiz, as a contemporary may do who has known it from beginning to end, the most striking feature in the survey is its sweet and steady consistency of excellence; and if one ask in what this chiefly consisted, the answer is plain, that she possessed, in larger measure than most persons, that quality which is the root of all the virtues, simplicity of heart. This kept her free from what is a common hindrance even of those with the best intentions, — self-reference, self-consideration. No one, I think, ever met Mrs. Agassiz without being helped into the pleasantest relations with her, through the complete absence on her part of self-consciousness. It was this forgetfulness of self which enabled her to discharge, without the strain of conscious effort, such difficult duties as from time to time it fell to her to perform.

The whole lesson of her life is a lesson of *character;* she was not a woman of genius or of specially brilliant intellectual gifts; what she did, what she accomplished, — and she did and accomplished much more than most women for the good of the society in which she lived, — was not so much due to exceptional powers as to the possession of certain not uncommon qualities in remarkable combination, all perfected by her simplicity of heart.

She represented indeed a rare and beautiful type of womanhood with singular completeness; for her naturally quick, tender and comprehensive sympathies, rendering her at all moments alive to the interests of others as if they were her own, were guided and controlled by a discerning and wise judgment, and animated by a courageous spirit. To this combination, a hardly less rare quickness of appreciation of whatever is beautiful or interesting in life, was added. A lover of music: with a lively interest in literature: and with an enthusiastic but not extravagant admiration for all that is heroic and noble in human character, her soul was always open to the best influences which the world can exert. The last time I saw her — not many months ago in her sitting-room upstairs — she was seated with a reading-desk before her on which lay open two books relating to the recent discoveries in Mars. She spoke of them with vivacious interest and intelligence, and our talk ran on naturally from the wonders of astronomy to the mysteries of the universe; mysteries which she confronted and accepted as simply as she had confronted and solved the problems of earthly life.

It is a great blessing for an institution, the life of which is to be measured by centuries, and which is as closely connected as Radcliffe with the highest interests of the community, to have for its founders men or women of such character as to make them contemporaneous with each successive generation, and exemplary from the possession of character such as all may imitate; admirable and inspiring men and women yet not removed from the common lot by unusual brilliancy of gift or marked superiority of intellectual power. Such was Mrs. Agassiz, delightful in life and in memory to all who enjoyed the blessing of her friendship. Whatever tradition may, in the course of centuries, gather around her person, she will surely stand as a noble figure of ever contemporaneous womanhood, modest, sympathetic, wise, sufficient for whatever duty.

PRESIDENT ELIOT

IT was fourteen years ago next spring that I saw Mrs. Agassiz appear before a singularly hostile audience attending a hearing before the Committee on Education of the Massachusetts Legislature on a statute establishing and defining Radcliffe College. Now the Committee on Education is not one of the most distinguished committees of the Legislature. It ought to be; but it is not. The ambitious and able members of the Legislature prefer service on the Judiciary Committee, the Committee on Metropolitan Affairs, or the Committee on Railroads. And so it happens almost every year that the Committee on Education consists of a number of remarkably plain men, or, we may say, of good common citizens of Massachusetts. It was so fourteen years ago next spring. Radcliffe College, successor to the Society for the Collegiate Instruction of Women, had come before the Legislature for its first charter.

I have said that the audience which collected in that spacious committee room was singularly hostile. It was largely composed of women; but the expression on their faces, as I looked at them, was not tender. It was set, and set in opposition to the plan that Mrs. Agassiz was to advocate. The greater part of the audience was of the opinion that either there should be a completely separate college for women in Cambridge, with its own corporation, government, degrees, and so forth, or that Harvard College should be opened to women on terms of complete equality with men. Either of these plans would have been acceptable to the great majority of the audience. The plan proposed was completely unacceptable.

It was necessary to have a public hearing on the law chartering the new college. I need not say that Mrs. Agassiz shrank from this public meeting. She never felt much confidence in her capacity to speak before a large audience. She always told me before the Radcliffe Commencement how much she dreaded her simple and dignified part in the ceremony. She thought she had no gift in public speech. She thought that the opposition would succeed. She knew that some members of the Committee had been primed by the opponents of the bill. The Chairman of the Committee had been the head of a Massachusetts High School, accustomed to treating boys and girls on an equality and carrying them together through the same programme. The plan proposed could hardly be congenial to him.

I went into the room with Mrs. Agassiz. On looking at the Committee it was plain that the task before her was going to be a difficult one. On looking at the audience the task seemed more difficult still. She felt the situation keenly. The case was opened by a lawyer retained on behalf of the petition. He stated his case clearly and succinctly, but produced no effect, so far as I could judge, on the Committee. Several gentlemen addressed the Committee, most of them on behalf of the proposal. I spoke myself, explaining the relations which Harvard University would maintain in the future with the proposed Radcliffe College. The case looked perfectly hopeless when Mrs. Agassiz arose. She first read a paper which she had written, describing the aims of the college, and how they would be fulfilled in combination with Harvard University. I was looking straight at the Committee, and the softening in the faces of the Committee was remarkable. Just her presence and her bearing changed the minds of those plain citizens of Massachusetts. The chairman of the Committee was visibly affected by her reading of her exposition and argument.

When her reading ceased, she said that she was ready to answer any questions the Committee might ask. Now that was really a terrible ordeal to her; but she felt it to be her duty and that it might prove a good way of serving her cause. And indeed it did. Her replies to the questions of the Committee were more effective than her paper. It was an effect produced by her personal bearing, by her speech, and by the absolute sincerity and disinterestedness of her petition. It was an effect of personality in public speech as strong and clear as I have ever seen. Before she ceased to speak, the case was won. The lawyer who was retained on the other side failed to make any adequate statement of the position of his clients. He was himself so impressed with Mrs. Agassiz's presentation of the case that he availed himself of a mode of retreat suggested to him by the counsel for the petition. He made no statement in opposition to Mrs. Agassiz. I suppose he did not feel equal to that task. I know I should have felt in that way, if I had been retained on the wrong side. Thereafter the petition for the establishment of Radcliffe College went smoothly on its course, and the needed bill was passed.

Mrs. Agassiz did not perceive at the moment the effect she had produced. She was agitated at the close of the meeting and felt that she had not succeeded; so I had the pleasure of telling her that she had succeeded, and that she had succeeded all alone.

The previous speakers have told of the womanly character of Mrs. Agassiz. She was cultivated, well-bred, and in her manner aristocratic, if you please, in the best sense; but there never was in this community a more influential woman, and in this case it appeared most clearly that her influence was of the strongest with common men. That is as it should be. I am sure those men said to themselves as they listened to her, "I should like to do just what this woman wants me to do. I will vote for the establishment of any college of which this woman is to be the head. I will vote for the establishment of any college which is going to give this woman an opportunity to bring up some women like her." That was just the effect she produced. Everybody in the room felt it. "Let us have the college which this woman asks for, and let us hope that she will train up in it women like herself."

INDEX

INDEX

Adams, Charles Francis, 268, 273, 274.
Agassiz, Alexander, 30, 37, 38, 45, 46, 56, 64, 93 ff., 171 ff., 175, 177, 178, 182, 185, 331, 372, 381, 387, 389, 396, 397.
Agassiz, Annie Russell, 64, 171, 172.
Agassiz, Cecile Braun, 30, 32, 37, 58.
AGASSIZ, ELIZABETH CARY (MRS. LOUIS AGASSIZ), ancestry and inheritance, 1 ff.; birth, 9; childhood in Brattleboro and New York, 9; life in Temple Place, Boston, 9 ff.; brothers and sisters, 10; life at Nahant, 15, 16, 39, 172, 183, 277 ff., 367 ff., 388; early education, 17; personal appearance, 17, 25, 35, 50, 218, 267, 401; her only misdemeanor, 18; girlhood, 18 ff., 30, 35; letters written in girlhood, 19 ff.; at a dance, 24, 25; in *The Waterman*, 26; letters from New York, 28, 29; first impressions of Louis Agassiz, 30, 31; meeting with Agassiz, 34; her life compared with that of Agassiz, 35, 165, 171; marriage to Agassiz, 35; life in Oxford Street, Cambridge, 35 ff.; in Charleston, 40 ff.; letter from Charleston, 41; on Sullivan's Island, 41 ff., 392; letter from Sullivan's Island, 42 ff.; letter from Washington, 44; ruse about a lost watch, 44; home in Quincy Street, 45, 172; part in the Agassiz School, 45, 46, 48 ff., 399 ff.; attitude toward the School, 66, 104, 105; notes on Agassiz's lectures in the School, 49, 400; assistance of Agassiz in his scientific work, 49, 51, 56 ff., 66, 69, 71, 81, 96, 113, 114, 118, 119 (*see also* below, Writings, *A Journey in Brazil*); on the fiftieth birthday of Agassiz, 54; interest in the Agassiz Museum, 56 ff., 92 ff., 372, 380, 381; summer in Europe, 58 ff.; first visit to Montagny and Lausanne, 59 ff.; letter from Lausanne, 59 ff.; letter from Montagny, 62; her father's death, 63; resemblance to her father, 8, 63; style in scientific writings, 64, 107, 110; journey in Brazil, 68 ff.; records of, 69, 71, 96 (*see also* below, Writings, *A Journey in Brazil*); dance at an Indian lodge, 69; intercourse with the Imperial family, 70, 73, 74, 78 ff., 102, 124, 177 ff.; letter from the Colorado, 71, 72; study of Portuguese, 72; letters from Rio de Janeiro, 72 ff., 101, 102; ascent of Corcovado Peak, 75 ff.; at lectures of Agassiz, Rio de Janeiro, 82 ff., 102; views on Brazilian women, 83, 89, 91, 92, 100; letter from Monte Alégre, 85 ff.; letters from Manaos, 88, 89, 93 ff.; letter from the Ibicuhy, 91, 92; tribute to, from the ladies of Manaos, 91, 92; letter from Pará, 95, 96; retrospect of Brazilian journey, 95, 96, 101; letter from Ceará, 96, 97; letter from Pacatuba, 97 ff.; ride to Pacatuba, 97 ff.; return to Cambridge, 103; visit to Washington, 110, 111; teas in Cambridge, 111, 112; summer in an absence of Agassiz, 112, 113; interest in the Humboldt celebration, 114; care of Agassiz in his illness, 115; at Deerfield, 115; letter from Deerfield, 115 ff.; on the Hassler expedition, 118 ff. (*see also* Hassler Expedition); record of the expedi-

tion, 119; letters written on the expedition, — at sea, 119, 120, 122, 123, 133 ff.; at St. Thomas, 120 ff.; Barbadoes, 122; Rio de Janeiro, 123, 124 ff.; Sandy Point, 126, 127; Monte Video, 127, 128; Bahia Blanca, 128 ff.; Port San Antonio, 130 ff.; Talcahuana, 145 ff.; Curicu, 152 ff.; Panama, 163; San Francisco, 164; return to Cambridge, 165; at Penikese Island, 166 ff.; bereavement in the death of Agassiz, 171 ff.; care of the children of Alexander Agassiz, 171, 172, 175, 182, 185; views on happiness, 173, 175, 176; membership on a committee for collegiate instruction for women, 192, 194, 196, 199, 201 ff., 403, 404; policy in regard to the aims of the committee, 205; elected president of the Society for the Collegiate Instruction of Women, 207, 404; negotiations for the affiliation of the Society with Harvard University, 231 ff., 243; consideration of the name "Radcliffe College," 241, 242; satisfaction in the proposed incorporation of Radcliffe College, 244; replies to criticisms of the incorporation, 245; policy toward Harvard, 245 ff.; at the hearing for the charter of Radcliffe College, 165, 249, 256, 257, 404, 405, 409 ff.; elected President of Radcliffe, 258, 404; desire for a dean for Radcliffe, 258, 259; ideals for Radcliffe, 261 ff., 326 ff., 338 ff., 357, 358; services to the college, 263, 324, 325, 404; loyalty to Harvard, 263, 265; views on the education of women, 264, 358 ff.; influenced by her life with Agassiz, 264, 265; Wednesday teas, Fay House, 266, 342, 343, 353; dread of Commencement exercises, 267, 318, 319, 343; family interests, 275; her mother's death, 275; interest in the Kindergarten for the Blind, 275, 276; visit to the Pacific coast, 279; year in Europe, 280 ff.; letters from Paris, 282 ff., 287, 288, 308; memories of Agassiz abroad, 282, 283, 288, 307; letters from Rome, 284 ff.; letter from Florence, 287; visit to Fontenay-aux-Roses, 287; letters from London, 288, 296; visit to Cambridge, 282, 289 ff.; at Girton College, 282, 290, 291, 298; at Newnham College, 182, 291 ff., 298 ff.; visit to Oxford, 282, 294 ff.; letters from Venice, 297 ff., 302 ff.; hears of first Radcliffe Commencement in Sanders Theatre, 302, 303; letter from Perarolo, 304, 305; letter from Cortina, 305 ff.; letter from Munich, 307; second visit to Montagny, 282, 307, 308; return to Cambridge, Massachusetts, 309; receives the Elizabeth Cary Agassiz scholarship as a gift, 309; correspondence in regard to the Radcliffe Gymnasium, 311 ff.; at the opening of the Gymnasium, 317; resignation as honorary president of Radcliffe, 341 ff., 347; called "President Emerita," 348; gratitude to President Eliot, 348; on Commencement Day, 1903, 350 ff.; illness, 356, 386; visit to Agassiz House, 358; notes for the opening of Agassiz House, 357; as an ideal for Radcliffe students, 358, 366, 408; visit to Harvard Observatory, 361, 382; occupations of later years, 367 ff.; at College (Brooks House) teas, 368, 382; sorrow on the death of her sister Sarah, 369, 371; views on old age, 371, 372; at the "Queens," 371, 374; ill health, 373; visit at Hamilton, 373, 377 ff.; reading of Carlyle, 373; views on Christian Science, 375; seventy-ninth birthday, 375; visit to the mu-

INDEX 417

seum of Mrs. John L. Gardner, 377; criticism of Richard Mansfield, 382; criticism of John Eliot, 383; invalidism, 386 ff.; at Arlington Heights, 388 ff.; failing strength, 393; death, 393; addresses in memory of, 394 ff.; article on, by A. Gilman, 193.

Addresses by: — for the Society for the Collegiate Instruction of Women, 211 ff., 223 ff.; at Commencement exercises, 218, 219, 221 ff., 227 ff., 261 ff., 314, 316, 358 ff., 360 ff.; at the State House, 251 ff.; at Bertram Hall, 326 ff.; announcing the gift of Agassiz House, 337 ff.

Characteristics: — 1, 8, 26, 35, 46, 48 ff., 55, 63, 64, 71, 172, 189, 205, 217, 223, 259, 263, 281, 282, 333, 334, 358, 367, 387, 391, 401, 404, 407 ff., 412; love of children, 81, 82, 90, 97, 367, 386 (*see also* below, Relations with grandchildren and great-grandchildren); love of flowers, 23, 122, 125, 126, 146, 149, 279, 387; love of Nahant, 15, 96, 282, 297, 298, 367, 388, 389.

Comments on books: — 42, 53, 54, 123, 372, 374, 376, 377, 379, 380, 383, 385, 387, 388, 392.

Letters of, to: — Associates of Radcliffe College, 343, 346; L. B. R. Briggs, 333; Mrs. L. B. R. Briggs, 353, 354; S. Cabot, 21; Emma F. Cary, 106, 350; Sarah G. Cary, 27 ff., 44, 52, 65, 75 ff., 93 ff., 106, 110 ff., 112, 115, 150, 166, 282, 285, 287 ff., 296 ff., 302 ff., 308; T. G. Cary, 19, 46; Mrs. T. G. Cary, 38, 55, 59, 62, 71 ff., 82 ff., 89 ff., 104 ff., 119 ff., 128 ff., 152; Elizabeth H. Clark, 369; Mrs. C. P. Curtis, 127, 174 ff.; C. W. Eliot, 231, 348; Mrs. C. C. Felton, 276; Louisa Felton, 350; Mary Felton, 164, 283 ff.; Mrs. J. T. Fields, 377, 389; friends who gave the Students' Hall at Radcliffe College, 339; A. Gilman, 205; Mrs. A. Gilman, 298; some graduates of the Annex, 245; J. C. Gray, 238; Mrs. A. Hemenway, 313; H. L. Higginson, 342; E. R. Hoar, 272; E. W. Hooper, 234; Agnes Irwin, 317, 319 ff.; A. Mayor, 185, 191; Cecile Mettenius, 184, 187, 375; C. E. Norton, 392; Grace Norton, 209, 280, 370, 371; Mrs. W. B. Richardson, 352; Mrs. W. B. Rogers, 190; the students of Radcliffe College, 286; Mrs. Q. A. Shaw, 81, 88, 126, 149, 163; O. Wister, 391.

Letters to, from: — L. B. R. Briggs, 332; C. W. Eliot, 239, 241, 347; A. Gilman, 197; G. S. Hale, 257; Mrs. A. Hemenway, 312; H. L. Higginson, 319, 342; E. R. Hoar, 268, 273; E. W. Hooper, 234; Agnes Irwin, 300, 318, 346; W. James, 335; H. W. Longfellow, 180; C. E. Norton, 322; Sarah W. Whitman, 330; Sarah B. Wister, 335.

Musical interests: — Comments on, Chopin, 391; *Fidelio*, 368; *Fiftieth Birthday of Agassiz*, setting for, 52; *Il Giuramento*, 28, 29; Mendelssohn, *Elijah*, 115; *Oedipus Tyrannus*, music for, 403; Rubinstein, 174; Von Bülow, 174; Wagner, 391; waltzes, 371. — Music lessons, 17, 19, 52, 53. — Musical tastes, 16, 22, 24, 26, 28, 29, 43, 116, 284, 334, 368, 371, 378, 381, 391, 403. — Singing, 13, 16, 52, 53.

Relations with: — Alexander Agassiz, 37, 38, 95, 171 ff., 175, 331, 332, 387; Ida and Pauline Agassiz, 37; the Agassiz family in Switzerland, 59, 60, 62, 282, 308; the alumnae of Radcliffe College, 352; the Braun family, 187, 188; L. B. R. Briggs, 334, 343, 390; Mrs. L. B. R. Briggs, 353, 354; Mary Cary [Felton],

INDEX

16; Mr. Christinat, 36; F. J. Child, 209; her colleagues at the Annex and Radcliffe College, 208 ff., 322, 323, 343, 346; Mr. and Mrs. Otto Dresel, 52; C. C. Felton, 17, 66; her grandchildren and great-grandchildren, 65, 81, 88, 105, 106, 172, 173, 175, 182, 372, 378 ff., 384, 386 ff. (*see also* Shaw, Louis A.); Agnes Irwin, 259 ff., 303, 317 ff.; Elizabeth Cabot Lee, 18, 108, 374; C. E. Norton, 209; the students of Radcliffe College, 254, 265 ff.; Sarah W. Whitman, 355, 356.

Writings of : — Manuscript Memoir of Thomas G. Cary, 3, 5, 63; *Actaea, a First Lesson in Natural History*, 64, 204; *Methods of Study in Natural History*, 66; *A Journey in Brazil*, 69 ff., 103, 104, 106 ff., 110, 112; *Seaside Studies in Natural History*, 93, 95; *An Amazonian Picnic*, 102; *A Dredging Excursion in the Gulf Stream*, 103; *The Hassler Glacier*, 119; *In the Straits of Magellan*, 119; *A Cruise through the Galapagos*, 119; *Louis Agassiz: His Life and Correspondence*, 181 ff.

Agassiz, George, 172, 182.

Agassiz, Ida. *See* Higginson, Ida Agassiz.

Agassiz (Jean) Louis (Rodolphe), early life, 35; in Munich, 307; in Paris, 283; arrival in Boston, 30 ff.; Lowell Lectures, 30, 31; at East Boston, 32; appointment to professorship at Harvard University, 32; life in Oxford Street, 32 ff.; Cambridge friends, 32; friendship with Longfellow, 32, 52, 180, 186; his wife's death, 32, 37; his children, 32, 37; meeting with Elizabeth Cabot Cary, 34; marriage with Elizabeth Cabot Cary, 35; zoölogical specimens in Oxford Street, 34, 38, 39; laboratory at Nahant, 39; professorship at Charleston, 40 ff.; lectures in Washington, 41; laboratory on Sullivan's Island, 40 ff., 392; library in Quincy Street, 45; part in the Agassiz School, 47 ff., 397 ff.; fiftieth birthday, 52; is offered a professorship in Paris, 55 ff.; summer in Europe, 58 ff.; friendship with Alexander Braun, 58, 187, 188; visit to Montagny, 59, 60, 62; *Methods of Study in Natural History*, 66; on the Thayer expedition to Brazil, 68 ff., 70, 71, 75, 81, 85 ff., 91, 93, 94, 96, 97, 99 ff.; lectures on the Colorado, 71; friendship with the Emperor of Brazil, 68, 72 ff., 78 ff., 102, 179, 180; lectures in Rio de Janeiro, 82 ff., 102; return to Cambridge, 103; failing health, 103; journey in the West, 103, 112, 113; expedition to the Gulf Stream, 103; his mother's illness and death, 104, 105; at the Humboldt Celebration, 114, 115; illness, 115; at Deerfield, 115 ff.; recovery, 118; on the Hassler expedition, 118 ff., 127, 128 ff., 137, 143 ff., 147, 151 ff., 160, 161; return to Cambridge, 165; school on Penikese Island, 165 ff.; failing health, 170; death, 170; biography of, 181 ff.; memory of, in Switzerland, 190, 191; memoir of, by Ernest Favre, 185; as a teacher, 264, 288, 351.

Agassiz, Maximilian, 172, 182.

Agassiz, Pauline. *See* Shaw, Pauline Agassiz.

Agassiz, Rodolphe, 172, 182, 378; daughters of, 378 ff., 384, 386.

Agassiz Museum, 56 ff., 92 ff., 372, 380, 381.

Agassiz School, 46 ff., 204, 264, 351, 394 ff.

Albatross, 130.

Alexander, Francesca, 282.

Alexander, Lucia S., 282, 287.

Amazon, the, 68, 59, 91, 95, 102.

Andes Mountains, 146, 156, 159, 162.

INDEX 419

Appleton, Thomas G., 112.
Association of Collegiate Alumnae, 245, 248.
Atlantic Monthly, 66, 102, 103, 119.

Boston, about 1840, 13 ff.; Globe Theatre, 116, 117; King's Chapel, 35; Pearl Street, 9; Temple Place, 9 ff.
Brattleboro, 4, 9.
Braun, Alexander, 58, 59, 187, 188.
Braun, Maximilian, 58.
Briggs, L. B. R., 173, 203, 333, 341 ff., 351, 352, 358, 366, 390, 394.
Briggs, Mary DeQ. (Mrs. L. B. R.), 173, 353, 354.
Brontë, Charlotte, *Jane Eyre*, 53, 54, 123; *Life of*, by Mrs. Gaskell, 53.
Browning, R. and E. B., *Letters*, 372.
Burkhardt, Jacques, 36, 43.
Byerly, William E., 202, 203, 207, 210, 249, 323.

Cabot, Elizabeth. See Lee, Elizabeth Cabot.
Cabot, Samuel, 21.
Cambridge, Massachusetts, 32, 33, 112.
Cary, Caroline. See Curtis, Caroline Cary.
Cary, Elizabeth Cabot. See Agassiz, Elizabeth Cary.
Cary, Emma Forbes, v, 10, 25, 39, 106, 110, 169, 350, 370, 381, 391; extracts from manuscript notes by, 10 ff., 24 ff., 45.
Cary, Georgiana S., 82, 90, 280, 368.
Cary, James, 2.
Cary, Margaret Graves (Mrs. Samuel Cary), 2.
Cary, Mary. See Felton, Mary Cary.
Cary, Mary Perkins (Mrs. Thomas Graves Cary), 4, 5, 7, 8, 9, 12, 13, 31, 275. See Agassiz, Elizabeth Cary, Letters of, to.

Cary, Richard, 10, 17, 25.
Cary, Mrs. Richard, 280, 281.
Cary, Samuel, 2.
Cary, Samuel, 2 ff., 46.
Cary, Sarah Gray (Mrs. Samuel Cary), 3, 4, 46.
Cary, Sarah G., 10, 20, 25, 26, 52, 54, 112, 257, 368. See also Agassiz, Elizabeth Cary, Letters of, to.
Cary, Thomas, 10, 25.
Cary, Thomas Graves, 3 ff., 7, 10, 12, 19, 39, 46, 62 ff.
Cary, William, 8.
Chanal, Madame de, 117.
Chantilly, 283.
Charlestown, 2.
Chelsea, 2, 109; Bellingham estate, the, "Retreat," 2 ff.
Child, Francis J., 207, 209, 397.
Christinat, Mr., 33, 34, 36.
Clough, Athena, 292, 293, 299.
Coes, Mary, 258, 346.
Conte d'Eu, 124.
Cooke, Mary H. (Mrs. Josiah B.), 196, 201, 323, 346.
Corcovado, Gulf, 145; Peak, 75 ff., 125, 145.
Coutinho, Major, 85, 97, 99, 100.
Curtis, Caroline Cary (Mrs. Charles P.), 10, 25, 34, 35, 127, 174, 177, 391; extracts from *Memories* by, 10, 16, 18, 48, 172, 263.
Cushing estate, Belmont, 22.

Darwin, Charles, 134, 137.
Davis, Andrew McF., 241, 242.
Dresel, Anna Loring, 52.
Dresel, Otto, 52, 53, 334, 385.
Duck, steamer, 143.

Eliot, Charles W., 194, 195, 199, 200, 204, 205, 231, 239, 241, 250, 310, 311, 321, 347, 348, 350, address by, commemorative of Mrs. Agassiz, 256, 409 ff.
Eliot, John, 383, 384.
Emerson, R. W., 14, 32, 388, 402.
Emmanuel College, 238.
Esperança, lodge of, 70, 163.

420 INDEX

Farlow, Lilian Horsford (Mrs. William G.), 196, 201, 207.
Fawcett, Miss, 293, 299.
Fay, Maria, 220.
Fay, Samuel P., 220.
Fay House, 220, 221. *See* Society for the Collegiate Instruction of Women.
Felton, Cornelius Conway, 17, 32, 34, 48, 65, 66, 180, 209, 264, 396.
Felton, Louisa, 350, 388, 389.
Felton, Mary Cary (Mrs. Cornelius Conway Felton), 10, 13, 16, 34, 39, 52, 371, 372.
Felton, Mary, 163, 280, 283, 292.
Felton, Una Farley (Mrs. Cornelius Conway Felton), 276, 277.
Fleming, Mrs. W. P., 361, 362.
Francillon, Marc, 59.
Francillon, Olympe Agassiz, 59, 60.
Froude, J. A., 123, 373.

Gallison, Mrs. H. H., 372.
Gambardella, 13.
Gardner, Mrs. John L., museum of (Fenway Court), 377.
Gaskell, E. C., *Life of Charlotte Brontë*, 53, 54.
Gilman, Arthur, 192 ff., 205 ff., 210, 220, 258, 259, 346; *Notes*, 192, 193, 195, 200, 204 ff.; article on Mrs. Agassiz, 193; articles on the Harvard Annex, 193; account of the hearing for the charter of Radcliffe College, 249 ff.
Gilman, Stella S. (Mrs. Arthur Gilman), 193, 195 ff., 201, 208, 220, 258, 259.
Gladstone, Helen, 292, 299.
Goodale, George L., 203, 249.
Goodwin, William W., 203, 207, 249, 256, 324; address commemorative of Mrs. Agassiz, 401 ff.
Gray, John C., 235 ff., 323.
Gray, Mrs. John C., 237, 239.
Greenough, James B., 194 ff., 198, 202, 203, 208, 323.
Greenough, Mary B. (Mrs. James B.), 194 ff., 201, 207.
Guanacos, 132, 134, 138, 139.

Gurney, Ephraim W., 208, 303, 397.
Gurney, Ellen H. (Mrs. Ephraim W.), 201, 207, 303, 402.

Hale, George S., 248, 257.
Harcourt, Lady (Lily Motley), 282, 288, 289.
Harcourt, Sir William, 289.
Hare, J. C., *Life of Sterling*, 42.
Harvard Annex. *See* Society for the Collegiate Instruction of Women.
Harvard Graduates' Magazine, viii, 193, 210, 230, 235.
Harvard University, 4, 32, 34, 40, 45, 192, 212, 216, 233, 237, 241 ff., 252, 255, 263, 269 ff., 368, 374, 382, 383. *See also* Agassiz Museum, Society for the Collegiate Instruction of Women, Radcliffe College.
Hassler Expedition: plan of, 118; life aboard ship, 119, 123, 126; at St. Thomas, 120 ff.; at Barbadoes, 122; at Rio de Janeiro, 124 ff.; at Sandy Point, 126; voyage from Rio to Monte Video, 128; dredgings, 128 ff., 136, 144, 151; at Port San Antonio, 130 ff.; in Gulf of San Mathias, 133; in a "pampiro," 135, 136; discoveries on Mt. Aymond, 137 ff.; Patagonian dinner aboard ship, 138; sunset on Elizabeth Island, 139, 140; Fuegian settlement on Elizabeth Island, 140; on Marguerita Island, 140 ff.; voyage from Otter Bay to Owen's Island, 142, 143; at Mayne's Harbor, 144; at Puerto Bueno, 144 ff.; in Corcovado Gulf, 145; in Port San Pedro, 146; at Ancud (San Carlos), 146 ff.; at Lota, 148; at Talcahuana, 149 ff., 160; expedition to Juan Fernandez and Valparaiso, 149; at ranch near Talcahuana, 150, 151; at Concepcion, 152, 153; road from Talcahuana to Tomé, 152; at Tomé, 153; at a Chilian *haci-*

INDEX 421

enda, 153 ff.; road to Chilian, 156; at Chilian, 157; at Sinarez, 158; road to Talca, 159; at Talca, 160; at Curicu, 152, 161; at Panama, 163; at San Francisco, 163.
Hemenway, Harriett L. (Mrs. Augustus Hemenway), 311 ff.
Higginson, Henry L., 64, 106, 207, 208, 319, 329, 332, 342.
Higginson, Ida Agassiz (Mrs. Henry L.), 37, 44 ff., 64, 106, 114, 329, 372, 382, 397.
Higginson, Thomas W., 57.
Hill, Thomas J., 118, 144.
Hoar, Ebenezer R., 268 ff., 402.
Hoar, Joanna, 269 ff.
Holbrook, John E., 40.
Holbrook, Mrs. John E., 40.
Holmes, O. W., 32, 107, 220, 385, 400.
Hoppin, Eliza M., 326.
Horsford, Lilian. *See* Farlow, Lilian Horsford.
Howe, Julia Ward, 382.

Ireland, Nathaniel, 220.
Irwin, Agnes, 259 ff., 300, 310, 317 ff., 324, 340, 341, 346, 351, 364, 390; Commencement address by, 364 ff.
Italy, 284.

James, Henry, *W. W. Story and his Friends*, 383.
James, William, 68, 72, 88, 195, 335, 336, 375, 383.
Johnson, Andrew, 111.
Johnson, Captain P. C., 118.
Johnson, Mrs. P. C., 118, 123, 130, 137, 144, 145.

Kimball, Mrs. David P., 316, 325, 326.
Kindergarten for the Blind, 275, 276.

Leach, Abby, 197, 198.
Lee, Elizabeth Cabot (Mrs. Henry Lee), 18, 28, 108, 374.

Lincoln, Abraham, 77.
Longfellow, A. W., 325, 341.
Longfellow, Alice M., 195, 201, 207, 276, 346.
Longfellow, H. W., 32, 107, 110, 178, 180, 184, 186, 188, 220; *The Fiftieth Birthday of Agassiz*, 52, 53; *Three Friends of Mine*, 180; sketch of his life by Norton, 392, 393.
Lyman, Miss (governess), 17, 113.

Manaos, 91, 336. *See also* Agassiz, Elizabeth Cary, Letters from.
Martineau, *Study of Religion*, 376, 377.
Mary, Queen of Scots, 295.
Mason, Ellen F., 207.
Mayor, A., 184, 185, 191.
Mettenius, Cecile, 59, 184, 187, 189, 190, 375.
Motier, 35.
Mt., Buckland, 127; Darwin, 127; Melimoya, 145, Osorno, 146; Sarmiento, 127.
Mowlson, Lady. *See* Radcliffe, Anne.
Mowlson, Sir Thomas, 242.
Müller, Max, 296, 297.
Müller, Mrs. Max, 296, 297.
Museum of Comparative Zoölogy. *See* Agassiz Museum.

Neuchâtel, 30, 35, 184.
Newman, J. H., *Apologia*, 388.
Norton, C. E., 207, 209, 238, 249, 322, 323, 374, 392; address commemorative of Mrs. Agassiz, 407 ff.

Peabody, Andrew P., 108.
Peabody, Josephine P., *Marlowe*, 354.
Pechet Harbor, 140.
Peck, Thomas Handasyd, 6.
Peirce, Benjamin, 118.
Peirce, J. M., 203, 207.
Penguins, 141, 142.
Perkins, Alice, 6.
Perkins, Edmund, 6.

INDEX

Perkins, Edmund (son of Edmund Perkins), 6.
Perkins, Elizabeth Peck (Mrs. James Perkins), 6, 7, 46.
Perkins, James, 6.
Perkins, John, 5.
Perkins, Mary. *See* Cary, Mary Perkins.
Perkins, Sarah Elliott (Mrs. Thomas Handasyd Perkins), 7.
Perkins, Thomas Handasyd, 4, 5, 7, 9 ff.
Perkins Institution for the Blind, 5, 7, 275.
Pourtalès, Count François de, 118, 120, 122, 132, 133, 137 ff., 140, 144.

Radcliffe, Anne, 241 ff., 252, 253, 269.
Radcliffe College, naming of, 241 ff.; proposed incorporation, 243 ff., opposition to its charter, 244 ff.; hearing for its charter, 248 ff.; incorporation, 258; reorganization, 258; officers, 258 ff.; relation to Harvard University, 245 ff., 261 ff., 265, 268, 271, 287, 301 ff., 344 ff., 349, 357, 390; the Joanna Hoar Scholarship, 268 ff.; halls of residence, 299, 301, 310, 311, 313 ff.; first Commencement in Sanders Theatre, 302, 303; needs in 1895, 310; purchases of land, 311, 314, 325; architectural scheme for its buildings, 313 ff.; Gymnasium, 311 ff.; library building, 315, 340; Bertram Hall, 316, 325 ff.; Associates, 322, 323, 343, 346; Students' House (Elizabeth Cary Agassiz House), 25, 329 ff., 336 ff., 341, 354, 356, 357, 394, 400; Whitman Room, 355; ideals and tradition, 358, 364 ff.; relation to the Agassiz School, 48, 394, 395, 400. *See also* Society for the Collegiate Instruction of Women; Agassiz, Elizabeth Cary.
Rancho, 98.

Revere, Paul, 6.
Ropes, J. H., 350, 351.

Schuyler, Georgina, address commemorative of Mrs. Agassiz, 49, 394 ff.
Seward, William H., 77.
Shaw, Louis A., 65, 66, 81, 82, 88, 94, 105, 110, 113, 114, 163.
Shaw, Pauline Agassiz (Mrs. Quincy A.), 37, 45, 54, 58, 64, 81, 88, 113, 126, 149, 163, 183, 280, 281, 287, 356, 372, 379, 380, 397.
Shaw, Quincy A., 64, 183, 281, 372.
Smith, Clement L., 207.
Sidgwick, Henry, 291 ff.
Sidgwick, Mrs. Henry, 291 ff., 299.
Society for the Collegiate Instruction of Women, formation and early activities, 192 ff.; published accounts of its origin, 193; founders, 194 ff.; relation to Harvard University, 194, 196 ff., 200, 206, 215 ff., 219, 225, 227, 228, 230 ff.; first circular, 200; officers, 202, 203; students, 202, 212, 213, 218, 224, 254, 364; rooms in Appian Way, 203, 219, 221; opening of its courses of instruction, 202, 203; list of its instructors, 203; called "Harvard Annex," 203, 206, 207, 212, 251, 252; becomes a legal corporation, 206, 207; adopts as name, "The Society for the Collegiate Instruction of Women," 206; signers of its Articles of Association, 207 ff.; officers, 207 ff.; raises an endowment fund, 211 ff., 219; development from 1879–1883, 211 ff.; from 1883–1884, 217, 218; purchases the Fay House, 220 ff.; enlarges the Fay House, 223, 224, 226, 227; purchases land and equips its first laboratories, 224; library, Fay House, 226; proposed change in its organization, 230 ff.; memorandum of its agreement with Harvard University, 240; adopts the

INDEX

name Radcliffe College, 241 ff.
See also Agassiz, Elizabeth Cary; Radcliffe College.
Spain, war of United States with, 370.
Steindachner, Franz, 118, 123, 131, 139, 144, 152, 160, 161.
Storer, Mrs. Robert, 401, 402.
Straits of Magellan, 118, 126, 130, 145.

Thayer, Nathaniel, expedition to Brazil, 68, 336.
Thayer, Van Rensselaer, 68, 72.

Venice, 297, 304, 305.
Vogeli, 111.

Wagnon, Cécile Agassiz, 59 ff.
Warner, J. B., 193, 202, 207, 230, 234, 249, 258.
Wendell, B., *Literary History of America*, 374.
Whiting, H., 214.
Whitman, Sarah W. (Mrs. Henry Whitman), 164, 323, 325, 330, 331, 351, 354 ff.
Whittier, J. G., 179.
Wilder, B. G., 58, 166, 168.
Wolcott, R., 373.
Women's Educational Association, Boston, 228.

Zell-am-See, 281.

Women in America
FROM COLONIAL TIMES TO THE 20TH CENTURY
An Arno Press Collection

Andrews, John B. and W. D. P. Bliss. **History of Women in Trade Unions** (*Report on Conditions of Woman and Child Wage-Earners in the United States,* Vol. X; 61st Congress, 2nd Session, Senate Document No. 645). 1911

Anthony, Susan B. **An Account of the Proceedings on the Trial of Susan B. Anthony, on the Charge of Illegal Voting at the Presidential Election in November, 1872,** and on the Trial of Beverly W. Jones, Edwin T. Marsh and William B. Hall, the Inspectors of Election by Whom her Vote was Received. 1874

The Autobiography of a Happy Woman. 1915

Ayer, Harriet Hubbard. **Harriet Hubbard Ayer's Book:** A Complete and Authentic Treatise on the Laws of Health and Beauty. 1902

Barrett, Kate Waller. **Some Practical Suggestions on the Conduct of a Rescue Home.** *Including* **Life of Dr. Kate Waller Barrett** (Reprinted from *Fifty Years' Work With Girls* by Otto Wilson). [1903]

Bates, Mrs. D. B. **Incidents on Land and Water;** Or, Four Years on the Pacific Coast. 1858

Blumenthal, Walter Hart. **Women Camp Followers of the American Revolution.** 1952

Boothe, Viva B., editor. **Women in the Modern World** (*The Annals of the American Academy of Political and Social Science,* Vol. CXLIII, May 1929). 1929

Bowne, Eliza Southgate. **A Girl's Life Eighty Years Ago:** Selections from the Letters of Eliza Southgate Bowne. 1888

Brooks, Geraldine. **Dames and Daughters of Colonial Days.** 1900

Carola Woerishoffer: Her Life and Work. 1912

Clement, J[esse], editor. **Noble Deeds of American Women;** With Biographical Sketches of Some of the More Prominent. 1851

Crow, Martha Foote. **The American Country Girl.** 1915
De Leon, T[homas] C. **Belles, Beaux and Brains of the 60's.** 1909
de Wolfe, Elsie (Lady Mendl). **After All.** 1935
Dix, Dorothy (Elizabeth Meriwether Gilmer). **How to Win and Hold a Husband.** 1939
Donovan, Frances R. **The Saleslady.** 1929
Donovan, Frances R. **The Schoolma'am.** 1938
Donovan, Frances R. **The Woman Who Waits.** 1920
Eagle, Mary Kavanaugh Oldham, editor. **The Congress of Women**, Held in the Woman's Building, World's Columbian Exposition, Chicago, U.S.A., 1893. 1894
Ellet, Elizabeth F. **The Eminent and Heroic Women of America.** 1873
Ellis, Anne. **The Life of an Ordinary Woman.** 1929
[Farrar, Eliza W. R.] **The Young Lady's Friend.** By a Lady. 1836
Filene, Catherine, editor. **Careers for Women.** 1920
Finley, Ruth E. **The Lady of Godey's:** Sarah Josepha Hale. 1931
Fragments of Autobiography. 1974
Frost, John. **Pioneer Mothers of the West;** Or, Daring and Heroic Deeds of American Women. 1869
[Gilman], Charlotte Perkins Stetson. **In This Our World.** 1899
Goldberg, Jacob A. and Rosamond W. Goldberg. **Girls on the City Streets:** A Study of 1400 Cases of Rape. 1935
Grace H. Dodge: Her Life and Work. 1974
Greenbie, Marjorie Barstow. **My Dear Lady:** The Story of Anna Ella Carroll, the "Great Unrecognized Member of Lincoln's Cabinet." 1940
Hourwich, Andria Taylor and Gladys L. Palmer, editors. **I Am a Woman Worker:** A Scrapbook of Autobiographies. 1936
Howe, M[ark] A. De Wolfe. **Memories of a Hostess:** A Chronicle of Friendships Drawn Chiefly from the Diaries of Mrs. James T. Fields. 1922
Irwin, Inez Haynes. **Angels and Amazons:** A Hundred Years of American Women. 1934

Laughlin, Clara E. **The Work-a-Day Girl:** A Study of Some Present-Day Conditions. 1913

Lewis, Dio. **Our Girls.** 1871

Liberating the Home. 1974

Livermore, Mary A. **The Story of My Life;** Or, The Sunshine and Shadow of Seventy Years . . . To Which is Added Six of Her Most Popular Lectures. 1899

Lives to Remember. 1974

Lobsenz, Johanna. **The Older Woman in Industry.** 1929

MacLean, Annie Marion. **Wage-Earning Women.** 1910

Meginness, John F. **Biography of Frances Slocum, the Lost Sister of Wyoming:** A Complete Narrative of her Captivity of Wanderings Among the Indians. 1891

Nathan, Maud. **Once Upon a Time and Today.** 1933

[Packard, Elizabeth Parsons Ware]. **Great Disclosure of Spiritual Wickedness!!** In High Places. With an Appeal to the Government to Protect the Inalienable Rights of Married Women. 1865

Parsons, Alice Beal. **Woman's Dilemma.** 1926

Parton, James, et al. **Eminent Women of the Age:** Being Narratives of the Lives and Deeds of the Most Prominent Women of the Present Generation. 1869

Paton, Lucy Allen. **Elizabeth Cary Agassiz:** A Biography. 1919

Rayne, M[artha] L[ouise]. **What Can a Woman Do;** Or, Her Position in the Business and Literary World. 1893

Richmond, Mary E. and Fred S. Hall. **A Study of Nine Hundred and Eighty-Five Widows Known to Certain Charity Organization Societies in 1910.** 1913

Ross, Ishbel. **Ladies of the Press:** The Story of Women in Journalism by an Insider. 1936

Sex and Equality. 1974

Snyder, Charles McCool. **Dr. Mary Walker:** The Little Lady in Pants. 1962

Stow, Mrs. J. W. **Probate Confiscation:** Unjust Laws Which Govern Woman. 1878

Sumner, Helen L. **History of Women in Industry in the United**

States (*Report on Conditions of Woman and Child Wage-Earners in the United States,* Vol. IX; 61st Congress, 2nd Session, Senate Document No. 645). 1910

[Vorse, Mary H.] **Autobiography of an Elderly Woman.** 1911

Washburn, Charles. **Come into My Parlor:** A Biography of the Aristocratic Everleigh Sisters of Chicago. 1936

Women of Lowell. 1974

Woolson, Abba Gould. **Dress-Reform:** A Series of Lectures Delivered in Boston on Dress as it Affects the Health of Women. 1874

Working Girls of Cincinnati. 1974